LANGUAGE AND LAW

'This book fills a vital need in the teaching of Forensic Linguistics. The content is well structured, chunked and contextualised to make it digestible for undergraduates, and readily integrated into lectures and tutorial sessions. I heartily commend Durant and Leung for putting this together.'

Paul Sidwell, *Australian National University*

Routledge English Language Introductions cover core areas of language study and are one-stop resources for students.

Assuming no prior knowledge, books in the series offer an accessible overview of the subject, with activities, study questions, sample analyses, commentaries and key readings – all in the same volume. The innovative and flexible 'two-dimensional' structure is built around four sections – introduction, development, exploration and extension – which offer self-contained stages for study. Each topic can also be read across these sections, enabling the reader to build gradually on the knowledge gained.

Language plays an essential role both in creating law and in governing its implementation. Providing an accessible and comprehensive introduction to this subject, *Language and Law*:

- ❏ describes the different registers and genres that make up spoken and written legal language and how they develop over time;
- ❏ analyses real-life examples drawn from court cases in different parts of the world, illustrating the varieties of English used in the courtroom by speakers occupying different roles;
- ❏ addresses the challenges presented to our notions of law and regulation by online communication;
- ❏ discusses the complex role of translation in bilingual and multilingual jurisdictions, including Hong Kong and Canada; and
- ❏ provides readings from key scholars in the discipline, including Lawrence Solan, Peter Goodrich, Marianne Constable, David Mellinkoff, and Chris Heffer.

With a wide range of activities throughout, this accessible textbook is essential reading for anyone studying language and law or forensic linguistics.

Alan Durant is Professor of Communication in the School of Law at Middlesex University, London.

Janny H.C. Leung is an Associate Professor in the School of English at the University of Hong Kong.

ROUTLEDGE ENGLISH LANGUAGE INTRODUCTIONS

SERIES CONSULTANT: PETER STOCKWELL

Peter Stockwell is Professor of Literary Linguistics in the School of English at the University of Nottingham, UK, where his interests include sociolinguistics, stylistics and cognitive poetics. His recent publications include *The Cambridge Handbook of Stylistics* (2014), *Cognitive Grammar in Literature* (2014) and *The Language and Literature Reader* (2008).

SERIES CONSULTANT: RONALD CARTER

Ronald Carter is Research Professor of Modern English Language in the School of English at the University of Nottingham, UK. He is the co-series editor of the Routledge Applied Linguistics, Routledge Introductions to Applied Linguistics and Routledge Applied Corpus Linguistics series.

TITLES IN THE SERIES:

Language and Law
Alan Durant and Janny H.C. Leung

Introducing English Language
Louise Mullany and Peter Stockwell

Pragmatics
(previously published as *Pragmatics and Discourse*)
Joan Cutting

Global Englishes
(previously published as *World Englishes*)
Jennifer Jenkins

Stylistics
Paul Simpson

Practical Phonetics and Phonology
Beverley Collins and Inger M. Mees

Discourse Analysis
Rodney Jones

English Grammar
Roger Berry

Researching English Language
Alison Sealey

Language and Power
Paul Simpson and Andrea Mayr

Language and Media
Alan Durant and Marina Lambrou

History of English
Dan McIntyre

Sociolinguistics
Peter Stockwell

Child Language
Jean Stilwell Peccei

Language in Theory
Mark Robson and Peter Stockwell

Psycholinguistics
John Field

Grammar and Vocabulary
Howard Jackson

For more information on any of these titles, or to order, please go to www.routledge.com/linguistics

LANGUAGE AND LAW

A resource book for students

ALAN DURANT AND JANNY H.C. LEUNG

Taylor & Francis Group

LONDON AND NEW YORK

First published 2016
by Routledge
2 Park Square, Milton Park, Abingdon, Oxon OX14 4RN

and by Routledge
711 Third Avenue, New York, NY 10017

Routledge is an imprint of the Taylor & Francis Group, an informa business

British Library Cataloguing-in-Publication Data
A catalogue record for this book is available from the British Library

Library of Congress Cataloging-in-Publication Data
Names: Durant, Alan, 1954- author. | Leung, Janny, author.
Title: Language and law : a resource book for students / Alan Durant and Janny HC Leung.
Description: New York : Routledge, 2016. | Series: Routledge english language introductions | Includes bibliographical references and index.
Identifiers: LCCN 2015042911| ISBN 9781138025585 (hardback) | ISBN 9781138025578 (pbk.)
Subjects: LCSH: Law—Language. | Semantics (Law)
Classification: LCC K213 .D86 2016 | DDC 340/.14–dc23
LC record available at http://lccn.loc.gov/2015042911

ISBN: 978-1-138-02558-5 (hbk)
ISBN: 978-1-138-02557-8 (pbk)

Typeset in Minion
by Florence Production Ltd, Stoodleigh, Devon, UK

HOW TO USE THIS BOOK

The Routledge English Language Introductions series consists of 'flexi-texts' that you can use to suit your own style of study. In this brief introduction, we outline the 'flexi-text' organisation, summarise this volume's main themes and point to their significance, and suggest some practical ways the book can be used in a course or for self-study.

Each book in the Routledge English Language Introductions series is divided into four sections:

A   **Introduction** – sets out the key concepts for the area of study. The units of this section take you step-by-step through foundational terms and ideas, carefully providing you with an initial toolkit for your own study. By the end of the section, you will also have a good overview of the whole field.

B   **Development** – adds to your knowledge and builds on the key ideas already introduced. By the end of this section, you will have a grasp of published work and issues in the field, and will be ready to embark more independently on your own exploration and thinking.

C   **Exploration** – provides examples of language data in context and guides you through your own early investigations of the field. The units in this section will be more open-ended and exploratory, and you will be encouraged to address unresolved issues, as well as to formulate answers to specific questions. The aim of this section is in part to prompt you to think for yourself, using knowledge and ideas acquired by reading material in sections A and B.

D   **Extension** – offers you a chance to compare your developing understanding and views with thought-provoking key readings in the area. These are taken from the work of important writers in the field, and are supported with contextual information and questions.

You can read any book in the series like a traditional textbook, straight through from beginning to end. This is, in effect, to read 'vertically' through the units (as in the grid that cross-references units in the table of contents): you read A1, A2, through to A10, followed by B1, B2, etc. This approach takes you through a broad field of study, starting with introductory concepts, moving through published literature and issues into more practical analysis and follow-up reading. The Routledge English Language Introductions are also designed, however, so you can read 'horizontally', across the numbered units (see grid), which then function as 'threads'. Units A1, A2, A3 and so on are closely connected with units B1, B2, B3, as well as with units C1, C2, C3, and D1, D2, D3. Reading all the As, then Bs, then Cs, then Ds will take you from key concepts in a specific area to a more advanced level of practical and scholarly engagement in the same area of the overall field. You can adapt your way of reading to how you feel you work best.

The index at the end of the book, together with the suggestions for further reading, will help to keep you oriented. Each textbook has a supporting website with extra commentary, suggestions, additional material and support for teachers and students.

LANGUAGE AND LAW

Language and law is an increasingly researched and studied interdisciplinary field. Currently, there are no fewer than seven international journals dedicated to its various strands of research. In this volume, we offer an introductory, practical guide to the field.

By way of introduction, we may say that there are four broad areas of inquiry in current 'language and law' scholarship (though these overlap and are often encountered in combination):

1 The language of the law

We examine language use in public sources of law (e.g. statutes, treaties and constitutions) as well as in private law documents (e.g. contracts and wills). Legal uses of language of this kind are commonly referred to as *legal language* (in English-speaking contexts, as *legal English*); they function as a seemingly distinct variety (or cluster of related varieties):

❑ Such use of language may be understood sociolinguistically as a register or sociolect (though we will see that precise linguistic classification is not straightforward).
❑ In the case of English, legal language developed through complicated historical changes involving at least three languages (Latin, French and English), as well as by responding to specialised professional needs.
❑ Legal language is used in a range of legal text types which exhibit distinctive structures that play important roles in how those texts achieve their legal effects.

Relatedly, we examine how written sources of law are drafted and interpreted, and how legal proceedings are conducted in a combination of written and spoken language:

❑ Each process in law enforcement uses highly conventionalised language practices (e.g. courtroom advocacy, cross-examination, jury instructions, judicial interpretation and law reporting).
❑ The specialised language practices used in legal proceedings may, however, bring about inequality and disadvantage to laypersons and vulnerable populations (such as children and second-language speakers); many people believe that language use in law generally could be simplified and made more accessible.

2 Law as language

Legal systems are brought into being by means of language, to a degree that differs from how language is used for most other professional purposes (e.g. when language is used in medicine or engineering, it constantly refers to a body of practices and standards established extralinguistically). In law, language is central in having:

❑ a performative dimension: it orders and transforms social relations, ownership and behaviour; and

❑ a constitutive dimension: it creates entities and relations, especially by means of linguistically formulated rules (we will also see that in the case of bilingual and multilingual jurisdictions, choice of official languages can have a profound impact on how legal systems are structured, including how law is written and read).

3 Language subject to law

General, 'non-legal' uses of language can become an object of legal analysis:

❑ Language may be introduced as evidence in cases that are ultimately about non-verbal behaviour (e.g. statements assessed in terms of whether they should be excluded as hearsay; expert forensic linguistic opinion admitted on topics including speaker or author identity, underworld slang, or degree of similarity between documents).

❑ Language use may itself be subject to legal regulation (i.e. by laws that deal specifically with language use) if it becomes disputed subject matter (e.g. in 'communication' crimes such as perjury, solicitation and threatening behaviour; or in civil actions involving defamation, trademark infringement or advertising language).

4 Interrelationship between law, language and wider society

This final category is not fully coherent because of the different possible ways in which law, language and society interact. Nor has it received much attention in the interdisciplinary field of language and law, though some of the issues have received treatment in cognate fields. We will not be able to cover all the topics that fall under this category, but here are some examples:

❑ language rights – claims that some specified use of language (e.g. as a medium of instruction) is a civil or human right (such claims can be particularly contentious among linguistic minorities);

❑ how legal systems cope (or sometimes fail to cope) with societal multilingualism;

❑ the penetration of politics and cultural values into law through particular uses of language; and

❑ representations of law in popular media.

Although these four types of intersection between language and law are often encountered in combination, they pose different problems in analysis. They have also been researched in different ways and to different extents. We explore each at various points in the 10 threads that follow. Together, the units that make up each thread show show how important language is in the formation and operation of law, and why studying language and law is thought-provoking and challenging.

It should however be pointed out that this rapidly growing interdisciplinary field is not without its identity crisis. Many topics in the book are concerned with reflecting the present stage of the field's development, for example, and foreground how linguistic methods and knowledge can be of service to legal practice. But it is reasonable to ask: to what extent is 'language and law' an *inter*disciplinary field, rather than an area of applied linguistics in which established linguistic methods and knowledge are simply re-presented in ways useful to another discipline? While the second of these positions does not limit the validity or value of work done in the field, it might nevertheless limit the field's growth, given a presumption that linguistic methods, paradigms and knowledge need to be stable before they can be *applied*. As this book shows, there are many interesting intersections between language and law that are not easily addressed by means of the stable body of what we already know; and some topics await even preliminary exploration.

Note: References to English law, US law and other legal systems in the book are illustrative. Our concern is with concepts and approaches more than with legal detail. No specialised knowledge of law is presumed on the part of a reader, but readers are encouraged to follow up relevant readings (guidance on introductory and other texts is given in a short section of 'Further Reading and Resources' at the end of the book).

CONTENTS

CONTENTS **CROSS-REFERENCED**

EXPLORATION

Analyses and Examples

EXTENSION

Engaging with Published Scholarship

UNITS

ACKNOWLEDGEMENTS

The authors would like to thank colleagues and students at their respective institutions, Middlesex University School of Law, London, and the School of English at the University of Hong Kong, for support and encouragement. Particular thanks are owed to a cohort of University of Hong Kong students who took ENGL2127, LLAW3190 and LALS3003 during 2014/15; their course was modelled on the book-in-progress and they contributed invaluable feedback. Modified in the light of their feedback and comments from other students and scholars (including a detailed read-through by Guido de Zordi), the book reflects the linguistic and legal contexts of the authors' working environments. Its international scope further reflects the fact that much of the planning discussion took place in a third location: Harvard University, where one of the authors was a visiting fellow; the authors would like to acknowledge support provided by the Harvard–Yenching Institute during that period. At Routledge, we would like to thank Nadia Seemungal and Helen Tredget for making possible a textbook that we believe brings together a fundamentally new combination of interdisciplinary content and pedagogic approach.

The authors and publishers would like to thank the copyright holders for their permission to reproduce the following material:

Extract from Constable, M. (1998) 'Reflections on law as a profession of words', in B. Garth and A. Sarat (eds), *Justice and Power in Sociolegal Research*, Northwestern University Press, pp. 19–35. Reproduced with kind permission of Marianne Constable.

Extract from Plain English Campaign, www.plainenglish.co.uk, reproduced with kind permission.

Extract from Goodrich, P. (1986) *Reading the Law: A Critical Introduction to Legal Method and Techniques*, Oxford: Blackwell. Reproduced with permission of Blackwell Publishing Ltd.

Extract from Heffer, C. (2005) *The Language of Jury Trial: A Corpus-Aided Analysis of Legal-Lay Discourse*, Basingstoke: Palgrave. Reproduced with permission of Palgrave Macmillan.

Extract from Burns, R. P. (2004) 'Rhetoric in the law', in W. Jost and W. Olmsted (eds), *A Companion to Rhetoric and Rhetorical Criticism*, Malden, MA: Blackwell Publishing, pp. 442–56. Reproduced with permission of Wiley.

Extract from Mertz, E. (2007) *The Language of Law School: Learning to 'Think Like a Lawyer'*, Oxford: Oxford University Press. Reproduced with permission of Oxford University Press.

Extract from White, J. (1985) 'Law as rhetoric, rhetoric as law: the arts of cultural and communal life', *University of Chicago Law Review*, 52(3): 684–702. Reproduced with permission of University of Chicago Law School.

Extract from Solan, L. (2010) *The Language of Statutes: Laws and Their Interpretation*, Chicago, IL: University of Chicago Press, pp. 64–6.

Extract from Danet, B. (1980) 'Language in the legal process', *Law and Society Review*, 14(3): 445–564. Reproduced with permission of Wiley.

Extract from Schauer, F. (ed) (1993) *Law and Language*, Aldershot: Dartmouth Press. Reproduced with permission.

Extract from Lidsky, L. B. (2000) 'Silencing John Doe: defamation and discourse in cyberspace', *Duke Law Journal*, 49(4): 855–945. Reproduced with kind permission of Lyrissa Barnett Lidsky.

Every effort has been made to contact copyright holders. Please advise the publisher of any errors or omissions, and these will be corrected in subsequent editions.

Section A

INTRODUCTION

KEY CONCEPTS

A1   'LEGAL LANGUAGE' AS A LINGUISTIC VARIETY

In this unit, we introduce the concept of legal language, perhaps the most obvious and traditionally debated intersection between language and law. The expression *legal language* designates what is often considered to be a recognisable linguistic variety, differing from other kinds of language use such as medical discourse, news reporting, Dorset dialect or underworld slang. But does a variety matching the name exist? And if so, what kind of variety is it: a dialect, register or something else?

In order to refine the concept of legal language, we introduce sociolinguistic concepts that help distinguish different *kinds* of linguistic variation. In related units, we extend our exploration of the concept: in Unit B1, we examine specific linguistic features associated with the variety, and in Unit C1 we examine contrasting views expressed about it. In Thread 2 (i.e. Units A2, B2, C2 and D2), we describe this complicated variety's historical development and the purposes it is thought to serve, as well as reasons why many people feel it is in need of reform if it is to achieve those purposes.

Scope of legal language

If you ask people what **legal language** is the language of, you will get different answers. Some say it is the language in which laws and legal documents are written: constitutions, treaties, statutes, law reports, wills or contracts. Others add courtroom and police language (spoken as well as written, and about legal topics generally or only when oriented towards litigation). Some also include non-professional use of language that is *about* law (e.g. in newspaper features), wherever discussion draws on legal terminology or style to represent a specific topic. Some maintain that 'legal language' is whatever lawyers say about law (including colloquial in-group talk), whereas talk on the same subject by other people is 'talk about law' but not legal language.

Whatever boundaries we adopt, what we call 'legal language' is a kind of discourse: a variably classifiable set of utterances with enough regularities to contrast fairly consistently with other kinds (e.g. with the language of parenting, cricket, menus or hairdresser talk). At the same time, legal language is evidently not a single, unified variety. Rather, it is a cluster of uses, distributed on dimensions that need to be disentangled. Merely aggregating these as 'legal language' constructs only a stereotype: part statute, part contract, part courtroom scenes from films, and drifting between historical periods and legal systems.

In a summary of research (including his own earlier work with Derek Davy on the language of legal documents in Crystal and Davy 1969), Crystal (2010: 374) describes the language of legislation as follows:

> [it] depends a great deal on a fairly small set of grammatical and lexical features. For example, modal verbs (e.g. *must, shall, may*) distinguish between obligation and discretion. Pronouns (e.g. *all, whoever*) and generic nouns (hypernyms, e.g. *vehicle, person*) help foster a law's general applicability.

Such formal description is suddenly far more precise, and can be extended by quantitative analysis of a corpus of representative texts. But some features of legislative language will also be found, in a different combination and with different frequency, in a contract or other private law documents. They will not be entirely absent, either, from the generally more discursive idiom of a judicial opinion as presented in a law report. One task in understanding legal language, therefore, is to differentiate *within* the legal variety as well as between legal and other varieties.

The term *legal language*

The phrase *legal language* is one among a cluster of terms used to describe a general field of study. Such terms include *language and law*, the reverse-order phrase *law and language, the language of the law* and *language in law*, as well as *forensic linguistics*. Both the order of terms and choice of preposition are live issues, as are the differences between *language* and *linguistics* and between *law* and *forensic*. The content of the resulting field, which Tiersma (2009: 11) describes as 'relatively fractured', is usefully summarised in Gibbons and Turrell (2008), as well as – slightly differently – on the website of the International Association of Forensic Linguists (www.iafl.org). At its broadest, topics in the field include written legal discourse (sources of law, and judicial declaration or interpretation of the law), spoken legal discourse (e.g. police and court interaction), linguistic evidence, legal education, translation and interpreting. Nuances between names and what they denote have been much discussed in the literature.

In countries where English is not the primary language of the legal system, legal language often goes under another name, partly because it is typically studied for different reasons. The phrase *legal English* (LE) is often used, for example, to mean competence in English for the legal workplace (Northcott 2013). Such approaches to legal language prioritise an applied, 'language proficiency' interest in how law works in English, an interest driven by a regionally varying combination of two forces:

❑　the international footprint of historically Anglo-American common-law legal systems in countries formerly colonised by or under the influence of English-speaking countries; and

❑　increased use globally of English as a legal lingua franca for commercial contracts and in formulating and enforcing public international law.

In these contexts, legal language, in English, is far less a variety absorbed during legal training, and is sometimes referred to as learning to **talk like a lawyer**; it is actively taught and certified (e.g. by assessments such as TOLES (Test of Legal English Skills) and ILEC (the International Legal English Certificate)). A good example of instruction in this idiom is Riley and Sours (2014).

Less attitudinally neutral than the terms above, **legalese** (along with *legal jargon, legal argot* and similar expressions) has a pejorative meaning: legal use of language that is clumsy, confusing or inefficient. Despite the apparent formality of legal discourse, lawyers are also sometimes said to use *legal slang*, an insider discourse between professionals.

While introducing terminology, we should note a further contrast implied by the term *legal language*: the contrast with 'illegal language'. Such language indicates use restricted or forbidden by specific laws, systems of extrajudicial regulation, and either binding or voluntary speech codes. We consider this rather different relation between language and law in Thread 8.

What *kind* of variety is legal language?

The term *variety*, to continue with writing by Crystal by referring to his *Dictionary of Linguistics and Phonetics* (2008: 372), signifies 'any system of linguistic expression whose use is governed by situational variables. Classification of different kinds of discourse may be made by reference to subject matter, the situation, or the behaviour of the speaker'. In some cases, Crystal continues, situational distinctness can be easily stated (e.g. as regards regional and occupational varieties). In other cases, perhaps especially in relation to social class, varieties are more difficult to define because they involve intersection of a number of variables (e.g. sex, age, region, class and occupation). Varieties also change according to purpose and over time (reflecting stylistic fashions as well as longer-term language change). What kind or kinds of variety, we should therefore ask, is 'legal language'?

Reflecting Crystal's point above, legal language appears to involve a number of variables. There are *professionals* (lawyers, judges, others) dealing with a *field* (or domain of activity: laws and their enforcement). Those professionals do so in certain *settings* of use (e.g. in a solicitor's office, in the courtroom), for specified *purposes* (to impose obligations, plead a case, issue a court order). One of the challenges in thinking about language and law, accordingly – and within that field, thinking about what constitutes the core concept of 'legal language' – is to understand how this variety relates to recognised axes of linguistic variation.

How lawyers talk and what they talk about

Linguists including Halliday have classified varieties by drawing a general distinction between variation determined by characteristics of the language user and variation related to situations of use.

❑ Variation by language user is known as **dialect** if variation is regional or determined by social structure; such variation includes grammatical and lexical distinctiveness, as well as pronunciation. It is known as **accent** if variation is regional or determined by social structure but restricted to pronunciation. The alternative term **sociolect** refers to a linguistic variety (a *lect*) defined on social rather than regional grounds.

❑ Variation associated with different topics, fields and contexts of use – including the relationship between participants – is known in stylistics and sociolinguistics as **register** (Halliday and Hasan 1976). Varieties of this type include registers of scientific, religious and academic English. In Hallidayan linguistics, because registers can be contrasted at different levels and in different ways, they are further classified on the basis of three aspects: their field (subject matter), their mode (the medium: spoken or written) and their manner or tenor of discourse (the relationship between participants). Some linguists (e.g. Biber and Conrad 2009) distinguish between register and **style**, while others (Crystal and Davy 1969) have used *style* with a wider meaning close to that of register (alongside the more familiar sense of a personally distinct authorial imprint).

In a useful online summary and critical account of legal language, Tiersma (2000) poses a central, provocative question in the form of a subheading: 'So what is legal language exactly?' He then answers his own question:

> Legal language has been called an argot, a dialect, a register, a style, and even a separate language. In fact, it is best described with the relatively new term **sublanguage**. A sublanguage has its own specialized grammar, a limited subject matter, contains lexical, syntactic, and semantic restrictions, and allows 'deviant' rules of grammar that are not acceptable in the standard language.

There is undoubtedly complex interaction between the variables. Legal language, Tiersma maintains, is not a dialect, but does have dialects of its own, since it varies according to place. Because of their differing legal systems, UK and US lawyers use different words for many similar concepts; and in countries such as India, legal English contains terms for indigenous legal concepts as well as terms imposed under British colonization. Legal language across all these places shows shared register characteristics, nevertheless. These include use of long and complex sentences, unusual word order, antiquated vocabulary, apparently tautologous expressions, passive constructions, ritualistic idioms and formal terms of address. There are also period-specific styles that make it feasible, despite the conservatism of modern legal language, to distinguish between documents written in different periods, and there are author-specific styles associated with particular judges, such as Justice Antonin Scalia in the USA or Lord Denning in the UK (usually judges presiding in a legal system's uppermost, apex court). In addition to these dimensions of variation, there are recognisable differences that correlate with different legal purposes (e.g. a constitution is formulated in broader terms than a statute or contract, and all of these differ from a law report), and there are differences between spoken or written monologues, such as a judge setting out his or her reasoning in deciding a case, and legal dialogue, such as argument that takes place during a closed hearing in a judge's chambers or during more abstract legal discussion characteristic of a Supreme Court.

Combine all these variables, and 'legal language' may well be a 'sublanguage' according to Tiersma's definition. Whatever it is called, the variety cannot be considered homogeneous. While a broad contrast can be made with language use in other fields, legal language involves finely shaded, overlapping styles that call for more legally situated, interdisciplinary analysis if we are to understand the interaction between language and law.

Does it matter what kind of variety 'legal language' is?

Distinguishing between user and use varieties is helpful descriptively, even if it is ultimately simplistic. Social markers (including age, region, class, job) intersect with situations of language use, especially in urban societies with considerable geographical and social mobility. Code-mixing and code-switching are extensive, both among bilinguals who switch between languages and among monolinguals whose style repertoire includes code-switching between varieties, some of which might traditionally be thought of as regional or class dialects. All these kinds of variation may be reflected in legal language.

Complications associated with what language varieties signify also matter. Speakers' varying ease in switching in and out of a class or regional dialect, when they wish to, in order to fit in with or adopt some other stance in relation to given settings can affect professional success. Some linguists prefer the dynamic term **repertoire** to the more static contrast between dialect and register in order to emphasise such significance. The relative difficulty involved in acquiring legal language as a variety also matters, because law is not simply a semantic field such as the weather or geometry, but a professional practice steeped in tradition, subject to intense educational selectivity, and respectful of accentuated hierarchy. Law as a field exhibits complex shadings of language use among different institutions, topics, practitioners and purposes. Such semiotic micro-variation signals professional and social relationships both within law and between the legal system and the wider public who are subject to law in a given legal jurisdiction.

A2 HISTORICAL DEVELOPMENT OF LEGAL ENGLISH

The four units that make up Thread 2 develop our exploration of legal language as a variety. In this unit, we outline the history of legal English; in Unit B2, we discuss specialised legal and social functions served by legal language; and in Unit C2, we consider arguments for and against reform of how legislation is written. The present unit introduces each of these themes by showing how the distinctive features of modern legal English are the result of sociolinguistic complexity during successive periods leading into the more stable situation of English, including legal English, from the late seventeenth century onwards. We suggest that modern perceptions of legal English are affected not so much by the variety's specific historical features (which are broadly consistent with the wider history of the language), but by the fact that historical substrata have persisted far more than in general usage, as collectively a marker of linguistic conservatism.

Key moments in the history of English
We begin by outlining key moments in the wider history of the English language, focusing especially on contact between different languages.

1   Although there is a complicated and interesting history of languages in the land mass that is now Great Britain prior to the eighth century AD, the impact of that linguistic history on modern legal uses of language was not significant. There is, for instance, little continuity between the Latin brought by the Romans in 43 BC

and later influence of Latin on legal English. When the Romans withdrew from Britain in AD 410, Latin almost died out and was only revived under the influence of St Augustine for use in Christian ceremonies after AD 597.

2 Almost immediately following the retreat of the Romans to defend Rome, Anglo-Saxons invaded Britain from north-west Europe, and introduced a Germanic language now known as **Old English** (alternatively, as **Anglo-Saxon**). This was the earliest, regionally varying form of 'English' in Britain. In contrast with the earlier period of Roman occupation, Old English existed in a predominantly oral culture.

3 Throughout the period AD 800–1050, another linguistic and political force contributed to the development of modern English, including legal English. Vikings from Norway and Denmark made incursions into north-eastern England and established a geographical jurisdiction known as the **Danelaw**: effectively a political and legal settlement dividing the country.

4 The most significant influence on legal English, however, follows the invasion of Britain by Normans from northern France in 1066. The Normans had themselves migrated to France earlier, as Norse-speaking invaders. But by 1066, they were speakers of Norman French. In England (but not Scotland), the language that then gradually developed was a contact language, **Anglo-Norman**. Norman French was the language of the aristocracy, used for government, administrative and military purposes. But it spread through intermarriage and adapted in response to the bilingual context. Latin was also in use as the language of scholarship and religion. Significant changes took place in Old English during this period, partly because the Normans became politically isolated from France during the thirteenth century, and partly as a result of increased mixing and trade between Normans and the Anglo-Saxon population. By the late thirteenth century, new forms of Old English, less inflected and more dependent on word order, were becoming prevalent and are now acknowledged as a distinct phase in the history of the language: Middle English.

5 **Early Modern English** is a name given to the language from the sixteenth century onwards. The Midlands (London) dialect had gradually emerged as a standard variety, especially following the introduction of printing in England by Caxton in the 1470s. Significantly, nevertheless, doubts continued into the early seventeenth century as to the status of English: whether the language was too impoverished for use in scholarship and other elevated purposes. English gained in prestige, however, because of several factors: the quality and popularity of literary writing (making it no longer seem inadequate compared to the humanist achievements of classical languages including Latin); reduction in the influence of Latin in the sixteenth century as a result of the Reformation; and hostility towards Latin during and following the English Civil War in the mid-seventeenth century.

6 These stages in the history of English emphasise invasion and colonisation of Britain by others, with **language contact** functioning as the main impetus to **language change**. Later phases involve a different direction of travel, quite literally. Britain invaded countries (including Ireland, from the seventeenth century onwards). American settlers who left Britain for religious and political reasons established English, initially alongside other languages, in what became, after

independence in 1783, the United States. Imperial expansion by Britain, at first commercially and then through settlement and political control, led to the imposition of English as the language of administration and education in the country's overseas possessions. The effect of such imposition during the nineteenth and twentieth centuries (along with Anglophone political, educational and legal institutions), combined with US political influence through the twentieth century, has resulted in worldwide influence of English as an international **lingua franca**, reflected in continuing use of the language in postcolonial national legal systems, as well as in international political and legal institutions and commerce.

Development of legal English as a variety

Surprisingly little reference to law is made in general histories of the English language, perhaps reinforcing a view that the language of law is somehow separate from more general processes of linguistic variation and change. However, the history of legal English calls for historical understanding that engages with wider sociolinguistic considerations as well as with language practices in legal institutions. A continuing need for interdisciplinary work on legal English emphasises the significance of pioneering historical studies such as Mellinkoff (1963) and Tiersma (1999), as well as earlier treatment of language in histories of English law (e.g. Pollock and Maitland 1895: 80–7).

Here are some of the main points in the history of legal English (inevitably greatly simplified):

1   Anglo-Saxon England was an oral culture and had no distinct legal profession. The society's ways of defining and enforcing social order involved practices many of which would now be considered superstitious or magical (e.g. trial by ordeal). Those practices included attributing special powers to words, requiring both those administering the law and those subject to law to remember legal phrasing exactly. The language of this ritualistic legal culture has contributed a large number of words to modern legal English (e.g. *bequeath, guilt, manslaughter, murder, oath, right, sheriff, steal, swear, theft, thief, witness* and *writ*), words that in many cases have narrowed or altered in meaning. Besides vocabulary, the Anglo-Saxon characteristic of giving significance to word-initial sounds, using **alliterative phrasing** to create memorable formulae, also left traces in legal English, especially after the shift in other varieties (including literary English) towards verbal devices such as rhyme: we still have *to have and to hold* (in marriage vows), *rest, residue and remainder, hold harmless* (in contracts), etc. In addition, Anglo-Saxon use of Latin after widespread adoption of Christianity in the seventh century forged an important connection between Latin as the principal language of religion and as the language of scholarship, with Latin emerging as the important language for legal thinking.

2   Far more important for legal English than the influence of Anglo-Saxon (or the minimal impact made by the Vikings' Old Norse) was the impact of French. The Norman Conquest in 1066 resulted in French-speaking Normans occupying virtually all positions of power in England. This made French the language of influence, despite Latin being, at least initially, the language of law. Two dates stand

out in what was historically a complex process. Around 1275, statutes began to appear in French, and by the early fourteenth century almost all Acts of Parliament were in French. In 1362, Parliament enacted the Statute of Pleading, which condemned the fact that parties in most legal actions could not understand the proceedings and required pleas to be made in English (Mellinkoff 1963: 111–12; Baker 2002: 76–9). However, since statutes in English only appeared later, from the late fifteenth century, ironically the Statute of Pleading requiring use of English was itself written in French.

3 Gradual resolution of the trilingual situation of Anglo-Norman Britain in favour of English gave rise to a much-debated anomaly in the development of legal English. Adoption of French in the legal system took place precisely when Anglo-French outside the legal system was in decline, yet at a time when a new legal profession was taking shape. So French became **Law French**, already a rarefied variety at the time it was adopted. This specialised variety survived successive efforts to abolish it (including a 1650 act for 'turning the books of the law, and all process and proceedings in courts of justice, into English', an act repealed at the Restoration in 1660) through to the final demise of French in law in the 1730s, nearly 300 years later. Features of Law French, which itself underwent changes during its long period of use, can be found in modern legal English, including: adjectives that follow rather than precede nouns (e.g. *attorney general, court martial, malice aforethought*) and a large amount of technical terminology (e.g. *appeal, bailiff, bar, claim, complaint, counsel, court, defendant, evidence, indictment, judge, jury, justice, party, plaintiff, plead, sentence, sue, summon* and *verdict*).

4 During the extended period of bilingualism and trilingualism, Latin also remained important for English law. Latin was used as the language of court records (as well as of writs, such as **habeas corpus**) long after it had been displaced as the language of legislation. Latin *versus* between the names of parties in cases (meaning 'against', and abbreviated as US *v.* or UK *v*) dates from this period. Because Latin was the principal language of scholarship of the period, learned English judges and lawyers incorporated literary quotations and maxims about law in Latin into their discourse (e.g. *caveat emptor*, rendered with Old English-style alliteration as 'buyer beware'). In view of the socially restricted proficiency in Latin of the period, however, such **Law Latin** began to include legal terms of French origin, as well as English words, whenever clerks and scribes were unfamiliar with the Latin they needed.

5 Three further characteristics should be noted from this transitional period:

❑ Use in modern legal English drafting and documents of long and grammatically complex sentences continues a practice of composing (and cultivated skill in reading) Latin prose from earlier periods, which had already influenced written French but was uncommon in Old English.

❑ **Binomial pairs**, or phrases consisting of two words linked by 'and' (e.g. *null and void, peace and quiet, breaking and entering, cease and desist*), which may be as much as five times as common in legal English as in other prose styles, typify a practice through which speakers responded to the existence of two simultaneously available streams of vocabulary: Anglo-Saxon or French in origin. Whereas the general effect on English vocabulary was for nuances to emerge between such terms (e.g. between *lawful*, *rightful* and *legal*), in law such phrases seem to have functioned more as formulae: they remained chained together as rhetorical synonyms, especially where they alliterated or showed some distinctive rhythmic effect (in a manner resembling Old English sound patterning, e.g. *last will and testament*).

❏ The period was marked by a complex shift in relation to **linguistic medium**. The advent of printing (Harvey 2015) resulted in wider dissemination of an increased number of uniform versions of legal texts, and legal proceedings changed in the balance they demanded between oral and written pleading. That seemingly small procedural change acquires far greater significance when it is remembered that oral pleading was conducted in French while the written forms from which 'counters' or 'narratores' made oral submissions were in Latin (Baker 2002: 76–9). Crucial for issues of legal authority, too, the shift from oral to written involved a change from viewing written documents as mere reports of an oral event or ceremony through to seeing written documents as the authoritative statements. Deeper still, fixation of discourse in writing consolidated the legal doctrine of precedent and introduced a textual and more interpretive, 'legalistic' dimension into adversarial litigation.

6 It would be simplistic to say that legal language has had a less eventful history since English became the language of law in Britain, with Latin and French merely persistent substrata. Legal English has been affected by massive expansion of vocabulary arising from its use in modern, industrial society, as well as by other factors. From the point of view of the variety's distinctiveness, however, the main, defining changes had already taken place. Many characteristics of modern legal English noted in synchronic studies (e.g. use of *hereinafter*, or complex prepositions such as *in the event that* rather than simply *if*) relate less to linguistic innovation than to persistence of features as archaisms. Legal language as a variety accordingly had a slightly anomalous relation to eighteenth-century arguments about 'ascertaining', 'fixing' or even 'purging' the English language. Its specialisation as a technical, professional language set it apart from other uses because of its conservative doctrinal values (especially treating prior judgments as authority on the meaning to be given to legal terminology). This characteristic may have made legal English resistant (though not immune) to further changes even in the face of criticism and almost continuous agitation for reform.

Past and present language?

The greatest influence on changes in legal English over the last three centuries has been massive geographical expansion in the spread of its use. English colonisers introduced legal English as part of introducing common-law institutions throughout the British Empire, and English became the language of law in the United States. English has also remained the language of law (or one language of law; see Thread 10) in many anglophone countries following decolonisation. Arguably, by comparison with the scale of variation evident in the general formation of New Englishes (e.g. Indian English, Nigerian English, etc.), the linguistically conservative tendency of legal English has acted as a brake on divergence. Perhaps as influential, however, as regards the footprint of legal English has been the extraterritorial reach of the English **common-law** system as the way to arbitrate international commercial cases, as well as the twentieth-century development of international legal bodies (the EU, UN, WTO and others) that use English as spoken or written and interpreted by non-native speakers who have no historical connection with Anglo-American common-law traditions.

LEGAL GENRES

In this unit, we explore another important kind of linguistic variation in legal discourse: variation by text type, or genre. Each different genre consists of interlocking elements that together allow it to fulfil a particular purpose. While genres can be found across all domains of discourse, in law specific genres serve precisely defined roles: they may prohibit something; impose duties or obligations; make promises; impose an order; advocate a course of action; or report the reasoning or findings of a court. Below, we outline the concept of genre and illustrate the most common legal text types. In Unit B3, we analyse how genres in law have developed historically, taking the example of the law report; and in Unit C3, we analyse generic features of a statute (what are sometimes called in legal skills courses 'the anatomy' of a statute; Finch and Fafinski 2011: 65–73). Our Unit D3 extract summarises some detailed empirical research into what is found to be a hybrid legal genre: that of jury trial.

Aesthetic and professional genres

To begin, it is necessary to clarify what we mean by **genre**, especially because the term carries connotations of aesthetic choice and artiness that seem out of place in the company of legal texts. Such associations may suit fiction and ballet but to many people seem inappropriate in relation to professional, especially legal, kinds of discourse.

In its most general sense, *genre* simply means sort, or type, of text. The word comes from Latin *genus*, meaning 'kind' or 'type' of anything, not just literary or artistic works. (*Genus* is still used in a technical sense to describe 'type' in the classification of species; and *generic* means 'broad' or 'with properties of a whole type or class', being related in this meaning to *general*.) In our discussion of legal language, we prefer the term *genre* to *text type*, since the latter seems to highlight formal rather than functional differences between texts.

Genre and register

In Thread 2, we discuss the concept of register as stylistic variation that applies across legal text types. By contrast, genre is concerned with the distinctiveness of legal text types within the overall class of texts that all display legal register.

Here is a brief comparison between register and genre. With register, relevant variable features tend to occur repeatedly within a text. Preference for passive grammatical constructions over active ones (*the meal was cooked by me* rather than *I cooked the meal*), idiosyncratic use of third-person *shall* ('the buyer shall . . .'), or presence or avoidance of contractions (*it's, they've, isn't*) recur in situations where a choice is available. Analysing register variation involves studying choices where relevant options were available to the writer or speaker (Biber and Conrad 2009). By contrast, genre markers are structural. Features that define a text – is it a recipe or restaurant review, a ballad or blues, a romcom or tragedy, or a will or wish list? – mostly occur only once, at particular points (often towards the beginning or end). Such features work together, usually serially (except in static forms such as photos and paintings), like a textual machinery or 'apparatus'. They imply movement and direction, propelling the text along a track that starts in one place and ends in another.

In documents, genre markers can be found in:

- layout, including **textual mapping** (e.g. section or chapter divisions, use of paragraph topic sentences);
- use of headings, titles and other ways of the text self-identifying as a particular kind of document;
- opening and closing statements that bootstrap the document into action and declare its purpose;
- types of material contained at successive stages; and
- closing statements outlining application or anticipated effect, signatures and dates where applicable.

Analysing genre is a process of checking for strategic markers of structure and purpose. This is because genre is to do with how things get done linguistically. Without essential elements, a text may cease altogether to function as an exemplar of the text type it is trying to be. In literature, music or film, that may not have any major consequence; it may even prompt new directions in creativity. With legal genres, however, the job to be done by the text, such as functioning as a will or a lease, cannot be accomplished unless essential, 'operative' elements are all present and relate to each other in the correct way.

The essential difference between register and genre can now be seen. One of its implications is that there may be many examples of the same genre that differ substantially in stylistic realisation while all achieving the same function. But if you take an essential genre feature away, although a text may still be in a register associated with particular genre, it may no longer function (e.g. as a job offer, letter of authorisation or will). The concepts of genre and register in this way contrast as dimensions of legal language, but coexist in any given text and often work in mutually reinforcing ways. Legal requirements for each clause in a contract will be realised in language with particular register characteristics (as well as jurisdiction-specific and period-specific legal dialect characteristics); and a preamble to a statute will have features that we recognise instantly as legal register but which also function as the preamble to a statute, not as a will.

Consider the interaction between genre and register in a **will**. A clause from a will (examined by Butt 2013: 303–4) states:

> Signed by the above-named Sarah Smith as her last will in the presence of us present at the same time who at her request in her presence and in the presence of each other have hereunto subscribed our names as witnesses.

Features of legal register are unmistakable here: 'hereunto' and 'subscribed' (the latter in the sense of 'written below'); the complicated coordination involved in saying the people were all there simultaneously; and the oddity of word order (adverbials placed between 'who' and its related verb). Butt's commentary, which is concerned with reform of legal drafting styles, proposes a simpler alternative: 'Signed by the testator in our presence and then by us in hers'. But Butt notes that alongside features of linguistic register, we must recognise another aspect of the clause: its essential role within the 'will' genre. The clause is an **attestation clause**: the will would have been invalid without a signature made by the testator in the presence of two or more witnesses present at the same time. A statement fulfilling this specification is not a matter of style (Butt in fact demonstrates that the will could have been written in a number of different styles). Rather, the attestation clause is an element in a specialised discourse 'apparatus' that has **performative effect**: it will bring about a transfer of possessions, but subject to the requirements of the relevant conventional legal genre, or text type, being met.

Legal text types

Genre is an important concept in relation to legal language. It is genre considerations that allow documents to perform, in a given instance, as operative **legal instruments**, carrying out acts rather than merely describing a wish or plan or reporting that changes have been brought about by some other action. The functions performed by genre also show why 'legal document' can be an object of analysis for a register study but not the name of a genre. 'Will' or 'insurance policy', by contrast, are such names, in that these are terms that indicate situated purposive behaviour.

There is no fixed list of legal genres, even though a set of prominent legal text types can be identified. The core types include:

- ❏ 'legislative' documents (e.g. treaties, constitutions, statutes, statutory instruments, by-laws (sometimes 'bye-laws'), regulatory codes);
- ❏ 'private law' documents (e.g. contracts, orders, deeds, wills, leases, conveyances, mortgage documents, building contracts); and
- ❏ 'procedural' documents (e.g. opening speech in a trial, cross-examination, summing-up speech, jury direction).

Each text type performs a specific legal task, or combination of tasks, and is governed by conventions that vary between legal systems. The first two categories are typically written genres (though contracts need not be). The third category consists of legal text types realised in speech, for example during court proceedings and at inquests and other tribunals. There are some text types again that can involve either speech, or writing, or the two in combination: **pleadings** (statements of case and related legal submissions such as skeleton arguments on which oral submissions will be based); and **judicial opinions**, as recorded in law reports (often written, sometimes with the assistance of a clerk, to be spoken, or written up after having been delivered orally and transcribed).

Moving beyond this core area of text types, other legal genres include expository documents explaining the law on a particular point or in a given area; there are also office memoranda, client advisory communications, and emails exchanged in case preparation. Moving outwards from courts and solicitors' offices into legal studies and public information, there are published **case notes**, law review articles, policy reports and reform proposals, as well as legislative materials in preparation (green papers, white papers, **travaux préparatoires**, transcripts of parliamentary debate), and many other kinds.

Genre is particularly important in relation to legal text types because legal systems function through a hierarchy of **authorities** ('authorities' here meaning statements made or reported in available document 'sources'). For the purpose of legal proceedings, some kinds of document will not be taken into account because they are inadmissible or not binding in a given context. More generally, sources are given different weight in legal argument. And while sometimes a single document may have its effect independently (e.g. an uncontested will), often documents occupy slots within an overall procedure that unfolds over time. Each builds on some previous document's specialised role within a larger 'legal machine' (e.g. a whole court case, or the complex process of legislation during which policy documents evolve into legislative drafting, are published as statutes or regulations, applied by courts, contested in litigation, and reported – all in ways that may result in later amendment and **codification**).

Contracts as an example

Consider the written **contract** as an example of genre. Contracts are private law documents that set out agreements between parties to perform particular actions. There is no legal requirement for a contract to follow a particular format; legal contestation will take not only the written document into account where there is one, but a range of other relevant circumstances and legal principles. Nevertheless, commercial contracts prepared by lawyers tend to follow a similar structure.

Simplified considerably (adapted here from Haigh 2015), a typical modern commercial contract follows a general structure and sequence of presentation:

- ❑ names and addresses of the parties;
- ❑ **recitals** (background information typically introduced by the register-specific term 'whereas');
- ❑ definitions;
- ❑ **conditions precedent** (i.e. conditions stated as being in place before the agreement);
- ❑ agreements;
- ❑ representations and warranties (promises that a given statement or set of facts is true, including promises that may give rise to a claim to damages if the contract becomes the subject of litigation);
- ❑ **boilerplate clauses** (standard statements of terms and procedures);

- ❏ schedules;
- ❏ signatures; and
- ❏ appendices.

Some steps or stages have general names that are recognisable from other kinds of text (even if some of these, such as 'schedules' meaning separate lists, or the phrase 'conditions precedent', which reverses the sequence of adjective and noun, may sound archaic). Other stages ('recitals', 'representations and warranties' and 'boilerplate clauses') use specialised names. Realisation, or fulfilment, of each step depends as much on legal requirements as on linguistic formulation, making genre a key area in which 'language and law' are not simply juxtaposed concepts, but intersect and create new, specifically legal meanings.

Some relevant legal requirements of a contract may be used in many different types of contract: e.g. effect of extraneous events (**force majeure**); service of notices; statement of governing law; basic interpretation principles; duration; what happens in the event of bankruptcy or insolvency; termination for breach; and dispute resolution. Others will be specialised to a particular type of transaction: e.g. lessor's powers and lessee's obligations in a lease; or a mortgagee's rights and remedies. All, however, are episodic features that characterise an operative legal genre. They bootstrap a document into existence as a particular kind of document; they define its purpose, scope and terms; they state its provisions; and they stipulate the circumstances of its application.

Each feature of a legal genre is accordingly both:

- ❏ conceptual (within the rule-governed system of what law requires and what the parties to the particular document want); and
- ❏ linguistic (expressed by means of a particular **speech act**: spelling out presumptions, requiring something to be done, undertaking to do something, stating agreement, etc.).

For each step, it is possible to move down a level, to see typical realisations that will satisfy what is needed for that step to be **legally binding**: for example, a particular clause may need to specify agency, or state exemptions or deadlines. Such clauses may be repeated, with relevant variation while retaining the elements required to be deemed operative. This contributes to the formulaic character of the genre as regards legal register.

Various shorthands are used in legal textbooks and training materials to describe document structure, including:

- ❏ COAL (how material should unfold in a contract): conditions, obligations, authorisations, limitations (Butt 2013: 119); and
- ❏ CLEO (a model developed primarily for students of legal English): claim, law, evaluation, outcome.

Reflecting on good and bad practice in legal drafting, Butt (2013) suggests that most (private law) transactional legal documents can logically follow one of three alternative structures that, weighed up from the point of view of anticipated reforms of legal language, he concludes have different merits:

1 a 'telescoping' form, front-loaded with essential information presented before less important information;
2 a 'thematic' form, dealing with each main topic in succession along with everything that relates to it; and
3 a 'chronological' form, following steps in a transaction in the order in which they would take place, like a narrative.

Scope for such variation in structure points to a significant aspect of legal document genres hinted at above: that already tested structures are usually followed. This conventional aspect of document patterns is reinforced on each occasion of use, reflecting and contributing to wider legal conservatism. Ready-made, 'boilerplate' material containing standard formulations (including **specimen clauses**) is available for incorporation into documents, within law firms and commercially, including increasingly online. Because of law's precise procedural needs, use of templates that require only filling in of standardised forms is not frowned on, but encouraged, although responsibility for understanding how a particular use of language relates to the law in a given set of circumstances will normally remain with the document user.

A4 PARTICIPANT ROLES AND SPEECH STYLES

Extending our discussion of genre in Thread 3, especially Heffer's analysis of jury trials as a complex, hybrid genre in Unit D3, we now describe the main determinants of spoken language styles used in courtrooms. Even within a specialised legal setting, we show, speech style co-varies with participant roles and with different stages in legal proceedings. We then examine the main speaking roles and associated styles likely to be encountered in court, identifying prominent features for further analysis in Unit B4. The speech styles used by advocates, which form a distinct kind of adversarial rhetoric, are introduced in Thread 5.

Who talks during a trial, at what stage and in what capacity?

There are major differences between different kinds of trial. So our brief introduction here involves considerable simplification (for a fuller description, see Mauet 2002; Zander 2015). The stages we outline are the main steps in an overall institutional process that is simultaneously procedural, conceptual and linguistic. The process is also adversarial, in common-law trials, and may last varying amounts of time. Not all steps are present in all kinds of proceeding, or at all levels in a court hierarchy, or in all jurisdictions. Our description of speech styles needs to be read with such legal variation in mind.

Here is a simplified list of the stages in a trial:

1   In jury trials, a selection process may be used to choose jurors. Some jurisdictions allow each party to raise challenges during selection; and where this is the case, such challenges may result in dismissal of potential jurors (a process known as **voir dire**, though this term has a wider meaning in some jurisdictions; Eades 2010: 41–2).

2   The judge instructs jurors on rules to be followed during the trial (these rules are known as **preliminary instructions**).

3   The prosecution or (in a civil case) the claimant's side presents an **opening statement**. This sets out their case and sometimes what witnesses will establish, leading to the main points in contention.

4   The opening statement stage is followed by presentation of evidence, in those hearings where evidence will be presented rather than purely legal argument. This phase is followed by the witness being cross-examined by the opposing lawyer, who asks questions to test that evidence. Witnesses who are present may be, but in most cases are not, re-examined by the lawyer who called them, in a bid to clarify or explain evidence that has emerged during cross-examination.

5   Next, the defending lawyer presents the defendant's case, seeking to refute the other side's claims. Defence witnesses also take an oath, are examined, cross-examined and possibly re-examined.

6   Each side presents a **closing argument**.

7   The judge instructs the jurors (where there is a jury) on the law applicable to the particular case; they retire to a private 'jury room' to deliberate. The jurors elect a foreperson to chair their discussion. They arrive at a verdict (either unanimously or by prescribed majority) that decides between restricted options prescribed by the court, and according to a given standard of proof.

The stages in this process (greatly simplified here) will mostly seem familiar from their representation in films and on television, though differences between actual proceedings and media representations of them should not be underestimated. What is important here is that the processes described above take place through the medium of language: mostly in speech, but supported as necessary by written documents and other evidence. Some stages involve exchanges between the judge and lawyers; others between lawyers; and others again lawyers and **laypersons. Cross-examination** (Stone 2009) is interactive, taking the form of questions calculated to elicit answers but constrained by precise rules. At other points, language is more standardised, for example in the form and content of **oaths** and **jury instructions**, which are recited monologues.

Discourse styles in the courtroom

Speech styles are relevant to court hearings because they combine to create a complex **speech event** type. Linguistic, and especially sociolinguistic, work on courtroom discourse makes possible more precise description of the different styles and of issues they raise (Gibbons 2003; Eades 2010).

Everyone's dominant speech patterns are connected, in sometimes complicated ways, to demographic categories (including age, gender, education level, socio-economic status and ethnic group). But people also typically speak differently in different contexts, hence the dynamic relationship between linguistic and social variables explored in sociolinguistics. Even within the same sociolinguistic setting, a person assuming a fixed role (e.g. as a judge) may adjust his or her speech depending on the audience and purpose of the interaction or stage in a particular interaction. Relatively stable **indexical features** of speaker identity (dialect and sociolect signalling regional and class formation, profession and status) interact in patterned ways with features of register (situational variation) and genre (variation of discourse structure by purpose) that we explore in other units.

Courtroom discourse follows procedural conventions that superimpose an institutional level onto such variation. Acknowledging such factors in courtroom behaviour can be important, however, if they affect what might otherwise be conceived as purely legal dimensions of proceedings. Even without presenting details, a number of introductory observations can be made about the roles and turn-taking rights of the main participants in courtroom interaction. In our concluding section below, we draw attention to some of the consequences of these structures.

Judges

The generic term *judge* is used to include roles at a number of ranks that are precisely differentiated in a legal hierarchy. Depending on the type of case, there may be more than one judge (usually an odd number in appeal hearings), who enter the courtroom through a private door and sit ('preside') on an elevated bench, symbolising their personification of authority in the 'hearing'; other symbols, in layout and ritual, reinforce judicial authority and the solemnity of the courtroom.

These aspects of physical context and procedure are reflected in **turn-taking conventions** as well as in speech styles. Being the most powerful persons in a courtroom, judges initiate speech whenever they wish. They can command behaviour (e.g. tell someone to stop talking or sit down; or draw a line of questioning to a close); they formally instruct the jury; they can interrupt proceedings in order to manage time or ensure proper procedure; and they deliver a judgment. Judicial decisions are presented as objective and almost inevitable because of the legal reasoning followed in arriving at them (Ferguson 1990). The judge is depersonalised as 'the court' or 'the bench', reinforcing his or her function as an embodiment of the judicial system (Gibbons 2003). Other courtroom participants address the judge as 'Your Honour' or 'My Lord' (depending on the type of court, and with variation across courts and between common-law jurisdictions; see Evans 1998). In some ritualised formulations, lawyers address the judge in the third person, as in the archaic introduction to a submission, 'May it please your Lordship'. The resulting interaction is a hybrid of second-person address and third-person reference (e.g. 'I don't know if your Lordship has had the opportunity to read ...'). Judges not present in the courtroom are commonly referred to respectfully as 'the learned judge' even in disagreement; and attention is drawn to disagreement only by suggesting that the learned judge may have 'erred' or 'fallen into error'.

Lawyers

Lawyers may also be known as 'attorneys' or 'counsel'. In the UK, they are divided into solicitors and barristers: the former do preparatory legal work and manage client relations while the latter argue in court (though professional structures are currently undergoing reform). No equivalent division is made in the USA or in some other countries of what is often referred to as the 'common-law family'. In this unit, we use generic 'lawyer' unless there is a reason to use a more specialised term; in this section, we focus on the **advocate** role (i.e. the role played by barristers arguing a case).

Lawyers normally stand while they speak in court but remain seated facing the bench when not talking. As regards speech style, lawyers switch according to addressee and other secondary but still intended audiences. Lawyers address or refer to each other as 'my learned friend' initially, subsequently contracted to 'my friend', conveying an assumption that they are a professional community (membership of which is reflected differently in interactional styles with one another outside the courtroom).

Where jurors are present, lawyers minimise apparent 'legalese'; and in examining witnesses, they orient themselves towards a coherent narrative linking the questions they ask. An opposing lawyer may occasionally raise objections by interrupting, in a formulaic **objection sequence** (in conversation analysis terms) that consists of the objection itself (e.g. 'I object' or 'Objection'), then the basis of the objection or claimed violation (e.g. 'Immaterial' or 'Calls for hearsay'), then the judicial decision. Such interruptions are rare, however, by comparison with television or filmic dramatisations of courtroom interaction (see also our discussion in Unit B5).

Witnesses

Witnesses come from all sections of society, so their speech styles vary greatly. Lay witnesses include complainants (or victims), eyewitnesses (or earwitnesses), character witnesses and defendants (though this last category may not be compelled to give evidence against themselves). Police witnesses may include the officer in charge of a case and an interviewing or arresting officer or officers. Expert witnesses are professionals (e.g. forensic evidence gatherers, industry experts or doctors) called to assist the **trier of fact**, subject to rules governing expert and opinion evidence. For technical reasons and to project authority, police and expert witnesses tend to adopt, even over-accentuate, features of their specialised professional language.

The **oath** taken by witnesses, we have said, is a ritualised, scripted performance. In their constrained answers to questions, witnesses then have little control over when to speak or what (or how much) to say, despite courtroom principles that evidence should be freely given, not coached and not biased by leading questions.

Unlike legal professionals, who are experienced users of courtroom language, police witnesses have been shown to engage in what is described as **copspeak**: a speech style characterised by jargon and over-elaboration (i.e. over-complex or unduly formal statement), possibly as a way of asserting authority (see Gibbons 2003: 85–7). For example, in a testimony cited in Maley and Fahey (1991: 8), a police sergeant is reported as saying, 'I was able to maintain the light being illuminated', meaning simply 'to keep the torch on'.

Juries

Traditional justifications for trial by a jury of peers include the aim of preventing abuses of power. In modern forms, this aim is symbolised by jurors entering through a private door and sitting in a box, signifying independence both from the parties and from legal professionals. As regards speech style, there is not much to say because juries do not say much. While jury members are the essential audience for courtroom discourse, they are almost entirely non-interactants. They cannot interrupt or ask questions; and their deliberations take place confidentially, weighing up what they have heard in a room that is closed to the public (and not directly researchable, to preserve the concept of jury integrity).

The role of juries in the delivery of justice is fiercely defended as a principle, particularly when linked to criticisms of alternative systems and especially as presumption of jury trial is gradually withdrawn. On the other hand, since juries do not interact with other court participants or report their dialogue, the degree of their comprehension of the judge's instructions to them, or of the detail of trials in which they are responsible for verdicts, is not easy to assess.

Other voices

Other courtroom personnel are also involved in the production, reception and reporting of speech in court besides these main protagonists. These other persons vary between types of proceeding, but typically include clerks, ushers and shorthand writers. Clerks speak in formalised chunks of discourse when handling procedural matters, such as announcing the judge's entry, juror selection or administering oaths; shorthand writers collect speech rather than speak. Observers sitting in the public gallery do not have any speaking rights at all, and may be imprisoned for **contempt of court** if they call out, applaud or take part in some other kind of disruptive behaviour.

The complexity of the speech situation constructed in courts in terms of roles, rituals and rights can be highlighted by introducing a further contrast, that between professional participation and participation by legal amateurs. Some litigants enter the discourse arena described above without legal representation (they are known variously as **self-representing litigants**, 'unrepresented litigants', **litigants in person** or **pro se litigants**). Such litigants attempt to participate in court interaction on the same footing as lawyers; but many enter the courtroom without any understanding of relevant speech styles or turn-taking, as well as ignorant of legal procedures and rules of advocacy or evidence. Such litigants often underestimate the contribution made to legal outcomes by speech event structure, trusting instead that they will be legally successful if or because they have a good case and will simply tell the truth. But since adversarial trial procedures have evolved as a complex, rule-governed discourse process, unrepresented litigants often struggle to adjust their speech to the continuous and subtle balancing needed between content, speech style and trial procedure, or to combine their narrative of disputed events with exposition of a legal problem. Because of limitations imposed by their **communicative competence**, some introduce strategies not permitted by legal procedures, such as calling names, exaggerating claims, or making additional, serious accusations or even threats. Judges may try to treat such discourse difficulties sympathetically, in order to ensure as fair a trial as possible, but can only do so by risking compromising judicial neutrality and creating a possible ground of appeal.

PERSUASION IN COURT   A5

In this unit, we introduce the topic of how advocates talk. We show how courtroom persuasion by lawyers is 'rhetorical' in the historical meaning of 'rhetoric', which combines eloquence with strategic patterns of reasoning and expected standards of proof. We conclude with an outline of moves and structures that together make up the advocacy involved in legal proceedings. This description serves as an introduction to closer analysis of linguistic techniques in the language of advocates in Unit B5.

Legal advocacy

Silver-tongued, probing eloquence by lawyers addressing the court is the familiar representation of a distinctive style of lawyer talk. This image of **advocacy**, however, is highly selective. It is also in some respects anachronistic. In English law, to take one example, jury trial has declined in frequency since the mid-nineteenth century fairly dramatically, despite its continuing popular endorsement as a democratising feature of the legal system (Zander 2015). Currently, less than 1 per cent of all criminal cases are tried before a jury; and access to **jury trial** in civil proceedings is restricted to a very small (and diminishing) number of causes of action. The reality of courtroom advocacy, where it occurs, is more one of strategic preparation, case management and variation in style adapted to hearings at different levels in the court hierarchy, rather than grand courtroom **oratory**.

In those cases where criminal courts are addressed by advocates in the presence of a jury, the common-law approach is adversarial rather than inquisitorial. The style of address adopted is ultimately combative, in that the advocate's aim must be to win on behalf of his or her client. Any obvious impression of gladiatorial engagement is offset, however, by professional politeness and etiquette. The merits of such an adversarial system have been widely debated in law, as well as in analyses of modern societies' overall discourse ecology (see Tannen's 1999 account of 'argument' cultures). The **adversarial system** is also defended by analogy with debating, where it is also put forward as the optimal way to discover truth through powerful statements made on each side of a question.

This is the context in which the modern language of advocacy must be understood: as simultaneously a vehicle for legal exposition and reasoning; a management task of eliciting anticipated evidence from witnesses and cross-examining them; and as strategic persuasion of a jury (if there is one), or encouragement of a judge or judges towards a favourable adjudication. Many practical manuals exist on how successful courtroom advocacy is achieved (e.g. Morley 2009); there are also accounts examining the historic-ally changing role and styles of advocates (e.g. Du Cann 1993). This unit links such insights to descriptive linguistic analyses that we explore further in Units B5 and C5.

Development of forensic rhetoric

Because modern courtroom speeches by lawyers are often still perceived as grand oratory or rhetoric, it is helpful to set the development of legal rhetoric in historical context. This is all the more important because the history points to close connections between formats of legal speaking and dialogue, on one hand, and systems of reasoning and democratic structures of political participation, on the other hand (Goodrich 1986: 168–208). The word **forensic** itself, for example, with its modern meaning of 'legal', derives from Roman 'forum', which simultaneously meant a political and legal assembly.

Among the earliest accounts of Western legal courts are those from classical Greece (though the wider, international context of other kinds of court should not be overlooked). Such accounts typically begin with Solon, in the eighth century BC, and with episodes in the Homeric epic poems. Recognisably legal hearings are known to have been held in Athens from about 400 BC. What amounted to an 'appeal court' in that period is striking by comparison with modern conventions: it involved an unregulated and often politically partisan equivalent of a modern jury consisting of up to about 500 people. Proceedings in such a setting encouraged recognition by defendants of the value of skill in verbal argument; and the gradually emerging field of **rhetoric** (the classical discipline concerned with techniques of public argument, evaluation and refutation) became a widespread feature of education among the political class in anticipation of a need to argue a legal case in that setting.

By the time of Aristotle's *The Art of Rhetoric* (about 350 BC), cultivation of public speaking had settled into three strands: deliberative (concerned with the future, and suited to political persuasion); forensic (concerned with things that had already happened, and suited to legal argument); and epideictic (concerned with praise, and suitable for ceremonial occasions). Each was characterised not only by verbal devices, but by specific forms of reasoning and proof deemed to be persuasive in the given setting. Aristotle's *Rhetoric* contains a whole section on litigation strategies, followed up in later sections outlining proofs, refutations and an analysis of what is usually translated as 'altercation', or techniques used in the face of contestation of rhetorical proofs by an opponent.

One important feature of the subsequent history of rhetoric was a series of philosophical controversies surrounding the role of verbal skill. One tradition, associated initially with a group of philosophers called the **sophists**, emphasised how far rhetoric allows a speaker to argue successfully on behalf of virtually any proposition. In a non-philosophical context, that view is sometimes echoed in modern questioning of legal advocacy (e.g. whether counsel genuinely believed clients they have vindicated or had acquitted in court). Philosophically, this view was attacked by Plato in his *Gorgias*. Plato considered it a fundamental problem of justice and democracy, hence the very different direction developed in his *Republic*. Another, contrasting tradition (associated in earliest forms with Isocrates) emphasised how far speech provides a basis for human civilisation, with implications as regards the structure both of politics and law. Each of these currents has persisted. So has a further divergence: how far the style and substance of verbal expression are necessarily interwoven; or, alternatively, whether verbal devices can be detached as simply ornament, independent of situated forms of reasoning of the kind propagated in political debate or law.

The divergence is hardly insignificant. Historians often note, for example, that rhetoric in both law and politics declined following the conquest of (largely) democratic classical Greece by Macedonia, and then how, after being revived in legal structures of the Roman Republic (e.g. by Cicero), rhetoric declined again during the Roman Empire. It underwent a further period of mixed neglect and renunciation in the Middle Ages, before being rehabilitated as part of a revival of classical learning during the Renaissance. Rhetoric then suffered another period of decline in the face of newer, 'scientific' views of the relation between language, persuasion and truth in the course of the seventeenth century. But by that time, rhetorical reasoning and eloquence had already been absorbed into specialised legal training and, partly fortified by legal conservatism, the combination of the two has continued in modified forms through to the modern period.

The absorption of aspects of the rhetorical tradition into legal advocacy is significant in relation to language and law for two reasons:

1   Legal advocacy emphasises the high value placed in legal formats on verbal submissions and the weighing of evidence as the appropriate means for achieving just outcomes. This sense of the value of skilled speech brings together different levels of legal thinking: from day-to-day courtroom pleading, through the structuring of legal hearings around formats involving verbal disputation (opening speeches, evidence, summing-up, etc.), to the fundamental formulation and operation of law in democratic societies.
2   Understanding legal reasoning as a kind of rhetoric involves acknowledging that styles of persuasion and argument necessarily adapt to different purposes and settings. Classical rhetoric identified and described specific lines of argument. But it also showed how stylistic register must be modulated for different purposes and audiences, and drew a distinction between high, middle and low styles of language suited to different kinds of speech event.

Changing styles of legal advocacy – from the now often parodied grand oratory of trials in some periods to the low-key interaction of other periods and other kinds of tribunal – reflect a practical connection in advocacy between purpose, style and outcome.

Changing styles of advocate speech

The contrast between legal rhetoric conceived as high oratory, and understood as strategic argument adapted to the needs of particular settings including courtrooms, can be seen more clearly by looking at a short, historical example. Below, we present an extract from Edmund Burke's opening speech in 1788 in a famous impeachment hearing against the Governor General of India, Warren Hastings. Burke's style of legal oratory was hardly representative even of his own period, and would be virtually impossible in ours. But it was widely admired, and offers a striking contrast with modern styles of courtroom speaking and questioning we consider in our related Units B5 and C5.

The crimes which we charge in these articles are not lapses, defects, errors of common human frailty, which, as we know and feel, we can allow for. We charge this offender with no crimes, that have not arisen from passions, which it is criminal to harbour; with no offences, that have not their routine avarice, rapacity, pride, insolence, treachery, cruelty, malignity of temper; in short in nothing that does not argue a total extinction of all moral principle; that does not manifest an inveterate blackness of heart, died in grain with malice, vitiated, corrupted, gangrened to the very core ... [. . .] As to the criminal, we have chosen him on the same principle, on which we selected the crimes. We have not chosen to bring before you a poor, puny, trembling delinquent, misled, perhaps, by those, who ought to have taught him better, but who have afterwards oppressed him by their power, as they had first corrupted him by their example. Instances there have been many, wherein the punishment of minor offences, in inferior persons, has been made the means of screening crimes of a high order, and in men of high description. Our course is different.

(Burke 2002 [1788]: 274–5)

Burke's style is clearly 'rhetorical' at a number of levels (look closely at the passage to find evidence for each of the points below):

1   It addresses its audience as an aggregated public rather than seeking to persuade specific addressees.
2   It adopts a 'high' style of long sentences modelled on Latin periods (far more common then than now).
3   It embellishes points with lists of cognate words and syntactic parallelism and antithesis.
4   It uses formal and unusual words and phrases ('malignity of temper', 'gangrened to the core').
5   It contains archaism ('wherein . . .') and word order inversion ('instances there have been many').
6   It is organised and punctuated to highlight prosodic patterning when delivered as bursts of eloquence.

Note, however, that despite the oratory and although the passage begins with a clear statement of its topic, 'the crimes', several hundred words later we still have no idea what crimes are being alleged.

The scale and architecture of Burke's speech (which concludes with 11 parallel structures, 'I charge him with . . .', and 5 'I impeach him in the name of . . .') are also notable. But Burke's closing techniques now sound excessive rather than forceful. His opening speech overall lasted four days (not in fact the longest opening speech in English law, which reportedly lasted over a hundred days). The impeachment hearing as a whole was also epic in proportion, lasting more than seven years. At the end of the proceedings, after rhetoric from both sides, Hastings was acquitted. But while the prosecution itself was unsuccessful, Burke's opening speech remains widely admired and is still included in anthologies of advocacy.

Burke's legal oratory seems extraordinary now, and would be impossible in any modern courtroom. That is not entirely surprising, given general changes in discourse expectation and because more active judicial time management has been introduced to control costs. The grand style of courtroom address has nevertheless not completely disappeared from either the occasional reality or more frequent cultural perception of legal advocacy. Modern linguistic descriptions of advocacy therefore offer the prospect of showing what stylistic characteristics are actually involved; which techniques, if any, have been retained from the earlier rhetorical tradition; and how residual features have been adapted to fit the modern structures and contemporary style of legal proceedings.

Current practice: style, moves and event structure

In the course of an analysis of a corpus of modern Crown Court jury trials, the British linguist Chris Heffer describes the role of an advocate, at least in criminal trials, in a manner that contrasts markedly with the role we infer from the Burke extract above:

> The counsel is above all a strategist engaged in acts of persuasion: persuading the jury of the guilt or innocence of the defendant: convincing the judge of the legal admissibility or otherwise of an item of evidence; coercing the witness into answering in a certain fashion.
>
> (Heffer 2005: 95)

The contrast with Burke here is not only between high-flown public monologue and strategic effort to engage with the jury in order to persuade them. It is also to do with an organisational rather than oratorical emphasis, requiring orchestration of the voices of others as much as projection of the advocate's own voice. And as in other situations, speaking cannot be disconnected from listening. A modern trial will also involve long periods during which the advocate listens, taking material into account in anticipation of making a response later rather than speaking straight away – hence the theatrical metaphor often invoked in relation to legal trials of a play consisting of a series of acts.

Advocacy is not just a texture of eloquence. Rather, it operates at a number of levels: there is the immediate stylistic level of choosing appropriate words and sentence structures to match the needs of courtroom interaction and expectations of relevant addressees; there is a speech act level calling for choices whether, and with what strength, to assert, ask questions, request clarification, object, exhort; there is a level of more complex discourse moves including crafted monologues, taking witnesses through their evidence, and interacting with opposing counsel and the judge(s); and there is the macro-strategic level of managing the trial's overall, combined narrative and expository schema (which we explore in Unit D3, D4 and D5).

INTERPRETING LEGISLATIVE TEXTS **A6**

Few issues are more important in language and law than how meanings are given to written legal texts. In this unit, we show how emphasis in law on singular, correct interpretation differs from the descriptive and explanatory approach adopted in linguistics. In Unit B6, we extend this discussion by considering the reasoning processes used in 'construction' (i.e. legal interpretation) to arrive at the meaning of problematic words and phrases in texts whose legal effect depends on their legislative purpose, not only on the meaning of individual words or grammatical relations between them.

Legal interpretation as a specialised approach

When we interpret utterances in everyday conversation or casual reading, we pay attention both to linguistic cues to meaning (e.g. choice of words) and to contextual cues as regards speaker intention. Legal approaches to meaning follow everyday strategies in interpretation, but in different ways. Three differences are significant:

1   Legal interpretation (often referred to as **construction**, from the word *construe*) takes a normative approach to attributing meaning. It ascribes singular, correct legal meanings by *deciding* meaning where there is doubt or disagreement.
2   The process of ascribing a meaning, which occurs spontaneously in everyday communication, often takes place through an explicit process of argument. The legal interpreter, usually a judge, takes into account not only linguistic meaning, but also legal considerations such as the purpose of the relevant legislation.
3   In litigation, legal wording may be tested in an adversarial setting. Common-law proceedings allow alternative interpretations to be argued, but require courts to follow specialised interpretive procedures in arriving at a legally correct outcome.

This specialised approach to interpretation in law can make the process baffling to someone who insists that **natural language processing** is always an instantaneous and spontaneous process.

Disputes over meaning

Although legal language is drafted as precisely as possible, courts often find themselves having to decide the legal meaning of disputed words before they can apply the law. In a world of alternative understandings of facts, ideas and values, as well as differing preferences as regards behaviour, law is often relied on as the social institution to 'fix' – in both senses of 'define' and 'resolve' – contested concepts in a society. Think, for example, of what words such as *marriage, extremist, indigenous, traditional, terrorist* or *life* mean. Inevitably, questions arise regarding what concept or concepts such words denote; what range of characteristics or behaviour they subsume; and how they are to be understood in different contexts of use. Those questions are amplified when the society in which the words are used experiences major change in terms of technology or values.

Interpretive difficulties arise not only with individual word meaning, but from the linguistic contexts in which the words occur. Syntactic ambiguity, uncertainty created by punctuation, collocation with other words in a list, combination with other words using the alternative connectives *and* versus *or*, and the grammatical scope of added modifiers: all these, individually or in combination, can create local interpretive difficulty.

For instance, if a will provides that money should be given to 'charitable institutions and organisations', the question arises as to precisely which people, conducting what kinds of activity, constitute an *institution* or an *organisation*; this question is tied to what kinds of activity are *charitable*. These are matters of lexical meaning. But the question whether, under the will, donations can only be made to organisations that are charitable, or whether it is only the 'institutions' that need to be charitable – and whether donations must be made to both kinds of body or only either one of them – are different kinds of question: these are questions to do with how the already problematic words are configured into phrases and sentences, and how those phrases and sentences should be interpreted in context.

Many interpretive difficulties in law nevertheless gather around contested individual words. Consider the following example:

❑   A UK case concerned with Hindu cremation (*R (Ghai) v. Newcastle City Council* [2010]) addressed the problem that cremation of human remains could lawfully take place only within a building. Hindu beliefs required, by contrast, that cremation should occur in a place where sunlight can fall directly on the body as it is cremated. Did a place for cremation consisting of roofs supported on pillars, with low walls and a connecting balustrade, satisfy the requirement of being a 'building'?

A question of interpretation of this kind is hardly rare, given the vagueness, polysemy and contextual variation in meaning of many if not most words. Hutton (2014) offers an analysis of a large number of such word-interpretation issues, chosen from cases in a number of jurisdictions. Was a racing pigeon a *pigeon*? Whether two deaths in the same incident were *coinciding*. Whether a Jaffa cake is a *biscuit*. Did a wiretap constitute a *search*? Is the Cherokee nation a *foreign state* in relation to the United States? Whether a post-operative transgender woman is a *woman* for the purpose of marriage.

Interpretive issues in law, as can be seen in these examples, can arise in relation to different word classes. Problems are not confined to nouns, but also occur with verbs (to *murder*, to *associate with*), adjectives (*alive*), and adverbs (*foreseeably, forthwith*), as well as phrases rather than single words (e.g. *best endeavours, in the vicinity*). Further, because law governs virtually all areas of activity (health, family, commerce, crime, sport, etc.), problems of word and phrase meaning are not restricted to a particular semantic field. An English prosecution of prostitutes who invited their customers from behind windows and from an upstairs balcony, for example, turned on whether they were soliciting 'in the street'. A US case discussed by Schane (2006: 38–9) turned on whether matching skirts and blouses were 'ladies' dresses' for the purpose of a lease protecting the exclusive right of a retail store to sell 'ladies' dresses, coats and suits' within a particular building.

Uncertainty of meaning

Words have a number of **dimensions of meaning**. These range from what concept or concepts the word **denotes** and what class of entities it can **refer** to through to **connotations** and other kinds of personal association. The full extent of a word's meaning varies between situations and language users. But because of the kind of judgments law is called on to make, it is the **scope of word meaning** that presents the most persistent legal difficulty: is X (a reported fact) a member of a (legally stated) superordinate class Y? To understand how fundamental this question is in law, we need to consider the sense relation of **hyponymy** and the concept of inclusion it conveys.

The so-called **classical model of categories**, often associated with Aristotle but reflected in modern semantic theories such as Katz and Fodor's (1963) system of semantic features, suggests that category membership is a matter of essential attributes (or necessary and sufficient conditions). For something to be a *bird*, it must be animate, not human, have wings and a beak, make a nest, lay eggs, and so on. The resulting system of categories has clear boundaries but also allows anomalies: birds that cannot fly or that lay eggs on the ground, etc. In contrast, Rosch's (1978) psychological theory of **prototypes** proposed fuzzier categories that allow for different statuses of membership, based on **goodness-of-exemplar** (GOE) characteristics. Her prototype approach, subsequently developed in psychology and cognitive linguistics, results in a spread of category members ranging from core exemplars through to marginal, borderline cases. While a *robin* might (in some cultures) be a prototypical bird, an *ostrich* is less representative of the category. This is not because it lacks the essential attribute of flight, but because it is a less frequently encountered example of the category: informants typically mention it later when listing members of the category and verify its membership of the category slower in experiments.

These alternative models of categories come into play in law in interesting ways. First, because laws are enacted as general provisions to be applied in varied circumstances, legal interpretation is almost continuously concerned with testing the fit between general concepts and individual persons, facts, and circumstances. In disputed cases, courts rule on whether borderline instances fall one side or the other of a category boundary. What, for example, are a medical patient's *needs*: do certain resources or treatments come within the meaning of *needs* or not? Hard legal cases are often concerned, among other things, with whether low goodness-of-exemplar entities should enjoy rights (or be required to fulfil obligations) associated with a category to which they appear marginal, or whether an action at the periphery of a category falls within that category for the purpose of a particular law. By deciding which side of a categorical line something falls, legal judgments assign to peripheral instances legal consequences seemingly more suited to dichotomous, or clear-cut, boundaries between categories.

One widely discussed legal example illustrates the complexity. What types of moving machine can be a *vehicle*? Conceptually prototypical vehicles, such as cars, move along roads. But other exemplars show different degrees of closeness to the prototype: from tractors and ambulances, through roller skates and buggies, tapering to a periphery of candidates including aeroplanes. Deciding, in relation to a public park that forbids vehicles, whether someone riding a bike, driving a lawnmower or entering by ambulance to assist an injured person is guilty of an offence depends in part on how the word *vehicle* is construed. Yet enforcement of an adverse judgment may involve penalties suited to more uniform membership of or exclusion from the category.

Difficulties surrounding *vehicle* have been at issue in a number of legal cases (including at least one about aeroplanes). Seemingly inspired by one of those cases (the US Supreme Court case *McBoyle v. United States* (1931)), the English legal theorist H. L. A. Hart discussed a hypothetical legal rule, **No vehicles in the park**, in his *The*

Concept of Law (1994 [1961]: 126–30). Hart argued that legal rules are formulated in general categories provided by ordinary language, but those categories, stated without reference to context, cannot be 'closed' in relation to the variety of possible facts. There will instead be a 'penumbra of uncertainty' at any given category's borderline, such that a kind of **open texture** emerges when general classifying terms are confronted with particular facts. (A theoretically contrasting, but not incompatible, discussion of *vehicle*, from a cognitive semantic perspective, can be found in Croft and Cruse (2004: 92); see also our discussion of legal problems associated with translation of *vehicle* in Unit C10.)

Figurative imagery used in legal discussion of meaning

Use of words and phrases such as 'open texture' and 'penumbra' to characterise word meanings and categories is figurative. Hutton (2014: 26–9) examines use of such figurative language in judicial reasoning, especially in frequent appeals to binary oppositions in determining a word's scope.

The term 'scope' itself, Hutton points out, is a visual-spatial metaphor. Below a top-level contrast between 'literal' or 'plain' meaning and 'purposive' styles of adjudication (which we consider in Unit B6), a number of metaphorical contrasts are commonly invoked. One contrast, Hutton shows, depicts meaning as conceptual space: 'narrow' meanings contrast with 'broad', 'wide' or 'expansive' ones. Another trope involves degree of permissiveness: 'strict', and 'restrictive', meanings contrast with 'liberal' ones. The 'letter' is contrasted with the 'spirit' of a text's meaning. 'Ordinary' and 'natural' meaning is contrasted with 'forced', 'strained' or 'artificial' interpretation.

Through mobilisation of such conceptual contrasts, an entity may be judged to 'fall within' or 'fall outside' a legal category. So, a wide meaning of *vehicle* might include a power-assisted bike or trolley, whereas a narrow meaning might exclude those modes of locomotion. A strict interpretation of *tomato* might insist it is a fruit, while a liberal meaning might acknowledge common reference to tomatoes as vegetables.

In law, a range of factors are taken into consideration in deciding word meaning. An 1890s US case concerned with what a *tomato* was found that trade usage did not differ materially from popular usage; and dictionary definitions (used as an aid to memory and understanding) did not lend support to the idea that tomatoes were fruit. How tomatoes are consumed also suggested they were vegetables, and the court decided to give the word that 'ordinary' meaning (Hutton 2014: 80–3). The matching skirts and blouses case referred to above also drew on **extrinsic evidence**, including commercial usage and evidence of practices in the relevant trade. The skirts and blouses were not dresses, and there had been no violation of the covenant; but the vendor was required to price the two garments individually to reflect this, and not to compel customers to buy a matching set (Schane 2006: 39).

In the Hindu cremation case, Lord Neuberger emphasised that while the meaning of *building* inevitably depends on context:

> it would not be right to take a somewhat artificially narrow meaning of the word, and then see whether the context justifies a more expansive meaning. It is more appropriate to take its more natural, wider meaning, and then consider whether, and if so to what extent, that meaning is cut down by the context in which the word is used.

A number of the terms and contrasts that we have seen are used to characterise legal meaning are in play here, alongside the semantically vague adjectives 'right' and 'appropriate' (which cut across procedural, legal and moral vocabularies). Lord Neuberger's conclusion was that *building* should be given 'its natural and relatively wide meaning', such that Mr Ghai's wishes in relation to cremation could be accommodated within the relevant regulations.

This approach may appear to make the interpretive process vague, especially as English courts are not obliged to repeat the construction of undefined words from earlier cases, or reflect how the same word is used in other areas of legislation (though they often do). The purpose of confining cremations within buildings differs in obvious ways from, for example, the aim of the Theft Act 1968 (where *building* is also defined and has been tested in numerous cases). The Theft Act highlights a combination of specificity and contextual variability required in legal construction of word meaning. In s. 9(3), *building* is defined to include 'an inhabited vehicle or vessel, and shall apply to any such vehicle or vessel at times when the person having habitation in it is not there as well as at times when he is in'. It is as much legal purpose as closeness to prototype that subsumes an uninhabited waterborne vessel within the meaning of *building* but still finds a partly sideless room with a roof problematic.

Word meaning in context

Reference in legal interpretation to purpose (e.g. as communicated by the long title of a legislative act; see Thread 3) is a reminder that although words function as concentrated nodes of meaning, they are shaded or modulated on any occasion of use by other factors. Those factors include: the other words around them (**co-text**); previous instances of the same word elsewhere in the same discourse; the situation in which they are used; and background knowledge likely to be drawn on by an interpreter. If we are to understand how word meanings are used and contested in legal settings, therefore, it is necessary to situate interpretive disputes in both the legislative text around the word and also in how we inevitably draw selectively on surrounding, contextual information.

A7   THE VOCABULARY OF LEGAL POWER

In this unit, we examine the relationship between language, law and power, a connection we touch on in different ways throughout the book. Here, we address the specific question whether legal concepts merely describe, actively give effect to, or obscure social power. First, we introduce two key concepts at the intersection between any society's political and legal spheres: *power* and *order*. Then we explain why use of such words is difficult to disentangle when thinking about legal language. Finally, we examine how language use may suggest different possible relationships that law can create between power and order.

Power, order and law

Law is often defined in terms of *power* and *order*. Both terms are **polysemous**: that is, they have various related senses. The multiple senses are used, and meaningful, in law in various ways; and this makes it potentially difficult to grasp fully how law is using them (because their meaning in a given context might involve one or other shading of meaning). The words *power* and *order* are prime examples of a general tendency in legal language: that while words appear to have precise senses, their meaning in a given context can only be gauged by understanding relations between some or all of the possible senses available.

Consider *power* first, which is a highly abstract term. *Power* has been used and understood in many different ways in social science (e.g. as military, economic and political power) as well as in other contexts. In social relations, *power* signifies force or capability that confers an ability to influence situations, events or people. Often, such influence takes place without cooperation from relevant other actors. Capability to influence, accordingly, extends to authority, control and coercion. By a **metonymic** shift of meaning, in international relations the (now count noun) *power* means a country (or social group) considered to possess power in the other sense (e.g. an *emerging power, regional power, great power* or even *superpower*).

For any such power or powers, the (uncountable) abstract resource, power, is built up in a number of ways: through ability to impose political will by military force; by commercial monopoly or supremacy; or by projected personal power ranging from charismatic leadership, symbolism and ritual through to direct domination and subordination of others. Some forms of power are in consequence 'hard', or coercive; others are 'soft', working by persuasion and influence. Operating in tandem with political and enforcement agencies, law exercises both hard and soft power: it imposes obligations backed by sanctions including imprisonment, bans and fines (and, in some countries, execution), and it gives effect to incentives, voluntary codes and other alternative regulatory measures.

Now consider *order* and *orders*. *Orders*, in a narrow sense, are commands given by someone in a position of authority to bring about a change in a state of affairs perceived as not going in the right direction: a state of affairs not being *in order*, in a different but related sense of the term. The first of these senses of *order* has specific applications in law, being used to refer to legal decisions and documents such as *court orders, formal orders* and *restraining orders*. The second sense of *order* is different: it is the meaning present in *social order* and also found in the common phrase *law and order*. The meaning of this phrase can either denote a specific characteristic or condition of a society (one that has both law and order), or, confusingly, if the words are read together, then as a description of law being used to maintain or even create order: law brings about order by containing disorder. A still more abstract and neutral sense of *order* refers to how things are arranged, as in *alphabetical order*. And a further, related sense of the word, now with a positive connotation, refers to a system in which everything falls in the right place and seems to run satisfactorily by itself.

Given this range of meanings, precisely what *legal order* means appears **ambiguous**. The phrase may be used to describe how law is organised (e.g. the *international legal order*). Rarely in academic publications but frequently in everyday usage, the phrase can alternatively carry ideological and moral content: the way things should be run as compared with the alternatives, for example in polemics concerned with imposing or restoring legal order.

The concepts expressed by the words *power* and *order* often interact in discourse about politics and law. Consider the following sentence taken from the economic liberal thinker Friedrich Hayek (1978: 128):

> The effective limitation of power is the most important problem of social order.

What this sentence means depends largely on tension created between the two contrasted words *power* and *order*, and contrast between the two terms is developed in the argument being made: that while government is indispensable in protecting a society against coercion and violence from others (by using power to maintain order), as soon as it acquires a monopoly over use of force (and so has too much unconstrained power), then government itself becomes a threat (to social order). As we will see below, law – specifically constitutional law – is often the mediator of tensions of this kind.

Metalanguage of law and social organisation

How law conceptualises the relation between power and order follows from the kind of social organisation in which a legal system is embedded. This is often reflected in the **metalanguage** used to talk about law. We can see this in three highly simplified forms of social organisation:

1   In some forms of social organisation, such as tyranny or despotism, the power of a sovereign may be unlimited (i.e. there is no clear constitutional order). While in some circumstances such social organisation might be thought desirable, in order to protect a population from war and fear (as in the analysis offered by the philosopher Thomas Hobbes in *Leviathan*; 2008 [1651]), the practical **discourse of power** adopted in such circumstances will consist of commands from a sovereign, and compliance, supplication and appeasement from everyone else. The ruling power need not always be an individual: authoritarian governments also present themselves under a shield of law. For example, the Nazi regime referred to their legal measures as 'Gleichschaltung' (meaning 'synchronisation', 'bringing into line', or 'a forced kind of coordination'). From a contrasting perspective, Pedro Albizu Campos, leader of a Puerto Rican independence movement during the 1930s, famously commented that 'When tyranny is law, revolution is order', critiquing what happens when power (both the count noun and the abstract resource) is presented falsely as law.

2   In modern liberal democratic states, power is shared out by forms of political participation, including elections. Government power is constrained by a constitution: a body of law that defines the powers of and relationships between branches of government. The constitution of such states typically maintains a **separation of powers** between three branches of government (the executive, judiciary and legislative body), a separation believed to provide checks and balances preventing abuse by any one of these 'powers'. In other words, in such societies,

law is used to structure political 'power' into a distinctive 'order'. The rhetoric (or use of language) involved in law, in this perspective, aspires to be 'socially constitutive' in the manner envisaged by James Boyd White (see Unit D5): a two-way traffic of ideas between specialised professional practice (involving legal training, rules and deliberation in particular cases) and a participative legal culture of explanation, debate and consultation.

3   **Marxist theories of law**, by contrast, and a range of non-Marxist critical approaches influenced by them, conceive law differently. Law, in such frameworks, is a 'superstructure' brought into existence by private possession of the means of production with its consequent division of society into classes. The two main social functions law then performs are accordingly to regulate relations of possession and to control the struggle between classes (Hirst 1979). Taking the form (in more recent European Marxist theories, such as the work of Althusser) of an **ideological state apparatus** supplementing repressive state powers including use of an army, law restates existing relations of production in the form of delegated powers and rights (especially property rights). In such legal restatement, it secures a structure of political domination. In order to rationalise social relations of power, legal uses of language in this context disguise economic and political inequality as equality under the law, mystifying the relationship that actually holds between power and population.

The contrasts emphasised here highlight alternative ways in which uses of language to describe law translate different types and degrees of political power into what we recognise as legal systems, converting power into legal order. Language used to describe law is in this context therefore not just language describing law, but language managing a complex relationship between law and a wider ideological system from which such legal language must translate.

The language of constitutions

The general importance of the points made so far is that different social organisations are based on varying configurations of law, power and order. Many such configurations are specified in written or unwritten **constitutions**, which prescribe how political power will be channelled into, and stated as, the legal system. Some countries (including the UK) have no written constitution, but consider themselves nevertheless to have one in the sense of a set of principles performing the same function. Where a constitution *is* a written document, or group of documents, it sets out what are regarded to be fundamental principles of its form of government. The constitution, sometimes described by a different rubric such as **basic law**, may prescribe how rulers are chosen and how they can be called to account or removed. It may also regulate the behaviour of the main political actors; and it may indicate what rights an individual has against abuse of power (see Adler 2007). Such constitutions are legal instruments promulgated at particular historical moments, often following a political upheaval such as a revolution, civil war, or decolonisation. Once ratified, however, a constitution will typically have entrenched status; this means it can only be properly amended or repealed by some special procedure.

From a linguistic perspective, what makes constitutions interesting is that providing a framework for even the most basic principles underpinning the structure and purposes of a whole society calls for a great deal of detail. Article 1 of the US Bill of Rights (signed 1789, ratified 1791) suggests that some sections may be conceived in this way:

> After the first enumeration required by the first article of the Constitution, there shall be one Representative for every 30,000 until the number shall amount to 100, after which the proportion shall be so regulated by Congress, that there shall be not less than 100 Representatives, nor less than one Representative for every 40,000 persons, until the number of Representatives shall amount to 200; after which the proportion shall . . .

Alongside highly specified measures of this kind (whose precise quantification nevertheless distracts from how contextually influenced the figures inevitably were), other measures are expressed in very broad terms. Contrast Article 1 above, for example, with Article 3, generally known as the First Amendment:

> Congress shall make no law respecting an establishment of religion, or prohibiting the free exercise thereof; or abridging the freedom of speech, or of the press; or the right of the people peaceably to assemble, and to petition the Government for a redress of grievances.

Each phrase of this article calls for (and has received) close scrutiny, not least because measures of this second type raise difficult problems of interpretation concerned first with how general they are, and second with how far they do or should reflect the thinking and values of the period in which they were written, despite being intended to remain in force for an open-ended future period.

Faced with major interpretive challenges of many kinds, the field of constitutional law in any given society queries and interrogates, as well as states, that country's legal form of organisation. An **apex court** such as the US Supreme Court must combine these two processes in judgments that clarify constitutive rules that distribute power within the society (of the kind illustrated above: 'there shall be one Representative for every 30,000') while ensuring that the society's regulative rules are complied with (e.g. 'shall make no law respecting an establishment of religion'). Interpreted and reinterpreted in case law, the US Constitution – to take this pre-eminent example – has prompted an accumulating record (a 'living document') of arguments exploring fundamental questions concerned with the intentions, presumptions and general meanings represented by written constitutional words.

Constitutions, commands and rules

Constitutional arguments and decisions are a public process through which law engages with and dispenses political power, while also limiting power according to the principles of a distinct legal order. That process may be contrasted with what happens in most legal disputes, which are not concerned with testing the constitutive rules of a legal system, but more narrowly with applying its provisions. These two processes engage different aspects of power and require different powers. Critical approaches to law tend to emphasise law's closeness to singular, homogeneous *power*. But most statutes and legal procedures are concerned with plural *powers*: compartmentalised packets of delegated authority and duty conferred on and exercised by different legal actors (e.g. police officers, bailiffs, judges, etc.).

All this makes the functioning of language in law harder to comprehend, partly because of the roles played by polysemy and vagueness in many of the keywords involved. Something of what *order* signifies, for example, that *power* does not, is a reconstruction of coercive power into a system of social regulation observing the **rule of law** (a principle subject to divergent interpretations but often functionally contrasted with the 'rule of man').

Nor does the effect of different uses of keywords in law end with power and order. Introducing the idea of the 'rule' of law in fact extends the semantic task, because implementing the 'rule of law' will only involve 'rules' if rules are how law works (since *rule*, as a general social condition, may be exercised either by a ruler who issues commands or by one who follows rules). *Rule* and *order* can both denote states of affairs, or 'systems', or they can mean what people do to influence the actions of others (as those others carry out commands or comply with general instructions). It is almost impossible to extricate law's relationship with power and order from conceptual problems inherent in the terminology involved. Yet beyond the questions of terminology, how power is exercised in language also depends on how, in practice, rules, commands and orders operate.

REGULATION OF LANGUAGE USE   A8

In this unit, we switch to a different perspective on language and law: how language used in situations other than 'legal' contexts – in general communication – is treated if it becomes the subject matter of litigation. Examples of when this happens include cases of alleged bribery, harassment, trademark infringement, insulting or abusive verbal behaviour, defamation, and actions in a number of other fields. How language is treated in such circumstances differs from interpretation of statutes (where the language was drafted in anticipation of being read according to legal norms). It also differs from how oral or written evidence is treated in court (because the significance of evidential language lies primarily in what is reported rather than in effects on an addressee or other person of what is being expressed). In the 'general language' situations we now discuss, the main legal focus is on the meaning and effects of communication in the field of regulated public behaviour.

Communications in trouble

To begin, we outline the many ways in which verbal communication gets into trouble with the law, either by constituting criminal behaviour (i.e. where prosecution may follow) or when disputed in a civil case (i.e. where one party, who alleges harm, sues another). We can clarify this range of uses of language, and why they are interesting, by listing the main types. Greenawalt (1989: 3) begins an analysis of the topic by asking an often-neglected question (which he argues is essential in clarifying the boundary of protected **free speech**):

> What is the 'speech' that is to be free and protected? Does it coincide with the category of verbal and written utterances, or is it possibly narrower or broader in some respects?

As a route into this question, Greenawalt lists the main ways in which (under US law) a person may be guilty of a crime committed primarily or exclusively by communicating. His list (Greenawalt 1989: 6–7) is longer than the list below; our point here is less the detail than the range:

1 Agrees with another to commit a crime.
2 Orders, requests or induces another to commit a crime.
3 Threatens harm unless another commits a crime.
4 Puts another in fear of imminent serious injury by physical menace.
5 Participates in a criminal endeavour by communicating (e.g. providing information that makes the crime possible or conveying false information or advice).
6 Warns a criminal how to escape from the police.
7 Threatens harm if someone does not submit to sexual intercourse or perform some other act he or she is free not to perform.
8 Offers to bribe someone or offers to receive a bribe for the performance of an act that should be performed, if at all, free of such inducement.
9 Successfully encourages someone to commit suicide.
10 Entices a child from custody.
11 Uses provocative or insulting language likely to cause angered listeners to commit crimes.
12 Engages in speech likely to lead those persuaded by its message to commit crimes.
13 Makes a false public alarm (e.g. the widely discussed example of falsely shouting 'Fire!' in a crowded theatre).
14 Acquires property or some other material advantage by deception.
15 Pretends to hold a position in public service with the aim of getting someone else to submit to pretended authority.
16 Uses language or representations that are insulting or offensive.

A second list can be produced of ways a person's communications may give rise to civil proceedings. A full list of this kind would be more diffuse and complicated than Greenawalt's, but might begin with categories based on topics in media and intellectual property:

17 Publishes a defamatory statement (i.e. a false statement likely to lower someone it refers to in the estimation of others, or cause them to be avoided or shunned).

18 Publishes or broadcasts an advert that contains false and disparaging comments about a commercial rival.

19 Engages in commercial activity using a verbal trademark sign that is identical to or resembles an already registered mark currently in use for the same class of goods or services.

20 Posts online a parody caricaturing the opinions and mannerisms of a celebrity, so precisely conceived and drafted that it appears to be a genuine post by the celebrity himself or herself.

A list of this kind would be extensive, reflecting the complexity of legal causes of action as much as different kinds of verbal action. A third list might also be produced, of kinds of utterance or text that fail to satisfy standards prescribed by **extrajudicial regulatory codes** (e.g. codes used to govern press, broadcasting and advertising standards); and further lists again could be compiled of communicative acts restricted by rules stated in institutional **speech codes** (e.g. corporate or campus speech codes). In legal terms, the lists would relate and overlap in various ways.

Linguistically, the categories of discourse behaviour listed above cut across channels, situations of use, topics or areas of social activity, genres, and types of communicator (the last of these including people engaged in conversation, social media posters, tweeters and bloggers, government, national broadcasters, and the communications divisions of multinational corporations). There is nevertheless a shared question in disputes related to all of them: what is the meaning of the allegedly offending or infringing utterance? Only when that meaning is determined can the law or relevant regulation be applied.

The meaning and effect of ordinary discourse

There is no reason in principle why laws and regulations should not be applied to communicative acts in the same way that findings of fact are made concerning other areas of human behaviour. In practice, however, being certain of the meaning or effect of a disputed communication is made more difficult by the exceptionally complex and nuanced character of language: its ability to talk about past, present and future events, as well as about hypothetical worlds and situations that didn't happen; its ability to convey meanings indirectly, saying one thing but implying another; and its capability to perform one kind of speech act (e.g. a question) in order to perform a different act (e.g. a request or apology). Much of the complexity in communicative behaviour results from our capability to imply something more or different in what we say by anticipating that the recipient will make relevant inferences.

In **content adjudication** (as proceedings related to the kinds of dispute above are known), meaning must often be inferred rather than taken from the words at face value. A standard textbook example in defamation law states, for instance, that while 'Mr X went into 158 River Street' is not in itself defamatory, it becomes defamatory if the relevant readership would be aware that the address in question is a brothel (for an introductory account, see Quinn 2011; for a fuller discussion, see Barendt *et al.* 2014). Defamation law, as we see in Unit B8, has developed sophisticated procedures for dealing with such implied meanings.

The issue of directly stated versus implied meanings also arises in other fields of law. In verbal exchanges during courtroom proceedings, whether someone commits **perjury**, or lying under oath, may depend on implication as much as explicitly expressed statement. President Clinton's famous denial during Grand Jury hearings in 1998 that he had 'sexual relations' with Monica Lewinsky appears more like a lie if the context and purpose of the question he was responding to are taken into account, rather than when interpretation of his answer is restricted to the phrase meaning of *sexual relations* (Solan and Tiersma 2005: 224). Writers including Tiersma (1989) have emphasised the importance of including implied meanings alongside literal meaning in interpreting courtroom answers.

Key questions in a number of otherwise largely unrelated areas of law concern how implied meanings can be precisely described, and how likely any particular indirect meaning is. Neither task is easy. Care must also be taken with utterance effect. One common challenge faced by courts, for example, is what speech act a given utterance is performing (Schane 2006). Some speech acts, as we have seen (e.g. conspiring, bribing, inviting a bribe, threatening), constitute crimes. But while often such acts may take an explicit performative form, in many cases they are more likely to be expressed indirectly. As Greenawalt himself notes throughout his study, borderline cases of protected speech are often created where indirectness is introduced into communications that might in explicit form be criminal speech acts. Indirectness creates the appearance of a statement or opinion that merits at least some minimal level of protection. Given the importance and complexity of indirect speech acts in sensitive areas, it is unsurprising that in jurisdictions hospitable to **expert linguistic evidence**, speech act analysis has been deployed to examine what constitutes a felicitous (or successful) speech act of a particular kind, whether performed explicitly or indirectly. **Bribery**, for example, has been argued to consist of a structure involving several moves, each of which may be realised in largely predictable ways: problem, proposal, completion and extension (Shuy 1993: 20–65).

Protected and unprotected speech

The central question prompting Greenawalt's enquiry into different uses of language concerned why some communications clearly merit and others do not merit protection as free speech, while some communications raise problems at the borderline (e.g. a ranting 'political' diatribe that stirs up angry and potentially vengeful feelings in its audience). Closer analysis should make it possible, Greenawalt claimed, to illuminate this question by relating it to the characteristics of different kinds of utterance.

The generic term Greenawalt uses for communication is *speech*. This is one of two conventional terms (the other being *expression*) used in discussions of the role of communication in democratic social structures. *Speech*, in this sense, is not in contrast with writing, but (as we note in Unit B1) with action or conduct. Varieties of such speech may be distinguished by a combination of topic (political, commercial, personal, etc.) and purpose (to convey new ideas, to discuss or critique other people's ideas or values, to expose, amuse, titillate or gossip, etc.). Different forms of speech, in this specialised meaning, may then be treated as meriting different degrees of protection on the strength of the contribution they make to the democratic and liberal political values on which the principle of **freedom of expression**, or 'protected speech', is based. *Expression*, often used almost interchangeably with speech, also means communication in general. In European law, it explicitly covers *receiving* as well as imparting information: Article 10(1) of the European Convention on Human Rights (ECHR), for example, states that 'Everyone has the right to freedom of expression. This right shall include freedom to hold opinions and to receive and impart information and ideas without interference by public authority and regardless of frontiers'. (For comprehensive discussion of the concept of freedom of expression, as well as how it is constructed in different legal systems, see Barendt (2005).)

Ultimately, Greenawalt's concern with communicative acts is legal rather than linguistic. The borderline between speech and conduct is important in his analysis because it is where many difficult legal questions arise in US First Amendment jurisprudence (where balancing is undertaken between the constitutional benefit of the speech and the harms to which it might give rise, with a presumption in favour of expression). The same is true in Europe, where free speech rights allow necessary and proportionate restriction on expression (as listed in ECHR Art 10(2)). Linguistically, however, what is interesting in Greenawalt's analysis is a central insight: that virtually all the kinds of communication whose restriction seems *not* to raise free speech issues are what he calls 'situation-altering utterances'.

Influenced by the work of Austin and Searle (see Thread 7), Greenawalt offers a generalisation based on speech act types and the expression value accorded to them legally. But he avoids a simplification that might have followed from simplistic contrast between **performative** and **constative** utterances. A contrast of that kind, Greenawalt recognises, would suggest that Austin's abandoned category of constatives (which state facts, describe states of affairs or articulate thoughts) convey ideas and are therefore candidates for legal protection, while 'performatives' are social actions for which language is simply a vehicle, and so should be treated as actions, not 'speech'. Even a simplified contrast of that kind, Greenawalt points out, helps to clarify the celebrated US judge Justice Oliver Wendell Holmes's explanation, in a US Supreme Court judgment, of why falsely shouting 'Fire!' in a crowded theatre brings responsibility for the false warning and enjoys no free speech protection. But it leaves the problem of indirectly expressed meanings that create the borderline cases in terms of constitutional protection.

The distinctions Greenawalt advances on the basis of his analysis of speech acts help to illuminate a central doctrine of US First Amendment thinking: that there is an important boundary between communications that add to a socially valuable **marketplace of ideas** by their expression or critique of ideas and values, no matter how unpalatable, and communications that are primarily kinds of conduct: acts of harassment, first moves in a fight, verbal actions of subordination, and subjugation or intimidation of others. That boundary has been repeatedly tested and examined through concepts including **fighting words** (as kinds of provocation, or **inchoate action**) and **speech plus** (communications embedded in threatening behaviour or incitement; for detailed history and discussion, see Kalven 1988). In a later work, Greenawalt (1995) examines how similarly difficult issues arise in **hate speech**; in that context, the concept and implications of 'performative' utterances – principally that, as actions, performatives may be regulated without interfering with free speech values – have been significantly, and controversially, extended by MacKinnon (1993) in relation to pornography, and more broadly in Butler (1997).

Language and freedom of expression

The concept of free speech or freedom of expression is, in the end, a political or philosophical topic more than a linguistic one (for a short introduction, see Warburton 2009). That topic, however, is central to understanding how language functions – and what its value is – in modern democratic societies. Where the boundaries lie between protected and unprotected speech depends on analyses that depend on linguistic assessments, whether the distinctions made are formulated in terms familiar in linguistics or in an alternative, separately developed legal **metalanguage**.

Freedom of expression has become particularly controversial over the last two decades, not only because of obvious political examples of its curtailment. The concept is crucial in understanding new forms of language behaviour on the Internet, especially given widespread misapprehension that language use online is not regulated in the way that face-to-face interaction, print publication, broadcasting or film exhibition all are. Online verbal communication poses major challenges to regulation, including at least the following:

❑   New kinds of **speech event** are being created, blending formats of one-to-one dialogue, centre–periphery publication, variable participant and overhearer groupings (McQuail and Windahl 1993).

❑   Current and archived discourse are accessible together to an unprecedented degree, flattening different historical contexts into a continuous present.

❑   Communicators and recipients may have vastly different belief systems and background knowledge, challenging face-to-face notions of mutual background knowledge.

❑   Communicators and recipients are often located in different legal systems, with sometimes very different norms and restrictions regarding what can and cannot, or should or should not, be communicated.

A9   **FORENSIC EVIDENCE**

This unit describes how linguistic knowledge can in some circumstances contribute to the functioning of law through an applied channel: that of forensic linguistics. There are two main ways this happens. First, linguistic evidence is sometimes presented in particular cases, assisting the police, courts and regulatory bodies. Second, analysis of language use in the legal system and insights that follow from it can help to improve **access to justice**. In this unit, we illustrate the variety of linguistic work that takes place under the heading **forensic linguistics**. In Unit B9, we exemplify techniques involved in forensic linguistic analysis in several fields. Our overall aim is to show how expertise has been brought to bear by forensic linguists on evidential questions. In doing so, we also note difficulties associated with use of specialist linguistic evidence in law.

What is linguistic evidence?

Most work in forensic linguistics is concerned with linguistic evidence. But in order to understand the significance of this statement, we need first to clarify what we mean by **linguistic evidence**, as there are different ways of understanding this phrase.

Several senses come together in relation to the phrase forensic linguistics. There is *linguistic evidence* meaning language data: text messages, letters, product warnings, trademark signs, etc. associated with a crime or dispute. These are evidence in the sense that such data – in principle equivalent in potential to footprints, blood samples or ballistics – will be interpreted, embedded in a legal argument, and later submitted as evidence in a legal case. But there is also a second sense of *linguistic evidence*, meaning the informed interpretation of such data (i.e. of the other kind of 'linguistic evidence') by an expert linguist. Such linguistic analysis may take the form either of a written report or spoken courtroom testimony; and it may have a direct impact on the outcome of a case. A third sense of *linguistic evidence* should also be noted: that of cumulative, published or publicly stated knowledge gathered through linguistic research regarding how language works (or sometimes fails to work). When this kind of evidence is brought to bear on problems in law, it can contribute to reform of legal institutions and procedures by informing public policy (e.g. by improving arrangements designed to assist protagonists who are not native speakers of the language used in a court system).

Forensic linguistics can be understood as a combination or layering of these notions of evidence. It brings expert analysis of language use, based on linguistic research, to bear within the legal system on questions that involve contested material consisting of utterances, texts or some other manifestation of language behaviour.

Four functions of forensic linguistic analysis

We have shown how forensic linguistics consists of different kinds of work. Those kinds of work are undertaken across different fields of language. So in order to illustrate the scope of forensic linguistics, we need to outline both dimensions of difference, which we do here by describing four main professional areas.

Assisting in police investigation

Language evidence that assists criminal investigation or is presented in court as oral testimony by an expert witness is the popular image of forensic linguistics. This perception is shaped by media imagery of other, different kinds of forensic science. But we can still usefully start with this image. Consider two hypothetical situations that might benefit from linguistic expertise:

(A) Police investigators propose to assume a fake online identity to hunt for a paedophile. How should a 40-year-old policeman talk online so he sounds like a teenage girl?	(B) The police have an audio recording of a bank robbery. Is it possible to tell from the speech attributes of the bank robbers in the recording whether they were using their first or a second language, or where they come from?

It is easy in both cases to see how linguistic expertise might make a contribution. Police officers are not trained to analyse language. When they investigate crimes where some piece of relevant evidence consists of an utterance or text (e.g. a voicemail, an allegedly fraudulent document or suspicious text message), a linguist might provide useful assistance based on research into how language is used. In other scenarios, a linguist might be able to verify the region of origin of asylum seekers by identifying their native language (Eades 2005); or be able to point to a class of likely suspects on the basis of their accent or dialect (Tanner and Tanner 2004); or help decode secretive **disguise language** such as gangster jargon (an example of how a secret language of this kind was decoded can be found in Gibbons 2003: 294–5). A linguist might be able to match someone's way of speaking during a phone call to a type of speaker through analysis of features of voice quality (note, however, that telephone quality may affect recognition accuracy; see Nolan *et al.* 2013); or a linguist might be able to attribute authorship of an anonymous document, using techniques we examine in Unit B9. Because problems related to the language used commonly occur in situations involving crimes and legal disputes, the range of situations in which linguistic expertise can be useful is very wide.

Resolving language crimes

Many legal problems take the form of people's verbal actions, including talking, shouting, writing, making phone calls and sending messages. A surprising number of speech acts, especially performatives, can accordingly become the subject matter of a legal action (see the list in Greenawalt 1989, summarised in Unit A8). In each area identified by Greenawalt (e.g. offering a bribe, extortion, encouraging someone to commit suicide, issuing threats), evidence provided by a linguist as to how an utterance realises conventions of verbal behaviour in the wider system of verbal communication could help clarify whether some particular form of words might fall within the scope of a defined illegal act.

Language crimes, to use the term adopted by Shuy (1993), attach different degrees of importance to the three levels of speech act investigated in linguistics (first distinguished by Austin 1962; see Unit B7): the **locutionary** level (the act of making the utterance); the **illocutionary** level (the force of the utterance); and the **perlocutionary** level (the addressee's uptake as prompted by the utterance). It is the locutionary act, for example, that leads to liability if someone divulges confidential information without permissible grounds. Most crimes, however, are concerned with illocutionary acts. Since such acts are often indirectly performed, and can differ vastly from the direct or canonical version of a given act, proving that an utterance performs a particular illocutionary act may be difficult. This is where linguistic analysis has on many occasions been found by lawyers to assist in presenting a case. For instance, it has been shown to be possible to threaten someone by making a seemingly innocent enquiry, 'How's David?', in the middle of a disagreement (David being the addressee's son, so putting David's well-being in question; Shuy 1993: 109). The flouting of the Gricean maxim of relevance by introducing David's well-being as a topic prompts an implicature that this enquiry is still in some way relevant to the disagreement, and contextually therefore a threat. In cases of defamation, the same author (Shuy 2010) has shown how certain kinds of illocution (malicious intent or negligence) and perlocution (damage caused) may be illuminated by systematic linguistic analysis.

A different class of legal cases is concerned not with the defendant's verbal behaviour but with how police officers may have distorted the meaning intended by interviewees by fabricating confessions or altering witness statements. Traditionally, no evidence is thought more convincing to a jury than a suspect confessing to having committed the crime. Coulthard's (2002) comparison of the wording of murder accomplice Derek Bentley's confession with a corpus of police language, however, suggested that some features of the confession (e.g. repetition of temporal expressions including 'then' and 'I then') resembled the sociolect of professional police officers far more than they resemble the idiolect of a mentally impaired 19-year-old.

Linguistic evidence in textual disputes

In the examples discussed above, the data examined for alleged illegality are potentially criminal speech behaviour. Many civil cases, on the other hand, are concerned with disagreement about the meaning of a word or phrase in a spoken or more usually written contract, and with breaches of such contracts (whether or not a promise has been broken). Such cases are handled as disputes between parties rather than as crimes. In such actions, linguists can potentially assist in establishing, with greater reliability than other, more informal means of argument, the most likely meaning or effect in a given communicative context of a particular statement, where that meaning or effect forms the crux of a legal dispute.

Similar kinds of linguistic analysis may also be used to clarify obscurity in texts or aspects of a text. In an insurance claim dispute, for instance, an insurance company declined a claim from parents whose child had died of sudden infant death syndrome (SIDS), on the basis that illness or disease was not covered in their accident and life policy. McMenamin (1993), a linguist, distinguished the meanings of *syndrome* and *disease* by researching medical dictionaries and related literature on terminology, as part of a successful submission that SIDS fell within the scope of an 'accident'.

Another area of textual dispute cases is litigation surrounding trademarks. Where such marks are verbal (rather than graphic marks or sounds), these are proprietary marks (names, other verbal devices, sometimes slogans) used as an identifier of the commercial origin of a product or service. Disputes typically surround whether a proposed mark can be legally registered as a trademark: many cannot, if they are held to be non-distinctive, or descriptive (referring to the origin, nature, type, value or quality of the product), or generic (referring to a general class of products). Among other difficulties, to register such marks as trademarks might confuse consumers as to the commercial origin (and quality) of goods and services they are searching for, and could restrict how other companies can market their own, competing products or services. In some cases, a further problem is of a mark potentially disparaging an already registered mark that has built up a reputation in the marketplace. Beyond initial registration proceedings, issues arise regarding whether one company has infringed another's proprietary rights; in such circumstances courts need to establish whether the junior or later mark is similar enough to create consumer confusion, or if the later or junior mark has taken unfair advantage of the senior mark. Businesses invest in designing and promoting their trademarks, and vigorously protect their proprietary rights in them against competitors. Linguists in some jurisdictions have acted, often alongside market survey researchers, as consultants providing reports and testimony examining similarity between signs in terms of sound, form and meaning. In one US case, for example, Butters (2008) testified that the pharmaceutical names *Aventis* and *Advancis* were similar enough to cause demonstrable confusion; and Shuy (2003) reports evidence he submitted in 10 other US cases.

Analysing legal consequences of communication failure

Given the centrality of language in legal procedures, how effective communication is can be a persistent issue (e.g. whether a participant or group of participants can understand an essential document, spoken question, or request). Communication failure may also occur, as we have seen, when lawyers communicate with non-lawyers because of the technicality (including obscurity) of legal language. Some population groups are particularly vulnerable in their encounters with the justice system, partly as a result of their **language competence**: prime examples are non-native speakers, the deaf or hearing-impaired, and children (related examples can be found in Unit C9).

Some challenges presented in law by communication are more fundamental. Jurors, as we have seen, are laypersons who (in serious criminal and some civil trials in common-law jurisdictions though rarely in civil law systems) decide on the facts found in a case. How much jurors understand of a trial, however, is inevitably affected by social factors, including level of education. Yet any process of jury vetting on the basis of demographics risks betraying the rationale for jury trial as 'trial by peers', since jury trials are not only a means of preventing abuse of power by the state, but also of bringing the justice system closer to the communities being served. Given the division of responsibility between judge and jury in a jury trial, it is essential that jurors understand what decision they are being instructed to make. Despite this, forensic linguistic research on jury instructions – which are sometimes presented in written form to ensure efficiency, consistency and legal accuracy (Heffer 2008) – suggests that they are frequently incomprehensible to the people who need to apply them.

Another site of comprehension problems in the legal system is communication between laypeople and law enforcers. Second-language speakers, juveniles and first-language speakers who have received relatively little education have been found to have difficulty understanding **police warnings**, sometimes with serious or even tragic consequences. Prescribed warnings are often literally that: drafted in advance in formal language, then simply read out. They sometimes contain long, complex grammatical structures and difficult words (Rogers *et al.* 2008), and many people receiving such warnings have been found to have waived their rights without understanding the information they have legally been given.

Another source of communication failure in legal procedures is invisible to most courtroom participants. It arises from how meaning may be lost in **translation**, when speakers of foreign languages interact with a court through interpreters. Research (e.g. by Berk-Seligson, analysing over 100 hours of tape-recorded US trials involving Spanish speakers; Berk-Seligson 2002 [1990]) shows how the quality of interpreters has a significant impact on how witnesses are perceived, and therefore potentially on how cases are decided. Translation inaccuracies are not only semantic. It has been shown that by inadvertently skewing the tone of testimony, interpreters can make a witness appear less cooperative, less likeable and less credible.

The forensic linguistic contribution

Not all forensic linguistic work is concerned with evidence used in criminal investigation or submitted at trial. Other forensic linguistic contributions examine and may critique the wider conduct or performance of law, and seek to assist in refinement or reform of legal procedures. While investigative and courtroom work is often commissioned as a commercial service by authorities or parties to a case, this broader, second kind of work concerned with reform or enhancement of legal procedures is usually undertaken by linguists who are proactive, socially engaged researchers. This kind of work may still have an effect on a given case (e.g. demonstrating communication failure as a potential ground for appeal); but it is more likely, if it does have an effect, to prompt review of a relevant policy or form part of a campaign for greater public awareness of problems regarding the fitness for purpose of some aspect of the legal system. Where analysis of how language works (and sometimes fails to work) in law is the main aim, forensic linguistic analysis can be found at any meaningful interface between language and law. In such circumstances, the term *forensic linguistics* functions as an alternative term almost interchangeable with the broader expression 'language and law'.

LEGAL ORDER AND LINGUISTIC DIVERSITY

A10

This unit introduces a topic implicit throughout the book but not directly addressed in previous units: how legal systems deal with speakers of different languages who come into contact with law, without compromising consistency of legal interpretation or fairness in proceedings. We describe the interaction that takes place between the idea of legal order and linguistic diversity, in arrangements known as legal bilingualism or multilingualism: the organisation of legal systems to function in two or more languages. Complications and challenges associated with such legal-linguistic structures are examined.

Law and multilingualism

Although the exact figure is disputed, it is estimated that there are over 7,000 living languages today (www.ethnologue.com). This number is all the more striking given that there are fewer than 200 independent states in the world (193 of them member states of the United Nations). Although the number of languages is not distributed evenly geographically, **linguistic diversity** is a fundamental human condition that virtually all states have to deal with in one way or another. States manage their linguistic diversity differently, however. Some, such as Belgium and Switzerland, adopt two or more languages as official languages for administration and in the courts; this gives rise to **bilingual and multilingual jurisdictions**. Others practise monolingualism, prioritising one national language as part of a nationalist identity or ideology and offering speakers who do not speak the **official language** only reduced rights (Pupavac 2012).

About one-third of sovereign states in the world now have two or more official languages. Some monolingual states also have two or more official languages in specific regions (Leung 2016). Due to the legacy of the British Empire and the rise of English as a global language, English is an official language in a significant number of these polities. To varying degrees, these polities may also have to function bilingually or multilingually in their law (a phenomenon known as legal bilingualism or legal multilingualism). This arrangement inevitably introduces additional complexity into all the language-and-law issues discussed in this book. Nor are the challenges confined to the bilingual or multilingual jurisdictions alone. All jurisdictions, whether multilingual or monolingual, need to deal with delivering justice to linguistically diverse communities, given the recently increased mobility of populations and frequency of transnational legal encounters.

Before we look at the challenges posed by multiplicity of language to legal systems, we need briefly to review how and why such issues have arisen. Some states are bilingual or multilingual because of linguistic diversity that existed at the time of the state's formation, whether by peaceful or military means. But the major reason legal systems today have two or more languages relates to European expansion and colonisation between the sixteenth and nineteenth centuries. Political boundaries were imposed for reasons that did not always respect language differences. Following decolonisation, a large number of postcolonial countries and territories in Asia, Australia, Africa and the Americas have retained legal systems imposed by colonisers; these legal systems are embedded in the former colonial languages, which continue to compete for status with local languages and, according to some, amount to a form of linguistic recolonisation or **linguistic imperialism** (Phillipson 1997). Examples of such postcolonial jurisdictions include Canada, Cameroon, Hong Kong, New Zealand and South Africa. Such jurisdictions may operate at a substate or state level. A third category of jurisdictions that operate multilingually consists of regional or global organisations that have created new kinds of globalised legal order, drawing on international law. Supranational bodies such as the World Trade Organization and the United Nations have their own judiciaries, which use multiple languages (predominantly English and French, sometimes also Spanish). The European Union, a political model for a new kind of transnational democracy, has 24 official languages from among its members states, partly because its laws are applicable not only to the governments of the member states themselves but also have direct effect on individuals and organisations within them.

Notwithstanding the obvious challenges posed by multilingualism to how a justice system operates (which we review below and explore in greater detail in Unit B10), granting enhanced status to **regional languages** has become increasingly common in Western democracies. Although it is difficult to weigh benefits against obstacles, political philosophers Kymlicka and Patten (2003: 5) observe that 'countries that have moved in this multilingual direction are amongst the most peaceful, prosperous, free, and democratic societies around'.

Representing law in more than one language

Legal translation is one of the first issues to arise when contemplating how to develop law in multiple languages. But translation is only one aspect of a more complex multilingual legal practice. Certainly, need for legal translation has increased, both nationally and internationally. But an important question beyond need or amount also arises: what status do translations have? In some jurisdictions, a translation of a law becomes more than a translation: it acquires the full force of law based on an **equal authenticity principle** that we consider below. In such circumstances, where both documents are operative, uniform application of law depends critically on quality of translation. If versions of law that are both deemed legally authoritative give rise to two or more different legal outcomes, then unfaithful or inaccurate translation of a legislative text may compromise the certainty of legal decision-making (a principle of consistency of legal effect known and valued as **legal determinacy**).

Problems with legal translation are particularly contentious in postcolonial jurisdictions. Many such jurisdictions retain their former colonial legal system, including foreign legal concepts and the former colonial language. Legal translation is a necessary step in introducing the local language(s) into the legal system and so elevating their status. In some countries, this was a legal imperative born in political struggle. But languages elevated in status this way are often criticised for lacking necessary vocabulary or the sophistication to function as a legal language, perpetuating a widespread colonial discourse of presumed superiority. Before inferring superiority or inferiority, it is, however, necessary to acknowledge that linguistic differences between a former colonial language and the native or so-called vernacular languages may contribute to difficulties in translation (for instance, as between English and Chinese in the former British colony of Hong Kong).

Translation problems extend beyond translation, if that practice is conceived narrowly. To translate is to interpret and to interpret is to translate. In this respect, the longstanding debate in translation studies as to whether a translation should be literal or free (idiomatic) runs in parallel with the 'letter versus spirit' debate in legal interpretation, which also concerns a choice between relying on a literal reading or construing the wider purposes of law (see Thread 6). Fidelity to a source text provides a guiding principle in general translation; but legal translation must be concerned ultimately with transfer of legal content rather than linguistic or cultural equivalence, so emphasis needs to be placed on equivalence of legal effect rather than on textual identity or similarity (Šarčević 1997). The legal translator must play the role of a comparative lawyer (Šarčević 2012) in their search for translation equivalents.

In recent years, methods of legal translation have undergone major transformation in order to ensure the quality of legislative texts written in different languages. Instead of translating law from one language into another, a number of advanced bilingual and multilingual legal systems have begun to employ **jurilinguists** (in Canada) or lawyer-linguists (in the EU): professionals who have a combination of language skills and legal knowledge, and who work together in drafting multilingual law. This method, known as **parallel drafting**, allows the co-drafters (who are no longer seen as translators) to preserve the original intent to be conveyed by a given law by working directly with the legislature, without the mediation of a source text in one particular language (Šarčević 1997).

Because of its 24 official languages, the EU has moved away from direct translation as a realistic approach. McAuliffe (2012) explains how instead an approach known as **pivot translation** has been developed in and for the European Court of Justice (ECJ, now usually known as the Court of Justice of the European Union, CJEU). Procedural texts such as written statements and oral submissions that are written in any one of the newer official languages are translated first into one of five 'pivot languages' (French, English, German, Spanish and Italian) and only then translated from that pivot language into other official EU languages.

Understanding legal texts written in two or more languages

Legal texts raise difficulties of interpretation as well as composition. Imagine a situation in which each language version of a particular law led to a different legal outcome. Lack of legal certainty would undermine public confidence. More importantly, the differing outcomes could result in chaos if implemented. Interpretation rules need to be devised specifically for multilingual situations.

Such rules raise once more the question of what status is to be accorded to each language version of a legal text. This issue needs to be clarified in interpreting multilingual legal texts before dealing with particular textual elements. Some jurisdictions, as we have seen (including Canada, Hong Kong and the EU), assign equal authority to different language versions, following the 'equal authenticity' principle introduced above (which is generally adopted in international law). Others specify that one language version will prevail where there are discrepancies (e.g. Maltese prevails over English in the laws of Malta; in Ireland, the Irish legislative text prevails over the English text). There is also a third possible relation between legal texts. In some circumstances, legal instruments are translated for informative purposes only, and have no legal authority. The German text of Belgian law is an example. One major difficulty associated with this treatment of two languages, however, is that citizens cannot rely fully on a version of the law that carries less authority than a version in another language. Whereas local discrepancy might not matter in many textual genres, with a legal text authority is perhaps the essential characteristic readers require.

Under the equal authenticity principle, all language texts of the law are presumed to carry the same meaning. Where discrepancies are found between texts, it is not permissible for an interpreter to assume that one language version better represents legislative intent, even if that version served at an earlier time as the source language for translation into other language texts (i.e. in a manner resembling appeal to legislative history in monolingual interpretation). Normally, interpretation of either text or both starts with **plain meaning**. If ambiguities are identified within a text (so-called intralingual indeterminacy), or if discrepancies are found between equally authentic texts (interlingual indeterminacy), then the putatively divergent language texts are compared for their respective levels of clarity and degree of meaning overlap. Sometimes the shared meaning, or meaning with less ambiguity, will be adopted. Where this way of resolving the problem proves unsuccessful, the ultimate criterion is legislative intent. In other words, a literal approach may in interpreting multilingual legislation need to be supplemented by a **teleological (or purposive) approach**, at least in some circumstances.

Where a jurisdiction has many language versions of its law, such as the 24 language versions available for comparison in the EU, a meaning carried by the majority of language versions may be given more weight. From the perspective of this kind of linguistic-democratic procedure, having multiple language texts may be an asset: a means of clarifying ambiguities contained in one language text by multiway comparison. It appears, however, that use of this strategy is relatively infrequent in jurisdictions with only two or three possibly divergent versions. In such circumstances, the more limited number of texts might create legal uncertainty by introducing interlingual indeterminacy, rather than converging on a shared meaning.

The question arises whether legal predictability is compromised in such procedures. Legal meaning, for example, is sometimes extremely difficult to determine even by close reading of one single, authoritative text of a given law. Yet even what constitutes that 'text' to be interpreted in the practices described can be uncertain, appearing to consist of a **mega-text** made up of all coexisting official language versions. The very fact of their coexistence raises practical issues. Can an average citizen, for example, living in a jurisdiction whose law is embedded in an amalgam of multiple versions, be said to understand that law if he or she relies on only one version? The 'mega-text' concept presumes an interpreter of multilingual law – not only a drafter – who is multilingual, and familiar with the renderings of law in different languages. Another practical issue is that comparison between languages is not an unproblematic concept. Do comparisons between language texts need to be made continuously, or only monitored periodically? It may even be the case that other language texts are only scrutinised when one party sees a strategic opportunity in doing so, and not otherwise. Some jurisdictions attempt to overcome this difficulty by routinely comparing different language texts of the law, even in the absence of any alleged discrepancy.

Linguistic access to legal procedures and practices

The challenges associated with translation between legal languages are formidable. Beyond translating authoritative sources of law, however, multilingual jurisdictions also need to ensure linguistic access to other forms of legal communication.

Spoken communication in the courtroom is an obviously important area. While some bilingual and multilingual jurisdictions offer the defendant a right to be tried in an official language of his or her choice, more often the question of which official language is used in proceedings is left to the court's discretion. For practical reasons, although many jurisdictions give official status to more than one language, few provide officially for use of more than one untranslated language in the same trial. Yet such de facto bilingualism does occur in the courtroom. A practice of **language alternation** in courtrooms in Botswana, Kenya and Malaysia is reported in Powell (2008), for example. Sometimes **code-switching** is also strategically employed by legal advocates, to foreground style shifting or in order to achieve calculated rhetorical effects.

Such bilingual discourse can be a source of significant difficulty for a court interpreter, and is rarely reflected in the court record.

Even in monolingual jurisdictions, it is usual for courtroom interpreters to be assigned to witnesses or litigants who speak a different language from the one used in the proceedings. Where this happens, original utterances rendered into the court language no longer have legal status. As we note in Unit A9, a sizeable research literature has documented the impact of court interpreters on the outcome of cases. But courtroom interpreting raises issues besides the quality of real-time interpreting itself: issues to do with **transcription** and recording. Where, as in many countries, no arrangement is made for audio and video recording of courtroom interaction, the written record captures only the interpreted, not the original, statements made by a witness. This makes it virtually impossible to retrace any injustice that may have occurred because of **misinterpretation**. An analogous problem arises when simultaneous rather than consecutive interpretation is used: words whispered by the interpreter into the witness's ear, for instance, are not normally picked up on the recording or heard by anyone else.

A further important but often neglected concern is access to legal materials. For a variety of reasons, multilingual jurisdictions tend to give more attention to translation of legislative texts than to making sure such texts are published, authenticated and disseminated in all the official languages. In common-law systems, there is also a further, substantial body of authoritative legal texts besides legislation: judgments communicated in law reports, which primarily declare but also contribute to developing the law. Making such reports available in multiple languages inevitably has a major cost implication that is not always taken into account alongside less tangible and sometimes abstract problems raised by language and law. But the extent to which such judgments and other legal reference materials are available also contributes to access to justice, especially given a recent, worldwide increase in unrepresented litigation.

Languages, law and policy

The complicated linguistic and legal situations discussed in this unit highlight important contemporary challenges in how language and law relate to one another. Some of those challenges are concerned with legal reasoning and judgment, informed by understanding of **cross-linguistic differences** and the rationale for the language policy adopted in a given jurisdiction. Other challenges involve practical issues of policy, education and investment. For example, legal education systems need to be planned and organised to deliver linguistically competent personnel. In Canada, fluency in both English and French is an essential requirement for appointment as a federal judge (except in the Supreme Court; Section 16 of the Official Languages Act 1988).

The issue of language competence applies to other courtroom roles, too, potentially including non-professional roles. Should language proficiency requirements be revised in relation to jury selection, for example, as has been debated in Wales (an issue we examine in detail in Unit D10)? Any such revision risks compromising a non-linguistic dimension of the fundamental rationale for jury trial: representativeness in the composition of a jury, based on random selection. Nor is training, in any obvious sense, an option. As yet, there appear no easy answers to many of the linguistic and legal dilemmas that arise in multilingual jurisdictions. While some jurisdictions currently require jurors to be proficient in the language of the proceedings, others prefer to provide interpreter services also for jurors. Whatever the best way of resolving such dilemmas, however, they undoubtedly foreshadow major challenges in legal systems of the future.

Section B

DEVELOPMENT

CONTEMPORARY APPROACHES

B1 LINGUISTIC FEATURES OF LEGAL LANGUAGE

In this unit, we look at the main features that have been attributed to the variety usually known as 'legal English'. We do this initially by working through Crystal and Davy's (1969) justly celebrated analysis of two examples of common legal documents: an endowment assurance policy and (what was then called) a 'hire purchase agreement'. Then we extend our discussion into a review of descriptive accounts by other influential scholars, including Mellinkoff (writing earlier than Crystal and Davy) and Tiersma (who later extended Mellinkoff's general approach). Once we have introduced key features of legal language, we raise questions of significance and method. Crystal and Davy's description of legal language predates large-scale corpus analysis in linguistics. We suggest some ways in which the analysis of legal language can be enhanced using such techniques.

The language of legal documents

Although Crystal and Davy (1969) do refer to historical forces at work in the development of legal styles, their account of legal language is mainly a synchronic one (i.e. a study of the language system as it exists at a selected point in time, usually the present). While their analysis is synchronic, however, it is no longer contemporary. Their chapter was published in an influential volume of 'investigations of linguistic style' that contrasted major situational varieties in English of the late 1960s. That is half a century ago – a long time, even in relation to a slow-moving linguistic variety such as legal style.

What is still valuable in Crystal and Davy's approach, however, is that the authors consider all the main aspects of language that play a role in creating style. Their analysis is guided by native-speaker impressions but builds up a picture by describing linguistic features: they start with questions of layout, work through sentence grammar and vocabulary, and conclude with general points about meaning. We can introduce the main areas of linguistic analysis of legal language by considering each of their categories.

Layout

The established perception of the layout of legal documents is that they are dense on the page, lack punctuation, and appear formal and archaic because they use fonts and devices associated with antiquarian styles of presentation and publication.

Some historical support for this view comes from the fact that much legal writing is not spontaneous, but copied from **form books,** or templates for writing documents that have evolved over centuries and been shaped by changing editorial and printing conventions. Such form books are either devised in-house by particular law firms or bought commercially. Important features of layout and design Crystal and Davy draw attention to include:

- ❏ solid blocks of text, sometimes a whole document consisting of one sentence, with 'few concessions to the convenience of the reader' as far as layout is concerned (Crystal and Davy 1969: 197);
- ❏ occasional, apparently ceremonial use of larger Gothic font;
- ❏ upper case used for first words of some paragraphs (e.g. WHEREAS, WIT-NESSETH) or words in the middle of sentences (e.g. AND), possibly echoing a decorative convention of the medieval manuscript tradition;
- ❏ capitalisation of particular words (mostly nouns), a practice that remains an established feature of modern German but was never consistent in English and became obsolete in general use by the late eighteenth century;
- ❏ no, or relatively little, punctuation; and
- ❏ some idiosyncratic spellings (e.g. legal 'judgment', rather than general English 'judgement').

Grammar

Crystal and Davy begin their account of sentence grammar with the observation that sentences in legal documents are often long and grammatically complex. Sometimes, a whole block of text may consist of only one sentence.

Their main insight is, however, a functional one:

> Reduced to a minimal formula, the great majority of legal sentences have an underlying logical structure which says something like 'if X, then Z shall be Y'. There are of course many variations on this basic theme, but in nearly all of them the 'effects' component is essential: every action or requirement, from a legal point of view, is hedged around with, and even depends upon, a set of conditions which must be satisfied before anything at all can happen.
>
> (Crystal and Davy 1969: 203)

Various formal features are capable of expressing, or being exponents of, this core rhetorical structure, whose function is to define legal relations. We can illustrate some of those formal features using a short sentence taken from a life assurance policy recently received by one of the authors:

(1) If the policy has not been dealt with it will be converted into a paid-up policy.

In a legal document, even a relatively straightforward but grammatically complex 'if, then' sentence of this kind is likely to be loaded with **adverbials** that specify conditions and concessions. Those adverbials may take the form of clauses (e.g. embedded *when*, *because*, clauses . . .), adverbs (e.g. *promptly*), or adverbial phrases (e.g. *in a reasonable period*). They may also be coordinated with one another by *and* or *or*, if there is more than one of them. Such adverbials tend to cluster at the beginning of sentences but may occur elsewhere in sentence structure.

Example (2) shows an adverbial towards the beginning of our illustrative sentence:

(2) If *at the end of the year* . . . the policy has not . . .

Example (3) shows that the adverbial may itself be modified:

(3) *If at the end of the year specified in (a) above* . . . the policy has not . . .

Example (4) shows an adverbial added elsewhere in the sentence, in this case after the main verb:

(4) If at the end of the year specified in (a) above the policy has not been dealt with *as in (a) or (b) above* it will be . . .

Incidentally, example (4) highlights, but deviates from, one of Crystal and Davy's other observations: typical avoidance in legal documents of **anaphora**. Anaphora means reference back to earlier discourse referents using pronouns or abbreviated forms (*he, she, it, they*, etc.). It is almost obligatory in most styles of English in order to avoid excessive repetition. By contrast, use of pronouns is extremely unusual in legal documents, in order to avoid creating ambiguity (the pronoun *it*, used in this example, is particularly problematic in this respect). Avoiding pronoun **coreference** conveys a distinct impression by creating a repetitive and mechanical form of cohesion within and between sentences. Instead of 'it' in example (4), the most likely legal choice would have been to repeat the noun phrase 'the policy':

(5) If the policy has not been dealt with . . . *the policy* will be converted . . .

Example (6) illustrates further complexity introduced into sentence structure by the fact that the main ('then . . .') clause also allows for added adverbials. Here is the second half of the example sentence in full:

(6) . . . it will be converted into a paid-up policy under provision 3 unless the conditions of that provision are not satisfied in which case a cash sum will be payable.

Note that here, an 'unless' clause adds another condition, which is in turn modified by a relative 'in which' clause. The resulting effect, of a kind usefully modelled diagrammatically by Crystal and Davy (1969: 203–5), shows complex relations of dependence, sometimes with several full or non-finite adverbials operating at the same, subordinate level. In this way, even relatively short sentences in legal documents, not much longer or more complicated than the one analysed above, may consist of, for example, the following functional elements:

If [Adv *and* Adv S V Adv *or* Adv], (then) Adv *or* Adv S V Adv *and* Adv.
Adv = adverbial
S = subject
V = verb

Part of the challenge in interpreting legal documents, which can be considerable, is to understand the logical structure of statements expressed by complex grammatical relations.

If we shift from functional analysis of relations within the sentence (subjects, objects, adverbials, etc.) to **constituents**, other patterns emerge:

> One of the most striking characteristics of written legal English is that it is so highly nominal; that is, many of the features in any given stretch are operating within nominal group structure, and the long complicated nominals that result are noticeable by contrast with the verbal groups, which are relatively few, and selected from a restricted set of possibilities.
>
> (Crystal and Davy 1969: 205)

Nouns tend not to be modified by adjectives (or premodified generally), and use of intensifying adverbs such as *very* in front of adjectives where adjectives do occur is almost never found.

By contrast, **postmodification** (i.e. use of adjectives, phrases or clauses after a word they depend on) is common. Sometimes such postmodification is highly detailed, and achieved frequently by reduced relative clauses: *the premium(s) in arrears together with any charge for loss of interest required . . ., payment will be made equal to interest on . . ., a rate decided from time to time.* Common within such **non-finite postmodification** (i.e. modification attached following the item being modified, and not amounting to a full clause) are examples that also show archaism: *herein contained, hereinbefore reserved, printed hereon.* Most distinctive of all is that postmodifying elements are inserted into sentences at whatever point offers the clearest indication of precisely what is being modified. An aim to achieve precision or avoid ambiguity, Crystal and Davy (1969: 205) observe in their discussion, 'always takes precedence over considerations of elegance, and unusual sequences are as a result common'.

Verbal groups in legal documents are notable for several characteristics:

- ❏ frequent negation (typically with a prohibitive meaning);
- ❏ a high proportion of non-finite forms (e.g. past participles); and
- ❏ high frequency of finite forms that follow the pattern:

modal auxiliary (usually *shall*) + BE + past participle

Shall is to be expected because this modal is used to express the obligatory consequence of a legal decision, rather than as a marker of future tense or to add emphasis (which are this modal's main functions in other varieties). Tiersma (1999) points out that unnecessary insertion of auxiliary verb form *do* is also common (e.g. 'I do appoint'), though both *shall* and AUX *do* are now discouraged in much current guidance on drafting.

Lexis
The most common perception about vocabulary in legal documents is that of **archaism**: both the use of fossilised forms (words and constructions no longer current in other varieties) and use of words and phrases that are still found but which retain specialised,

older meanings in law. Crystal and Davy (1969: 207) highlight WITNESSETH and *aforesaid* in their two sample documents. Combined with archaism is a preponderance of words of French origin, or of Latin origin via French, by comparison with words of Anglo-Saxon origin (a phenomenon discussed in Mellinkoff 1963). Similar imbalance occurs in other varieties of English concerned with learning or science, but results in a marked stylistic feature of legal English: that of **etymological doubling**. Such doubling, or chaining, involves collocation (i.e. juxtaposition) of synonyms or near synonyms coordinated by *and* or *or*: examples include *made and signed, breaking and entering, terms and conditions, able and willing*. Tiersma (1999) suggests that legal draftsmen simply got into a habit of using **word-pairs** in order to ensure inclusion of something, even if the reader was unfamiliar with one or other of the words used for it, rather than because some legally significant nuance had developed between the two words. The practice, Tiersma argues, survived simply because of legal conservatism.

Etymological doubling of this kind differs from another, ultimately more significant feature of legal documents: the (much criticised) particularisation of any given general concept by means of a long list of alternative words within the same semantic field, in an apparent effort to ensure mention of all possibilities (e.g. *the tenant shall affix to the wall no painting, hanging mirror, clothes hook, decoration, device, accoutrement . . .*); such listing tries to be exhaustive but can have a very different effect: that of drawing attention to any item missing from the list, and opening up each word in the list to legal dispute as to its meaning and scope (see Thread 5).

Vocabulary and meaning

More significant than either of these local features, however, as regards how style intersects with meaning, are the different kinds of vocabulary found in legal documents. A very wide range of terms is inevitable since almost anything can become a topic for legal stipulation. Within this very wide vocabulary, however, there are four notable kinds, each of which may be interpreted differently. The boundary between the four types is not precise or static (and our description here involves some simplification); but broad differences between them need to be recognised as creating an important field of contrast within legal language that does not exist in most other varieties:

1   Like other professions, law has its own specialised **terms of art**. These are technical words and phrases (such as *rescission, abatement*) whose use is restricted to law, and which have fixed, often complex legal meanings. Some are borrowed from Latin and Law French (e.g. *mens rea, estoppel*). Such terms cannot usually be replaced by other words without losing some essential aspect of their accumulated legal meaning and significance.

2   Closely related are words (e.g. *consideration, convenient, extortion, emolument, objectionable, provenance, promise, summary, trust, relief, instrument* and many others) that have a technical meaning in law but also one or more non-technical, different meanings in wider usage. Tiersma (1999) calls such words **legal homonyms** (in a sense of homonymy that does not require separate etymology, but is based on distinct meanings associated with two or more domains of use). Disambiguation of legal homonyms depends on context and register. Use of such

words can appear anomalous to a layperson, suggesting they must convey some different meaning from their meaning in other varieties of English.

3   Many other words function technically in certain legal texts but are not legal homonyms because they have not acquired a stable and distinct legal meaning. Definitions are often offered for such terms in a 'glossary of terms' or 'definitions clause' in the relevant document. But such definitions are not like definitions in a descriptive dictionary, which reflect usage. Rather, legal definitions are prescriptive guides to meaning, supported by authority to dictate what meanings will be accepted. By convention, such defined terms are often either capitalised or written in boldface in contracts and other documents, to indicate which ones they are.

4   Words and phrases not in any of these categories are generally referred to as **ordinary words** (of English). Such words include *building, dress, street, biscuit, foreign* and many others. Because legal statutes and private law documents concern all kinds of people, objects, events and processes, such words come from almost any sphere. Most never become the crux of an interpretive dispute. But if they do, it falls to the courts to decide what their correct meaning is for the purpose of the legal proceedings in question (through a process of 'construction' that we discuss in Thread 6).

The status of some expressions within this classification may be unclear. Some seemingly fundamental words of law, such as *beyond reasonable doubt*, are held for legal reasons to be 'ordinary words of English' even though they may sound like technical terms. Some idiomatic phrases are first used by an individual judge but become by frequent repetition quasi-technical expressions: the *innocent bystander* in contract law; *bane and antidote* as characteristics attributed to an allegedly defamatory statement; or *a shield not a sword* as a characterisation of promissory estoppel. What makes the four broad categories important in a description of legal English is how each is treated differently in tackling a problem of interpretation; solutions to such problems range from prescriptive definition through to cumulative modulation of a disputed word's meaning over time as a way to evolve the best (*convenient*, to use a legal homonym) match to a complex mix of facts and legal requirements (Hutton 2014).

Alongside this complication of several different *kinds* of vocabulary items, Tiersma (1999) also notes that semantic relations that hold between vocabulary items in a given semantic field can be specific to legal language. For example, legal discourse can create oppositions through **antonyms** that are not opposites in general usage. One of his examples is *speech* and *conduct*, two terms that overlap in ordinary language. Generally, speech appears to be a kind of conduct; if the word has an opposite, then that word would be *writing*. American courts, by contrast, will typically treat *speech* and *conduct* as opposites: if something is 'speech', First Amendment free speech protection applies; but if behaviour is deemed to be 'conduct', then such protection will not be available. Tiersma points out that this contrast can be confusing to a layperson, for example when burning an American flag is held to be free 'speech'.

Style and typicality

Crystal and Davy conclude their 1969 analysis with an essential observation: that much in the style of legal documents is not ornamental, but functional. Tiersma

(1999), for example, draws attention to the fact that legal style differs depending on whether it is spoken or written for several reasons: partly because spoken language, even oral courtroom argument, is less highly structured and formal than writing; partly because hurried interaction between legal professionals in speech creates an insider-style, clipped, telegraphic, and full of abbreviations; and partly because mixed spoken–written styles such as that of judicial opinions generally adopt a more reflective, discursive style than contracts or wills.

The question accordingly arises: how far are features identified in any given analysis of legal language 'typical'? And what are they 'typical' of? The vocabulary and grammar of a constitution or a treaty will differ from those of a will, phone contract or law report. Page layout is not dense on the page of a modern statute, or unpunctuated in the way it may be in a tenancy agreement. Within 'courtroom discourse', style varies between different legal participants and at different stages of a trial.

Crystal and Davy, of course, did not present their account as a description of legal language, only of legal documents. Their study offered generalisations based on data – their examination of actual texts – combined with **native-speaker intuitions** and understanding of the historical development of legal discourse. For their chapter, the selected data consisted of two private law documents, which they considered 'reasonably central in a linguistic sense' even though they recognised that 'like any other variety, the variety analysed is blurred at the edges and changes imperceptibly into something else' (Crystal and Davy 1969: 195).

Research into legal style is now more likely to use a larger **corpus**, especially a corpus in which texts are tagged, or labelled, for both qualitative and quantitative analysis by subtypes reflecting legal function (will, statute, contract), jurisdiction (which country a document is operative in), and date. Inevitably, an element of idealisation will still enter into any attempt to describe 'legal language'. That is inherent in deciding the corpus of texts that provides the data set from which generalisations will be made. Broad contrasts can be ventured between text types at a high level of generality (e.g. 'legal documents differ from novels or history books'). But the limits of such general statements are exposed if equivalent generalisations are made within either of the fields compared.

Forty years after Crystal and Davy, Coulthard and Johnson (2007: 35) begin their discussion of 'the language of the law' with the statement that 'anyone who hears the term legal language thinks immediately of grammatically complex, sparsely punctuated, over-lexicalised, opaque written text'. But for them, this is a starting point rather than a conclusion. Equipped with modern **corpus linguistic techniques**, they are able to go beyond induction from small samples of data to investigate linguistic patterning far more confidently than would have been possible earlier: 'is the characterisation accurate', they ask, 'and, if so, how did it come to be so?' (Coulthard and Johnson 2007: 35). Researching legal style now, either using search tools developed in an existing legal database (such as Westlaw, JustCite or Lexis) or by searching a linguistically constructed corpus of selected legal texts is likely to adopt a more quantitative approach than Crystal and Davy's pioneering summary (for discussion and illustration of corpus methods in relation to registers, genres and styles, see, for example, Biber and Conrad 2009).

FUNCTIONS OF LEGAL LANGUAGE

In this unit, we consider the functions served by legal language, rather than describing what it looks or sounds like. Because *function* has different meanings in different subfields of linguistics (and still more meanings in social theory), first we disentangle the word's relevant meanings. Then we outline accounts given by two influential writers on legal language of the goals and functions served by specific features of legal style. Some aspects of each of these accounts celebrate the effectiveness of legal language; others imply that unless legal language continues to be reformed away from its historical stylistic conventions, it will remain to some extent dysfunctional. We consider arguments on each side. In Unit C2, we consider contemporary campaigns for reform of legal language more directly.

Legal language from a functional perspective

Answering the question *why* legal language is idiosyncratic by comparison with other varieties is complicated by the uncertain meaning of the word *function* across its varied use in linguistics and social theory.

In linguistics, **functional** often means essential in creating a signifying contrast at a relevant level of linguistic structure. For example, there are many aspects of sounds articulated by speakers, but only some of those sounds enter into significant contrast with others (e.g. distinguishing /p/ from /b/ at the beginning of *pat* or *bat*). At sentence level, form and function are also distinguished. A basic English sentence may consist, in terms of form, of a noun phrase followed by a verb phrase: NP VP. But the functions served by those constituents in creating meaning must be characterised in different, functional terms, such as SVO (subject, verb, object). At the communicative level, functions have also been categorised. For example, Halliday identifies three 'macro' functions realised by a range of formal elements: **ideational**, **interpersonal** and **textual**. The detail and complexity of function in linguistics have been extensively discussed in a whole tradition of linguistics: that of functional or functionalist linguistics (for examples, see Jakobson 1960; Halliday 2004).

In connecting linguistic forms and functions with wider social structures, the role of a particular use of language may be considered 'functional' in further ways (and in sociology there is also a much examined field of 'functionalism').

❑ A dialect or sociolect may signal membership of a regional, class or occupational group. It may function to affirm membership of that group or to contrast with (or if there is no mutual intelligibility between varieties, potentially exclude) other social groups of speakers.

❑ Use of a particular linguistic register may not only reflect, but actively create, the relative technicality, formality or intimacy of a situation: the relationship between conversational participants may be shaped over time by strategic register choices, rather than determined in advance by a pregiven register requirement associated with a given situation.

❑ The function of a language variety *as a whole* might be viewed as creating, maintaining or altering social relationships. For example, ways of talking to or about women or minorities may function to dominate or subordinate such groups. Legal language might create and maintain a benign system of social order or serve the interest of an existing ruling class.

Language use contributes to social relations in various ways, including by functioning as a kind of **symbolic capital** (Bourdieu 1992). If we wish to discuss legal language from a functional rather than formal perspective, therefore, we need to keep different dimensions in mind, including whether we are talking about the function of particular words, speech acts (e.g. issuing an order or giving a verdict), courtroom language rituals, or the whole linguistic variety in comparison with others. Given long-standing acknowledgement of the idiosyncrasies of legal language, we should also be alert to the issue of possible dysfunction, which we return to at the end of this unit.

'Fit for purpose' depends on views of purpose

The most influential, scholarly accounts of legal language as a variety share an important starting point. They recognise that understanding the variety's functioning requires looking at legal language as **situated social action**: choice of forms cannot be understood independently of what those forms are used for. Each account starts with formal description of linguistic features and patterns, but moves to observations about functions served by the linguistic features identified. Because such functions inevitably combine communicative, legal and wider social considerations (e.g. the place of law in a democracy), there is often a speculative dimension. Inevitably, linguists must frequently acknowledge their lack of familiarity with the professional functioning of the discourse they are analysing, for example what a will, pleading or statute must accomplish in order to have legal effect and be 'functional' in a legal as well as linguistic sense.

Once specific functions are identified, further questions need to be asked, including whether those functions could be achieved equally, or more effectively, by a different style of discourse. Accounts of legal language accordingly often combine linguistic description with evaluation: occasionally admiration for the effectiveness of legal language, given the difficulty of the challenges it faces, but more often criticism and polemic advocating new levels of clarity to be achieved by 'plain language' reforms (which we consider in Unit C2).

Below, we outline arguments made by two influential US lawyer-linguist scholars, David Mellinkoff and Peter Tiersma, who link:

❑ what legal language is like (description);
❑ why legal language is like that (explanation, usually historical);
❑ what roles legal language performs (functional account); and
❑ what effects it has (professional and social assessment).

Mellinkoff's The Language of the Law

Mellinkoff (1963) is widely considered the first major study of what 'the language of the law' is (though he himself acknowledges antecedents in various fields). Mellinkoff outlines nine main characteristics, related principally to vocabulary and grammar. In addition, he devotes a separate chapter to what he calls 'mannerisms of the language of the law'. These are distinctive features that have investigable historical origins but appear less easily explicable in terms of modern legal function. Such mannerisms include legal language being 'wordy, unclear, pompous, and dull'. Together, these and other aspects give legal language what Mellinkoff calls its 'uncommon touch': they set legal language apart from other discourse styles despite the English and US legal systems he is describing being, with a specialised meaning Mellinkoff alludes to, 'common' law systems. For Mellinkoff, legal English is 'a zone where the language of law loses contact with speech'.

As regards how legal language functions, there are two steps in Mellinkoff's reasoning:

1   His first step is to contextualise stylistic choices (e.g. a form of words was introduced when English law was conducted largely in Law French, or Latin, or a combination of both languages with English; or some aspect of legal language is a carry-over from a period of widespread illiteracy in which there was a different balance between oral and written proceedings).
2   His second step assesses the continuing significance or consequences of such stylistic choices. These can be either within the law or how the legal system fits into society. One example is that selection of linguistic forms based on an earlier tradition of usage fits with the dependence of legal reasoning on previous interpretations and judgments (because of the common-law system of **legal precedent**). A contrasting example is that particular forms may be chosen to mystify some aspect of law, so that it remains incomprehensible to many people who are nevertheless subject to law.

Among the characteristics of legal language emphasised by Mellinkoff is law's attempt at 'extreme precision'. This, he suggests, results in unusual word order when phrases are inserted into a sentence less to be idiomatic than in order to minimise risk of ambiguity. But he also makes a contrasting observation: that law's use of language is intentionally **vague**. Legal language, he argues, favours expressions that are sufficiently flexible in meaning that they can be interpreted in new and unforeseen situations, as the social facts with which law has to deal vary. Tension between such contrasting aims leads to complex consequences. The linguistic conservatism suited to the development of law by means of authority and precedent can make communication between lawyers and their clients difficult, if members of the public perceive archaic forms as a closed, insider discourse suited to use between lawyers but which excludes outsiders.

Tiersma's analysis of legal language

The other especially influential thinker on this topic has been Peter Tiersma. Tiersma's analysis ranges across a number of specialised research studies; his general position is encapsulated in *Legal Language* (1999), summarised in Tiersma (2008), and available in condensed form on his website www.languageandlaw.org (which has, however, not been updated since his death in 2014). Tiersma acknowledges his debt to Mellinkoff and by way of background provides a succinct account of the origins, historical development and characteristics of legal language as a variety or cluster of varieties. Later stages of *Legal Language*, however, focus on why that variety is difficult to understand and how it can be reformed (in fact, some of the reforms he advocates have begun to be introduced since publication of the book).

Tiersma reviews arguments in favour of the distinctiveness of legal language. He emphasises need for decontextualised written communication if the law is to be applied consistently and authoritatively. Broad and impersonal statements of legal rules, he observes, help project the law as impartial, especially if expressed using **passive voice** (which creates an impression that legal acts are accomplished without the intervention of a fallible human agent). Formal, archaic and ritualistic language separates legal proceedings from ordinary life, marking them as special and important, particularly if the legitimacy of courts is enhanced by ritual language that suggests they are unchanging, ancient institutions.

In the course of his account, Tiersma significantly develops Mellinkoff's historical explanation of features of legal language: that they had their origins in a transition from an oral to a written legal culture. Noting the emergence of an English legal profession during the same historical period as the transition into a writing-led legal culture, Tiersma suggests that professional monopoly produced a 'conspiracy of gobbledygook'. 'Talking like a lawyer', in his account, allowed lawyers to mark themselves as members of a profession, and continues to function as a commercial display, attracting custom. The technicality, even incomprehensibility, of legal style he suggests helps command high fees; and use of template documents (e.g. preprinted standardised forms) whose interpretation has already been tested in adversarial proceedings in court is economically efficient. Each of these arguments is commonly invoked in current debates about further review and reform of legal use of language.

A practical challenge: legal drafting

An interesting, complementary approach to how legal language functions can be found in guidance on legal drafting. In a study of international common-law practice, Butt (2013) asks: what influences the legal drafter? His answer is that the main influences are:

- ❏ familiarity and habit, based on security achieved by adopting forms and words that have been used before;
- ❏ conservatism, both general and allied to common-law reliance on past judicial decisions;
- ❏ fear of negligence claims, because of the required standards of professional advice and duty of care to clients;
- ❏ constraints on how legal documents are physically produced;
- ❏ pressure to conform to professional norms, including deadlines and clients' demands;

❏   desire to avoid ambiguity;
❏   the mixture of languages from which law in English has drawn its vocabulary;
❏   payment by length of document and time, reducing incentive to minimise the task
    or time taken to complete; and
❏   a litigious environment and risk that documents will come under hostile scrutiny
    from other lawyers.

Emphasising the practical implications of his discussion, Butt illustrates each of these factors in detail, showing how aspects of legal documents ranging from length and layout to phraseology and exemplification are determined by technology available (including in earlier periods of legal development), by commercial pressure and professional community norms.

Legal language and culture

There is, however, another, often neglected approach to how the seeming oddity of legal discourse can be understood in terms of function: a view put forward by some legal scholars and anthropologists of the variety's symbolic and ritualistic aspects (alluded to by Crystal and Davy in their suggestion that ceremonial features of legal usage such as archaism amount to a verbal performance 'directly equatable with wigs'; Crystal and Davy 1969: 213).

Ritual aspects are central to Berman's (2013) celebration of legal language as providing 'effective symbols of community'. Berman's analysis was written in the 1960s, but only published posthumously 40 years later. As well as discussing formal features and applications of legal language, Berman argues that legal discourse styles function not only to impose obligations, communicate legal argument, persuade, or adjudicate, but also create what he calls a 'liturgy of legal procedure': a set of elaborate and in his view dignified verbal rituals suited to dealing with highly charged or impassioned situations that need to be settled by legal proceedings. To describe the combined process through which language (and symbolism) shapes society and communicates ideas, Berman coins a new term for how he believes legal language functions: 'communification', a combination of communication with the creation or development of communities and values. Berman's claims as regards the functioning of legal language can seem over-optimistic when viewed alongside extensive criticism of the very features he celebrates. But his concern with legal language as embedded in deep patterns of cultural behaviour engages with a valuably broad understanding of language's symbolic as well as narrowly communicative functions.

Functions or dysfunction?

In this unit, we have used 'function' in a descriptive way, rather than as necessarily implying effective or successful operation. The distinct but related question of how far the internationally varied and changing styles of English used in law are fit for purpose is not easily resolved. What is clear, however, is that the demands made on legal discourse are intense and sometimes contradictory. As Crystal (2010: 374) puts it, legal discourse is:

pulled in different directions. Its statements have to be so phrased that we can see their general applicability, yet be specific enough to apply to individual circumstances. They have to be stable enough to stand the test of time, so that cases will be treated consistently and fairly, yet flexible enough to adapt to new social situations. Above all they have to be expressed in such a way that people can be certain about the intention of the law respecting their rights and duties. No other variety of language has to carry such a responsibility.

GENRE ANALYSIS OF LEGAL DISCOURSE

Unit A3 introduces the concept of genre partly by contrast with linguistic register. Both kinds of variation, we point out in that unit, contribute to the overall characteristics and suitability in a given situation of a text or stretch of discourse. In this unit, we look more closely at how discourse genres function in law. We distinguish between synchronic (systemic) and diachronic (historical) aspects of genre and illustrate how legal genres have developed by reference to the history of law reporting. In Unit C3, we look at features of another legal text type: the statute.

Directions in genre analysis

Genre has been studied extensively since ancient times, both as an aesthetic category (e.g. the distinction between tragedy, epic and lyric in Aristotle's *Poetics*) and in treatments of public rhetoric (e.g. the contrast between forensic and political styles of speaking in the same philosopher's *The Art of Rhetoric*). A range of classificatory systems can be found, including ones based on formal properties, conventional purpose, occasions of use, and anticipated effect. Although training manuals have always existed offering instruction in different styles of writing and speaking, it is relatively recent that questions raised by differences of discourse type have been viewed as a distinct field of research: **genre analysis**.

Modern linguistic theories of genre

In his study of genre analysis as a way of understanding English in academic and research settings, Swales (1990) summarises different approaches to genre thinking, including accounts in folklore studies, literary criticism, rhetoric and linguistics. Central to his own understanding is a concept of 'discourse community', or group of language users narrower than a sociolinguistic speech community who are all concerned with shared purposes in an organised, social or professional practice. Building from this starting point, Swales develops an approach to analysing genre based on the following propositions:

1   A genre comprises a class of **communicative events**; such events share communicative purposes that are recognised by expert members of the discourse community and provide the rationale for the genre.

2   Genre can only be realised in complete texts (or text that can be projected as if complete), because genre does more than specify codes to be found within a group of related texts; it specifies conditions for beginning, continuing and ending one particular text.

3   While linguistic register imposes constraints at the levels of vocabulary and syntax, genre imposes norms at the level of discourse structure. Genres may have their own 'complementary' registers, however, and communicative success may require some appropriate relationship between systems of genre and register.

4   Genre is socio-rhetorical in character; it performs social action in the form of text production and reception.

5   Genres show stability in conventions of different kinds and are named or labelled, sometimes using an informal metalanguage, by participants or users in the relevant discourse community.

6   Genre involves **content schemata** (i.e. frameworks of knowledge, values and an orientation towards the topic), as well as **formal schemata** (i.e. how something should be told or narrated). Participating in a discourse community may entail some assimilation of its world view in order to communicate successfully.

7   Texts in a genre exhibit family resemblances in structure, style, content and intended audience. Texts are exemplars or instances of genres, which vary in their degree of prototypicality.

Current research and application

Swales's work has been influential in many fields. Co-researchers and others have extended his conception (sometimes referred to as **textography**) while retaining the main themes. But relatively little work has been done, for reasons we discuss below, on legal genres. Available contributions include work by Bhatia (1993: 207–18), who has applied genre considerations to the 'easification', or simplification for ease of use, of legal discourse, and Heffer (2005), an extract from whose work is reproduced in Unit D3.

Applied linguistic analysis of legal genres raises at least two significant challenges:

1   The *purposes* served by legal genres are embedded in specific and changing kinds of professional interaction and transaction. So if we merely say that legal discourses aim to create, implement and enforce laws, such a general observation will fail to capture the essential differences between legal subgenres. On the other hand, if we try to grasp the difference between legal subgenres in terms of purpose more precisely, we cannot do so exclusively by linguistic methods. Most of the relevant considerations will be specifically legal, taking the form of rules, reasoning and outcomes. Research into such differences accordingly requires an interdisciplinary perspective.

2   In linguistic studies of genre that compare different professional fields, genre functions as a *descriptive* category. In professional (including legal) settings, by contrast, genre is a prescriptive or normative category: it groups features and expectations based on explicit or tacit rules regarding what *should be* incorporated into writing or speech in a given set of circumstances. Even aesthetic forms such

as fiction, music and film are regulated by normative constraints (e.g. audience expectations that need to be met, and marketing categories); but with legal genres, the constraints are actively imposed and enforced (not least because requirements must be fulfilled for a text to be operative). A combination of procedural rules, legal training and contestation ensures conformity with norms.

Legal genres as constructs

We can look at legal genres either synchronically or diachronically. Synchronically involves analysing a number of factors: the configuration, at a particular time, of the community of users of legal discourse; the types of text they produce, use or expect to encounter; and normative pressures on what they do and believe. Such analysis is likely to consist of investigating the rhetorical organisation of texts as types, coupled with contextual study (e.g. through ethnographic methods) of user expectations and values. Studying genre diachronically involves investigating the historical development of genres and the combination of linguistic and institutional forces acting on the processes of change that affect them. For law, the two kinds of study are closely connected; this is because the process of historical development in law directly involves the past imposing its imprint on later genre structure.

Case study: law reporting

Genres do not form a fixed list, but are an evolving range. They emerge, develop and become residual in ways that depend on their usefulness to a relevant community of users. In addition, because genre is concerned with patterns of thought and values associated with a given discourse community, not only with aspects of form, the historical development of a genre is simultaneously both the development of a field or practice and the development of a language style or format.

One result of such complex interaction between discourse forms, users and social context is that genre requires a different *kind* of history from the history of register (as described in Unit A2). The history of a legal genre must describe changing communicative needs and purposes, within changing legal institutions. We illustrate these points below with a brief history of **law reporting**, taking English law as our example (adapted from Durant 2012; for further legal detail, see Zander 2015). The account we present should make it possible to see how far the history of language use in law is simultaneously the history of legal thinking in action.

Here is a short history of law reports:

1   In England, the earliest court decisions were only stored in the minds of judges and court officials. But there has been a recognisable genre of law reporting from the thirteenth century onwards, growing out of early medieval **plea rolls**. The rolls, literally rolls of parchment, recorded decisions and were kept to establish the rights of the parties in a particular case, as well as to assist with enforcement of decisions.

2   During the period between the late thirteenth and mid-sixteenth centuries, law reports take the form of what are now known as **Year Books**. These were handwritten, first in Law French and Latin, then later in English. Such reports show a shift of purpose: they were no longer addressed only to the court and parties

directly involved, but also to a public beyond consisting largely of law students who were less interested in the details or outcome of a case than in the reasoning applied in it (since this could offer a more general picture of the system of law and might be useful in arguing later cases).

3   From the mid-sixteenth century onwards, law reports are known, especially after 1578 (the date of a collection by Edmund Plowden called *Commentaries*), as **nominate reports**. These reports were commercially published, and of variable accuracy. They were called 'nominate' reports because they were known by the names of their authors: Plowden himself, Sir Edward Coke, slightly later James Burrow and others. The nominate reports took a more expansive, 'commentary' form, elaborating on the earlier and narrower recording of stages of litigation and decisions.

4   Although the nominate reports circulated in a rapidly expanding law profession, there was still nothing resembling a public *system* of law reporting, with a standardising influence over the genre of the kind that now exists. Over time, however, reports increasingly recorded judicial decisions as sources of legal authority. This new emphasis responded to a need, in the rapidly expanding field of law, to explain decisions. But in doing so, it blurred the distinction between a historical record of judicial decisions and statements of what the law was. Only later, during the second half of the eighteenth century, were conventions to be followed in reporting actively sought. When adopted, such conventions related to who could write reports (authorised reporters), what the process of publication and circulation should be (to minimise delays in publication), and what topics should be covered (essentially, which cases should be reported).

5   From the 1860s, the *Law Reports* series ('Judicial Decisions of the Superior and Appellate Courts in England and Wales') conferred greater authority on published reports. They also incorporated advocates' arguments and opinions, revised by judges. The second half of the nineteenth century also brought further standardisation and institutional oversight: the *Incorporated Council of Law Reporting for England and Wales* dates from this period, followed by the *Weekly Law Reports*, *Times* reports (with antecedents in *The Universal Register*), and later *All-England Reports*. In principle, any report of a judicial decision could be cited in court, but law reporting gradually became a specialised profession; and a rule of **exclusive citation**, under which preference was given to authorised reports, was adopted and periodically restated.

6   Following further nineteenth-century reforms, English law reports came largely to resemble modern reports. Even now, however, in a period of online access to decisions of courts of record, less than 5 per cent of English cases are reported in an authoritative, published form. Even *Law Reports*, the most official reporting channel, and so a mouthpiece of legal authority, covers only about 10 per cent of that 'less than 5 per cent' reported overall.

Modern law report structure

This brief history provides necessary background for understanding the modern genre of a law report. Further detail along such lines would help clarify the circumstances in response to which particular new features of the genre were introduced.

But now switch from diachronic to synchronic. Allowing for variation in different types of publication, the list below indicates how a modern law report typically sets out its material:

- ❑ Names of the parties, court where the case was heard, names of the judges, date.
- ❑ **Catchwords:** compiled by the law reporter (rather like keywords in a research article).
- ❑ **Headnote:** summary of the facts of the case, questions of law, decision (in the USA, known as **syllabus**).
- ❑ List of cases cited in judgment.
- ❑ List of other cases cited in argument.
- ❑ Details of the proceedings: short history of the case.
- ❑ Résumé of counsels' arguments.
- ❑ Judgment: the facts, legal issues, and outcome (in the highest courts, this may consist of several opinions, including dissenting opinions).
- ❑ **Formal order** (i.e. outcome, such as 'appeal dismissed').

These largely standardised stages are now the main genre conventions of law reporting in terms of layout. Fuller understanding of them would involve taking drafting considerations into account, analysing who reports are read by, and what use is made of them (e.g. in preparing for and during legal proceedings). During the twentieth century, reports have been increasingly presented in layouts that make searching, skimming and citation easier, with simplified vocabulary and sentence structure, and clearer signposting of speech acts (e.g. reflecting moves from summarising earlier proceedings, through narrating facts of a case and developing legal arguments, to delivering judgment and handing down a verdict).

What makes legal genres worth examining in this way is that they are not simply fixed receptacles of legal procedure, but discourse forms that have responded and continue to respond – even if at a slower pace than other discourse styles – to changing needs and priorities. Conventions in law reporting vary between jurisdictions, and change both for legal and ergonomic (user-related) reasons. For example, the shift to online reporting has modified the convention of referring to page numbers and led to adoption of a system of paragraph numbering, now accepted as a proper form of citation. More significantly, decisions of the European courts (which hear some cases, and to which **preliminary questions** are referred by national courts in other cases before judgment) are reasoned and presented in a manner that differs from traditional English law reporting, and there is a tendency towards accommodation between the two. Trends in law reporting will continue to respond to shifts of form and expectation; and because of the institutional structures and conservative culture of law, as conventions evolve, normative practices develop around them, along with an instructional literature.

Examining the genre of the law report brings different rewards depending on the perspective from which such reports are viewed. For law reporters, understanding the genre guides how to write reports (a task of modelling to which applied linguistics could contribute); for law students, familiarity with the genre involves specialised reading skills (i.e. it is a field of applied comprehension); for judges and judges' clerks, facility with the genre guides the drafting of opinions suitable in content and style for incorporation into a now sophisticated document style that originated as simply an aid to judicial memory. To the linguist, law reporting presents the challenge of understanding the development, functioning and style of a discourse form more institutionally constrained and complex than genres such as the conversational anecdote, the prayer, the detective novel, or the scientific research article.

SPEECH IN THE COURTROOM

Fields including conversation analysis (CA) have shown that everyday verbal interaction is highly structured and rule-governed. How far, we ask in this unit, does courtroom discourse simply transpose structures from everyday verbal interaction into a new setting? Or does it alter patterns and expectations that underpin communicative behaviour, creating a distinct and specialised kind of interaction? Trials have often been characterised as a battle, contest, performance, or process of storytelling. All these descriptions capture important insights. But in this unit, we aim to describe courtroom discourse more precisely, by looking at how the verbal interaction involved consists of specific moves and sequences. Then we consider the higher-order organisation of courtroom discourse into episodes, as an overall genre. Finally, we explore how different levels of organisation of courtroom discourse are connected and why this matters.

Courtroom interaction

An early description of courtroom speech patterns, drawing on the then emerging field of **conversation analysis** (Hutchby and Wooffitt 2008), is presented in Atkinson and Drew (1979). Two characteristics distinguish Atkinson and Drew's approach from an ethnographic study. First, they do not only focus on obviously unusual speech patterns; rather, they seek to establish basic rules and patterns that constitute a whole, given area of observed behaviour. Second, their analysis avoids dependence on subjective reporting by conversational participants; instead, they offer an account based on linguistic evidence, including especially uptake by other parties in an interaction.

Atkinson and Drew's description suggests a mix of similarities and differences between courtroom talk and everyday conversation. For example, in examination of witnesses both the order of **conversational turns** and the types of turn permitted are highly constrained. In CA terms, the question–answer **adjacency pair** is the primary pattern of exchange. But other, locally managed sequence types are embedded into this unit of exchange including sequence types known as **challenge–rebuttal** and **accusation–denial**. More generally, Atkinson and Drew's study suggests a hierarchy of levels of structuring, with systems of local subroutines ordered by higher-order structures and purposes.

Different types of interaction at different stages in proceedings

Popular images of a courtroom trial tend to highlight two contrasting organisations of language use in terms of participation. One is a kind of institutionally orchestrated theatre: a drama of speeches between characters in different roles. The other focuses on extended monologues, either by lawyers making submissions or by a judge delivering his or her judgment. Given this polarisation, it is useful to describe (allowing for the sorts of simplification we acknowledge in Unit A4) the different kinds of language use in a trial, including which stages consist of monologue and which consist of dialogue.

Heffer (2005; see extract in Unit D3) explains the distinctive characteristics of courtroom interaction in terms of participant roles and strategic goals. In everyday conversation, he suggests, it is usually clear who the speaker, listener or overhearer are for a given verbal interaction. But consider, by contrast, a courtroom question and answer sequence involving a lawyer and a witness. Interaction in such circumstances requires a more multilayered account of speech event roles, for instance a **framework for participation** along the lines described in Goffman (1981), subsequently developed in Levinson (1988). When a lawyer asks a question, Heffer (2005: 48–50) notes, he or she relates to what is said on a more complex **footing** than in ordinary conversation. The lawyer is the speaker of the question (in Goffman's terms, simultaneously the 'author' and 'animator'), but also the legal spokesperson for his or her client (Goffman's 'principal', here the person being represented). The witness is the apparent addressee and is expected to respond with answers. Yet the judge and jurors (where the latter are present) are the main **intended targets** for the entire sequence, since the purpose of the examination is to communicate facts and an overall impression to them. (Quite commonly, ahead of examination, lawyers in fact instruct their witnesses to look at the jury if there is one when answering, rather than at the lawyer asking the question). An opposing lawyer is also listening: a **ratified hearer** in Goffman's term, overhearing in a non-technical sense but with a legitimate, albeit adversarial purpose: exercising where necessary a (procedurally granted) right to interrupt, and preparing cross-examination or refining later submissions to the court in the light of what he or she hears.

The involvement of numerous participants in a courtroom interaction shaped by defined hierarchical roles and a complex framework for participation inevitably results in a highly ritualised discourse genre. Heffer suggests that the trial genre in fact includes three subgenres, which he describes as procedural (e.g. juror selection and instruction); adversarial (e.g. opening, examination and cross-examination, and closing); and adjudicative (e.g. deliberation and judgment). Cutting across the sequence and purpose of each subgenre, however, is an important further contrast: between sections that consist of **dialogue** and sections that consist of **monologue**. The verbal exchanges (dialogue) are themselves of several types: interaction among lawyers (typically on points of law or procedure), interaction between lawyers and witnesses (in examination and cross-examination), and interaction between lawyers and the judge(s). While these subtypes differ from each other in the legal status of their participants, as well as in their content and style, there is a stronger contrast between them collectively and other stages of the trial that resemble monologues: instructions, opening and closing statements, verdict and sentencing. In these monologue subgenres, what is distinctive is precisely that no verbal response is expected. The complexity of different types and levels of contrast is partly why Heffer gives his chapter on the topic the title 'The trial as a complex genre' (Heffer 2005: Chapter 3).

Difficulty in analysing courtroom discourse is increased further by the fact that neither the monologue nor the dialogue stages are purely one or the other. During examination of witnesses, for example, whatever 'dialogue' takes place is highly controlled. Witnesses appear to engage in dialogue, in that they respond to questions using their own words. But from the perspective of a lawyer taking a witness through his or her evidence, witnesses function almost as animated objects: they verbally produce content, evidence, which the lawyer either knows already or strategically anticipates; they are then dismissed once the relevant content has been elicited. Because lawyers normally have access in advance to essential matters to be presented at trial, courtroom presentation and testing of evidence in an adversarial system may to this extent be viewed as a controlled performance for the benefit of the judge or jurors more than an inquisitorial process of eliciting information, or a dialectical enquiry into truth. The appearance of dialogue, for all its richness of detail and texture, is an incorporation of voices by an overarching, dominant voice, an impression reinforced in the final handing down of the court's judgment as described by Ferguson (1990): the judge synthesises courtroom interaction, absorbing contributions into an authoritative monologue.

Different kinds of structure, as might be expected, may be identified at different levels of courtroom discourse. There is a level of microanalysis of sequences and moves (a level that raises questions of the purpose, typical form of realisation, and effect on different participants of those moves and sequences). Moving up a level, there are relations of dependency among such moves as they constitute episodes in a trial: opening statement, taking of evidence, summing-up. Above these are macro-structural **characteristics** of the courtroom genre, in which a trial's discursive features are in contrast with other forms of legal discourse (e.g. inquests or police interviews), as well as with other kinds of institutionalised, multi-voice discourse (e.g. religious services; weddings and funerals; administrative and political meetings; sessions of parliament; and news broadcasts).

Courtroom discourse and its functions

It is arguably the macro-level perception of courtroom discourse that, beyond the sphere of law, conjures up the images of battle or contest, performance or storytelling (each of which picks up a genuine but selective aspect of trials). The micro-level of styles of address, specific wording and objections, by contrast, is what is often recalled by participants most vividly. A full account of this complicated form of adjudication-by-interaction is likely only to emerge from descriptions that can connect observed details of interaction at different levels with the higher-order functions that trials serve.

In this context, there are links to be explored further between several approaches: the microanalysis of courtroom interaction as developed by authors such as Drew and Atkinson; the account of courtroom discourse offered by Heffer; and participant-focused observations about witness behaviour made by researchers such as Conley and O'Barr (2005), which we discuss in Unit A4. Heffer's (2005) account of the language of jury trial, for example, is part of a larger argument (which we consider in more detail in Unit D3): that such discourse shows a tension between two different ways of talking about (and in fact conceptualising) what is going on, use of narrative and legal exposition. For Heffer, what is important is that these two kinds of discourse together produce the 'complex genre' he describes, addressed simultaneously to two different audiences. But Heffer's general account may turn out to be more suggestive if considered alongside participant-focused observations about witness behaviour of the kind made by Conley and O'Barr (2005). They argue that how different litigants structure information can be categorised as being either **rule-oriented** or **relational**, based on informant interviews or analysis of conversational moves and sequences. What is significant from their point of view is that legal proceedings are receptive disproportionately to the former. If the contrast they put forward is justified, then there may be implications that go beyond the scope of any one of the studies described above on its own concerning the effectiveness of the justice system as a whole.

Such implications can be seen more clearly if findings from the different kinds of study are brought together. In their deliberations, for example, judges restructure relational accounts into legally relevant categories in order to pursue their own form of reasoning. In an empirical study conducted by Conley and O'Barr, however, members of the judiciary 'described relational litigants as hard to follow, irrational, and even crazy, while praising the straightforward efficiency of rule-oriented accounts' (Conley and O'Barr 2005: 73). Opposing that preferential treatment, Conley and O'Barr maintain (on the strength of sociolinguistic findings and research on reasoning in other fields) that relational accounts are not illogical, but simply follow a different kind of logic from the sort of reasoning a court can easily accommodate. For Conley and O'Barr, issues regarding courtroom discourse are in this way not only questions for scholarly analysis, but matters calling for practical reform, if litigants with legal claims of equal merit fare differently because they show different kinds of communicative competence. Their research (e.g. O'Barr and Conley 1990) shows a strong connection between witness background, greater satisfaction and less frustration with the (US) justice system when witnesses are able to use more narrative forms in small, informal courts or in tribunals or **alternative dispute resolution** (ADR; usually mediation) settings.

B5   LINGUISTIC STRATEGIES USED BY LAWYERS

In this unit, we introduce and discuss the main features of courtroom persuasion. We examine a series of examples of rhetorical techniques deployed at different stages of a trial in Unit C5.

Awareness of audience

Persuasion involves 'a deliberate effort to change a person's attitude' (Bradshaw 2011: 1). To persuade judges and jurors successfully, lawyers must combine attention to their message with attention to how they present that message, including by means of **non-verbal communication** such as facial expressions, gaze, body language, silences and physical distance (Burgoon and Bacue 2003). Advocacy manuals deal with all these considerations from a practical, experience-led point of view that reflects law's preference for tradition, cumulative wisdom, and experientially proven outcomes. In this unit, we bring together such understandings of advocacy with other approaches based on linguistic and related research.

Advocacy is often regarded as a matter of performance. But it cannot be reduced to performance entirely, since it is never unidirectional. Rather, advocacy involves implanting an idea or altering an existing idea in someone's belief system, in a courtroom context an idea or ideas that can form the basis of an important later judgment. To maximise the effectiveness of their advocacy, lawyers accordingly seek intuitively and through training to understand human **cognitive bias**, which influences judges' or jurors' perception of information presented to them. This practical approach combines with awareness of different audiences; so, in order to reflect necessary differences between legal and lay communication, lawyers adapt their persuasion strategies to different situations, adjusting in particular to whether a case involves a jury trial or a **bench trial** (i.e. proceedings overseen by one or more judges but no jury). Audience awareness (Bradshaw 2011) and the related principle of **recipient design** (structuring a message to reflect the priorities of its recipient rather than the needs or wishes of the speaker) are as a result central to advocacy.

Permissible strategies in advocacy vary between jurisdictions. For example, **objections** based on the manner or purpose of the language used (e.g. on grounds of vague or ambiguous questions) are raised more often in US courts than in other common-law jurisdictions, largely because in American courts any ground for appeal will be treated as having been waived if an immediate objection was not raised (Evans 1998). In an increasingly international media environment that potentially elides important jurisdictional differences in procedure, interactional differences can surface in unexpected ways (e.g. in one of our examples in Unit C4, an unrepresented litigant in Hong Kong may have been influenced by American courtroom dramas when seeking to raise an objection in an impermissible way).

Speech attributes and style

In many walks of life, a good public speaker is, at least partly, one who can manipulate **prosodic features of speech**, including pitch, tempo and loudness, intonation, and tone of voice, in order to reinforce other stylistic choices. Such characteristics also feature in courtroom advocacy. For example, **intonation** – including sometimes slightly exaggerated, 'stage' intonation – may be used to express irony or incredulity. The advocate may vary **tempo**, slowing down to let an important point sink in. Rapid questioning, on the other hand, may be used to put pressure on a witness. Such features are sometimes calculated for effect in a given courtroom situation, and at other times appear to be conventional effects that have been acquired from manuals and mentors.

Stylistic selection is not a matter purely of one-off choices. One highly regarded advocacy skill is an ability to switch between formal and informal register depending on topic and target audience. Jurors may fail to attend to or understand – or may even appear bored by – evidence presented to them. One requirement of verbal communication to jurors is therefore simplicity, despite the complexity of the subject matter and legal framework governing what has to be communicated.

Most published work on advocacy consists of guidance by and for practitioners. Some studies, on the other hand, such as Findley and Sales (2012), claim to analyse 'the science of attorney advocacy', and relate practical advice to more general observations and evidence. Chapter 3 of Findley and Sales (2012), for example, presents a digest of recommended verbal techniques collected from a range of documents, suggesting the following as the main techniques to be adopted: use of familiar language, simple words with few syllables, short and linear sentences, attention to thesaurus alternatives, and care with figurative expressions. Among more general recommendations, they include: avoid 'legalese' and baby talk, humanise the client, and insert what they call 'memorable impact words' and details.

Perhaps surprisingly given the adversarial nature of the speech event overall, one effective persuasive strategy according to advocacy manuals is to be polite and likeable. This is recommended both for lawyers and their clients. Researchers such as Cialdini (2008) conclude that we are more persuaded by, and display more trust in, people we like. In a courtroom context, one way of appearing likeable is to **accommodate** linguistically to jurors, since psychological research suggests that people like people who resemble them. In analysing one US trial, Fuller (2009) showed how lawyers manipulate properties of language to communicate messages they would otherwise not be permitted to express. She documents how some Southern black attorneys switch from Standard US English to African American Vernacular English (AAVE) in order to convey solidarity and alignment with African American jurors and in order to show humility. Fuller concludes that such style switching is a frequent and clearly marked usage.

Apart from likeability, credibility is another, more obvious requirement in courtroom persuasion. The relationship between speech style and credibility has been studied by researchers such as Erickson *et al.* (1978), who found that testimonies containing frequent use of **powerless speech attributes** such as **intensifiers** (*so, very, surely*), **hedges** (*kinda, I think, I guess*), **hesitation forms** (*uh, well, you know*), **questioning intonations** (e.g. use of rising, question intonation in a declarative sentence), **polite forms** (*please, ma'am, thank you*) and **hyper-formality** (e.g. use of bookish grammatical forms) are perceived as less credible. Such 'powerless speech' features are commonly used by laypersons (such as witnesses) but avoided by legal professionals.

Control and coercion in questioning

In order to influence what jurors think, advocates seek to gain as much control as possible over what witnesses say (and, subject to professional and ethical restrictions, also what they do not say). Such control is achieved through strategic questioning, often by taking advantage of the **power asymmetry** in the lawyer's verbal interaction with witnesses. Lawyers are generally not allowed to ask leading questions during examination-in-chief, but are permitted to ask leading questions during cross-examination (for comparison with UK law, see Monaghan 2015; for US law, see the American Bar Association website at www.americanbar.org). Other restrictions also apply: for example, in the UK, lawyers must not ask questions merely to insult, humiliate or annoy a witness.

Evidential rules in these and other ways limit the types of questions lawyers can ask. But lawyers still control topic, pace and duration (e.g. they can put fewer questions to a powerful witness and more questions to a weaker one). Lawyers can also use **coercive question forms,** loaded with information that the answerer may find difficult to accept but also difficult to refute. In Australia, improper questions (e.g. questions that are misleading, confusing or unduly annoying) are prohibited (s. 41, Evidence Act 1995). But Cooke (1995: 73) nevertheless reports attempts to 'upset, unsettle, confuse, confound or otherwise intimidate' witnesses 'through an aggressive barrage of questions' in Australian courtrooms. Permissibility aside, appearing over-aggressive can backfire. There may accordingly be a dynamic trade-off between (as well as rhetorical combinations of) the characteristic of being aggressive and being likeable.

Degree of coerciveness may be highly context-sensitive but it can be described in general terms. A typology of coerciveness in questioning is offered, for example, by Danet and Kermish (1978), based on how far lawyers control witnesses' answers during cross-examination. **Leading questions** consisting of a declarative sentence plus tag question (e.g. 'You walked into the room, didn't you?'; see Unit C4) are considered highly coercive: they strongly suggest and limit the answer that can be given, typically to 'yes/no'. A witness would be under increased pressure if he or she gives an unexpected, non-compliant and linguistically 'marked' answer. **Open-ended questions,** such as ones that start with *who, what, where, when* and *why,* are considered less coercive. The researchers found that the more coercive the questions, the shorter the answers they elicit.

Dunstan (1980) argues that analysis of coerciveness needs, however, go beyond surface linguistic forms (such as question type) and must investigate the contextual function and significance of an utterance. Analysing examples in context, he notes that cross-examination questions rarely request information. Instead, they counter arguments, display incredulity, repair initiations and pre-sequencers, and are to this extent primarily forms of accusation. For example, after receiving an unfavourable answer, a cross-examiner may pose a follow-up question challenging the previous answer (e.g. by pointing to inconsistency, as in 'But in the police interview, didn't you say that the car park was dimly lit?' or by requesting justification; Atkinson and Drew 1979). Alternatively, following a witness's answer, a lawyer may comment 'I hear what you say' before turning to the next question, implying disbelief (Evans 1998). Another strategy involves **reformulation** of a previous answer in different words, to make the answer fit the questioner's overall theory of the case. A hypothetical example of this is discussed in Danet and Kermish (1978): the witness testifies (in a case in which a car accident causes injury to a young person) that she 'saw a little girl crossing the street and a car struck her'. The cross-examiner then asks, 'Now this little girl darted right in front of the oncoming car, didn't she?' Substitution of 'darted' for 'crossing' deflects responsibility from the defendant and draws attention to a presumption of erratic behaviour by the child. Note, though, that in such examples, the underlying conflict between speaker and hearer remains concealed. Even more directly aggressive questions are typically masked in polite forms: 'Would you please, if you possibly can, answer my next question "yes" or "no". You did not report the donation to your superior, correct?' Examples of further questioning techniques are explored in Unit C5.

Pragmatic and discourse strategies

Techniques for indicating reference can also subtly alter a witness's testimony and jurors' perception of events being reconstructed in the trial narrative. For example, lawyers can manipulate personal pronouns to designate **in-group and out-group boundaries**, by including the jurors in a 'we' construction while referring to the other side in the case as 'they'. **Modals** can also be employed to unsettle a witness's appearance of certainty. For example, a witness can be made to sound overconfident when presented with a forcefully phrased question: 'Is there the slightest possibility you might have misheard what he said?' The status of a witness may also be strengthened or diminished by adjusting the **form of address** used towards them (e.g. the contrast between 'John' and 'Doctor'; Gibbons 2003).

Other pragmatic techniques adopted in courtroom advocacy include strategic use of **interruption** (especially when a witness is saying something damaging to the case the advocate is seeking to establish); **repetition** (often with a raised intonation contour to cast doubt on an answer that has been provided); **overlapping speech**; and dramatic **silence**. Pausing after an answer can appear to demonstrate respect for the witness, while also giving judges and jurors more time to digest that particular section of an utterance.

Lawyers may also build credibility by emphasising information that fits into the audience's belief system before gradually introducing arguments that they may find difficult to accept if presented in isolation. In jury trials, since opportunities for verbal interaction with jurors are limited (except during **voir dire** in some jurisdictions), lawyers make educated guesses about their audience based on professional experience and intuition.

Storytelling

With an accumulation of evidence and competing accounts surrounding the crux event or events at issue in a trial, jurors construct a **mental model** of what happened, typically in the form of a story (Berg 2005). For courtroom purposes, a successful story shaped by the lawyer offers a theory of the case that is simple, consistent and compelling; such a story is also one that highlights the strengths of the case as perceived from one particular point of view, minimising weaknesses. The story leads to an obvious conclusion but allows jurors to feel they have solved the puzzle themselves (see Bradshaw 2011 for discussion of storytelling techniques in the courtroom). As well as in opening and closing speeches, such stories can be created through questions: how lawyers can tell a story through a series of questions, rather than by means of more conventional narrative techniques, is illustrated in Unit C5.

The audience for a courtroom story must be able to visualise and imagine it easily. Research suggests that a moment-by-moment narrative recounting a crime, in a criminal case, is more believable than an abstract statement about the relationship between the defendant and the physical event (e.g. probability of DNA matching). As in many novels, stories are commonly narrated in the **historic present tense** in courtrooms. Heller (2006: 266) argues that 'jurors do not decide whether to convict by calculating probabilities or by scrutinizing inferential chains'; instead, he suggests, they decide whether a narrative 'possesses the "lifelikeness" that appears to mark it as true'. The potential criticism that other lives are reduced in such advocacy to jurors' own expectations, or even prejudices, is countered by the requirement of supporting evidence and the fundamental principle of judgment by peers.

The proposition that it is easier to impress jurors with stories than with statistical information is based on empirical evidence. Wells (1992) reports how, when a mock jury was told that 80 per cent of tyres of the Blue Bus Co., but only 20 per cent of the alternative Grey Bus Co., matched the tracks of a bus that had killed a dog, few (around 10 per cent) found the Blue Bus Co. liable for damages. With a different mock jury group, an eyewitness took the witness stand and testified that he saw that the bus was blue. Even though the jurors were told that eyewitness accounts have been shown to be only 80 per cent accurate in making such identifications, a significantly greater number of mock jurors (around 70 per cent) found the Blue Bus Co. liable in this condition of the experiment.

From one perspective, rhetorical strategies are extralegal factors that should not affect the outcome of a case in an ideal, rational legal system. On the other hand, legal advocacy provides ammunition for lawyers to use, at least in common-law adversarial systems, in the knowledge that the outcome of each case will be determined by the court after competing submissions and evidence have been presented as coherently and vigorously as possible by the respective parties. In this sense, an adversarial (rather than inquisitorial) structure for trials depends on competitive testing of arguments and evidence followed by detached judgment, even if a different balance of legal, factual and emotional components is likely to be found as between bench and jury trials, and in other adjudicative forums.

PRAGMATICS AND LEGAL INTERPRETATION

Unless there is a reason not to, legal interpretation presumes that legislative texts are optimal in conveying a legislature's intention, even if in practice word meaning will vary because it is inevitably context sensitive. 'Construing' a legal text, as a result, involves pragmatic aspects in addition to the semantics of language and the specialised forms of reasoning associated with legal rules. In this unit, we outline the role of contextual interpretation in legal meaning. We also consider alternative judicial approaches to legal interpretation. In conclusion, we broach the question of how closely approaches to interpreting legal texts should be expected to resemble linguistic understanding of the ways meaning is created in everyday language use.

Semantic and pragmatic aspects of meaning

Legal indeterminacy that results from **linguistic indeterminacy** (such as ambiguity and vagueness) seems at first to be concerned with semantic dimensions of meaning: with the denotational meaning of words and syntactic relations between them. As we see in Unit A6, however, determining even the meaning of isolated words and phrases (*building, in the street, dresses*) also involves pragmatic considerations.

Pragmatic theories (e.g. Gricean accounts of meaning, and relevance theory; Sperber and Wilson 1995) show how discourse interpretation proceeds in part through contextual inference. The reader or hearer fills out an incomplete, encoded semantic representation using cues given by co-text, accessible background knowledge and inferred purpose. Pragmatic studies investigate a cumulative process of **inferential enrichment** that widens, narrows and approximates linguistically **encoded meaning** according to context, as the reader or hearer seeks to understand the intended meaning of an utterance (Wilson and Carston 2007).

Legislative intent

Legal interpretation is similarly concerned with ascertaining intended meaning (though in law this is a complicated assumption, as we will see). The meaning looked for in a law is the meaning intended by the legislature and conveyed by the words used in the statute. But the phrase 'conveyed by' here obscures major complexity, because the interpretive process takes place in a different context (the courtroom) from that of the enacting legislature (the lawmaking assembly and related drafting bodies).

Claiming that the meaning attributed by a court amounts to the legislature's *intended* meaning faces several major difficulties that any approach to legal interpretation must overcome:

1   If meaning is understood literally (in law, as the 'plain', 'ordinary' or 'popular' meaning, or as **natural signification**), interpretation requires judges to assume that the drafter created an autonomous document: one whose meaning does not depend on contextually varying inference or extrinsic evidence.

2   Allowance needs to be made for the **collective authorship** characteristic of a legislature (as contrasted with a single lawgiver); collective 'intention' must be ascribed to a body of legislators who have different political agendas and convictions. Legislation, including the choice of enacted words, is often a result of negotiation and compromise.

3   Intention must be differentiated between: (i) meanings anticipated to apply to all conceivable situations; and (ii) attitudes, values and lifestyles specific to the historical moment or social situation in which the legislation was passed.

4   Some kind of resolution needs to be achieved between the subjective intention of particular, historical authors, and an objective intention 'modernised' by others in ways that adapt the narrow linguistic meaning to contemporary norms or sense of legal purpose.

A great deal of legal scholarship has been devoted to examining approaches that result from different ways of viewing these problems, especially literal and purposive statutory interpretation (see Barak 2005). Although all interpretation of legislative language is influenced by contextual factors, the significance of pragmatic interpretation is more evident in purposive reading of the law (for discussion, see Durant and Leung 2016).

Approaches to legal interpretation

The name given to the process of ascertaining meaning for a statement of law is legal construction. Efforts made to control meaning, and so embody the rule of law by achieving clarity and consistency, superimpose on spontaneous processes of discourse comprehension a range of additional interpretive measures. These include rules of interpretation (Bennion 2001; Barak 2005); and also, reflexively, rules governing rule handling itself (Twining and Miers 2010).

Historically, questions surrounding interpretation have been complicated in common-law systems by the sometimes overstated primacy of **literal interpretation**, an approach that flourished in the second half of the nineteenth century and early twentieth century, and which has enjoyed renewed influence in contemporary variants described as **textualism** (advanced in US law especially by Justice Antonin Scalia; Scalia and Garner 2012). However, emphasis on strict interpretation of particular words has been marginalised in English law in recent years by approaches that attach increased importance to context, intention and purpose: **purposive interpretation**.

Basing our description here on Manchester and Salter's (2011) comprehensive discussion of statutory interpretation in English law and the recent influence of European law on common-law approaches, we now summarise the two broad approaches.

Literal interpretation and the golden rule

A 'literal' rule (sometimes known as the **plain meaning rule**) requires word-for-word reading of the law, through which words are given their natural or ordinary meaning. Judges base such meaning either on their own understanding, or their understanding of how words are comprehended by others in the population generally or relevant groups of people. Judges may consult a dictionary definition in arriving at such a meaning.

The legal term **golden rule** (which originated in mid-nineteenth-century English legal judgments) refers in its varied formulations to decisions to depart from literal interpretation where a court decides not to give words their ordinary signification because such a meaning would result in 'manifest absurdity' that could not have been the legislature's intention. In applying the golden rule, the court 'takes the whole statute together', appealing to meaning in the word's immediate legal context.

Purposive interpretation and the mischief rule

While usually distinguished from one another in law textbooks, and associated with different historical periods, the purposive approach and the **mischief rule** both seek to establish legal meaning as the meaning intended by the legislature (for English law, by parliament). In contrast with the literal approach and golden rule, which emphasise words in their immediate linguistic context, the mischief rule and purposive approach take account of legal purpose. They give more weight to the idea that legislative intention might not be adequately conveyed by the words themselves (e.g. because not all new situations can be foreseen in drafting provisions).

The notion of a mischief rule has its origins in a 1584 English case, *Heydon's case*. In that case, the court resolved that 'for the sure and true interpretation of statutes', four things 'should be discerned and considered': what the common law was before the making of the act; what the mischief and defect was for which the common law could not provide; what remedy parliament 'resolved and appointed to cure the disease of the Commonwealth'; and the need for judges to interpret words so as to suppress that mischief and advance a remedy. There was no indication in *Heydon's case* that the mischief rule should only be used in cases where the meaning of words is ambiguous; but the rule has mostly only been invoked in such circumstances.

Constraints on legal interpretation

Laws are written by draftsmen to embody the intent of a legislature; but once they have been enacted, they are interpreted and applied by judges in particular cases independently of the legislature that formulated them. Legal rules, as well as being stated in statutes, are in this way polished – in some circumstances, arguably modified – by judges in deciding cases where there are matters not covered by the relevant statute or when the applicable meaning of some word or phrasing in a statute is uncertain.

This process of judicial decision-making is constrained, however, by relevant propositions of law (what is called the **ratio decidendi**, often abbreviated to 'ratio') developed in earlier decisions. Such legal propositions do not necessarily take a clearly stated form (e.g. being found in a specific sentence), because the legal proposition emerges in relation to particular facts of the particular case. Nevertheless, the ratio creates a precedent that may be binding, depending on the relative position in the court hierarchy of the court establishing the rule and the subsequent court contemplating its use. Detailed rules guide the application of precedent cases; but the process overall amounts to a kind of cumulative interpretation, as courts build on decisions made by earlier courts. This is known as the doctrine of **stare decisis**: in specified circumstances, later courts are required to stand by decisions made by earlier ones.

What are the practical consequences of this complex procedure of legal interpretation as regards how meaning is actually attributed? Two aspects stand out.

Different notions of context

In pragmatic theories, such as Gricean accounts of implied and inferred meaning, meaning is arrived at by a hearer making inferences that combine what is explicitly said with contextual inferences in order to arrive at the relevant meaning. Context typically includes features of the immediate speech situation (including participants and their relationship) plus a wide range of accessible assumptions about the world that can be activated with different amounts of processing effort. Pragmatic theories based on notions of cognitive effort and reward, such as relevance theory, focus on spontaneous effort made by hearers to find relevant meaning when an intention to communicate with them is signalled.

Hermeneutic models for ascribing legal meaning differ in significant respects, not least in that the interpretive effort made is typically methodical, conscious and rule-governed rather than spontaneous. When courts go beyond the literal meaning of words, their allowance of contextual inference is highly constrained, limited to taking account of precisely specified features of context, either 'intrinsic' or 'extrinsic' to the statute in question.

❑ So-called **intrinsic material** may include other provisions within the statute, as well as marginal or side notes, headings, any preamble, and the long title (but not the short title, which is provided for reference purposes only). Use of such aids as practical guidance in understanding what a statute means underscores the communicative significance of genre conventions in legal texts (see Thread 3).

❑ **Extrinsic material** may include explanatory notes published in tandem with (recent) legislation; other statutory provisions, whether in the same field or in other fields of law; general common-law principles; parliamentary materials; some classes of pre-parliamentary publication (e.g. law commission reports); international treaties and conventions; and in some circumstances policy considerations (effectively the judge's view of what the best policy for the law to adopt would be).

Appeal to maxims

In addition to use of such materials, courts also rely in interpreting on general presumptions, some of which relate directly to language and some to the conceptual nature of legal rules.

These interpretive presumptions take the form of **canons** or **maxims**. They are interpretive rules, but resemble accumulated wisdom rather than collectively forming a principled rule system or psychologically realistic model of processing. In practice, judges do not refer to which rule they have applied, if any; and the complexity of fit between rule, wording of the law in question, and the fact situation to which the rule is applied may also obscure how (or even if) a particular rule has been followed.

Such maxims often have Latin names. These include **expressio unius (exclusio alterius)**: a maxim that presumes that expression of one thing implies exclusion of another. This presumption has the result that where one thing is mentioned within a class, this mention by implication excludes other things in the same class. Another maxim is the **contra proferentem** rule, which requires that if ambiguity in a clause or document cannot be resolved in any other way, then the words should be construed against the interests of the person who put the clause forward. Another is the rule of **lenity**, which requires courts to decide meaning in favour of the defendant if a different, specific meaning has not been expressed in the relevant provision. Others are the rule known as **eiusdem generis**, which stipulates that a word should be given a meaning that is of the same kind or nature as other words listed with it; and **noscitur a sociis** is a rule requiring that the meaning of a word or phrase should be guided by words or phrases associated with it.

Other established presumptions are less like practical wisdom gained from interpretive experience than deeper-seated assumptions. These include a presumption that a statute creating criminal offences should require a blameworthy state of mind (**mens rea**) on the part of the defendant; that a statute linked to possible imprisonment should be interpreted strictly in favour of the individual; that a statutory provision is not intended to make changes in existing law beyond those expressly stated; and that a statute will comply with a country's obligations under international treaties and conventions.

Law as an interpretive social institution

The combination of careful legislative preparation and drafting, rules governing statutory interpretation, and cumulative development of legal interpretation through case law creates a complex and rigorous procedure for examining meaning and for monitoring meanings that have been ascribed. At the same time, the process retains flexibility, which allows legal interpretation to respond to changing circumstances. Manchester and Salter (2011) in fact devote a substantial proportion of their analysis to looking at what they call the **dynamics of precedent**: essentially how words, concepts and rules based on them evolve over time in difficult areas of law, including unlawful *detention* of mental health patients, *equal* pay and marital *rape*.

International variation

So far, our exposition in this unit has been based on English law, though the general principles apply across common-law systems. Since the interpretive processes as we have described them are a normative set of procedures governed by legal institutions, their detail varies both over time and between legal jurisdictions. The English approach to legal interpretation outlined above, for example, has gradually changed since the coming into force of the Human Rights Act 1998, in the direction of interpretive practices developed in non-common-law systems in Continental Europe.

The gradual accommodation to changing styles of interpretation in English law has not, however, precipitated anything like the controversy to be found in US law over the relative merits of textualist and intentionalist approaches. According to textualists, the first rule of interpretation must be, as with a literal approach more generally, fidelity to ordinary meaning; judges should not speculate about what lawmakers intended to say or achieve in enacting a legal text. The major proponent of textualism, the eminent US judge Justice Scalia, has argued that 'The text is the law, and it is the text that must be observed', echoing a warning expressed in an earlier period by Justice Oliver Wendell Holmes (1809–1894) that 'We do not inquire what the legislature meant; we ask only what the statute means' (Scalia 1997: 22–3).

This complex controversy between different approaches to legal interpretation in US law will continue. But there is another changing horizon also to be considered: that of international, 'world' law in fields including international trade, human rights, and criminal behaviour, including war crimes and genocide. In public international law, to take one area, a cluster of key words and phrases (including *self-determination, indigenous, sovereignty, torture, slavery, aggression, piracy, genocide, occupation* and *security*, among others) have shown themselves to be exposed to contested interpretation in forums, including international courts, tribunals and treaty negotiations. Tensions over the meaning to be given to such terms are exacerbated not only by differences between national legal systems, but by differences between the languages in which international law is expressed, since complex meanings are carried across but shaded differently in different languages. Such tensions, it appears, present new interpretive difficulties with important global ramifications.

Laws as a unique form of linguistic expression?

Legal enactments are undoubtedly communicative acts, not only literal statements. But in some views, they are more than either. According to Greenberg (2011), enactments are rules expressed in words and embodied in documents, but conceptually distinct from the either the words or the documents in which they are expressed. Rules, including legal rules, can after all be unwritten, tacit or implied (a theme explored in Twining and Miers 2010). It might therefore be the rule, rather than the language in which a rule is expressed, that should be examined for meaning. Greenberg argues that **communication theories of law** (i.e. frameworks for interpreting legal texts based on likeness to principles underlying general communication, especially personal communication) cannot provide a satisfactory account of how statutes contribute to law's content or effects.

Legislative systems, Greenberg argues, have aims that are not reducible to their communicative content as analysed according to linguistic (including pragmatic) standards and principles. Rather, what is distinctive about laws may be precisely that they use linguistic means for unique, normative and symbolic purposes. Those purposes, Greenberg notes, range from specifying conceptual rules and ensuring that legal standards will be enforced and complied with, through to advancing justice, fostering the legitimacy of the legal system, preserving the status quo, and promoting a particular ideology. Because laws operate in these combined ways, he concludes, the legal 'meaning' of statutes and other legal instruments is only partly communicated by the words in which they are expressed; legal meaning is not reducible to those words – or to our customary ways of understanding most other kinds of language use. We pursue these fundamental questions in Unit D6, as well as more generally in Thread 8.

LEGAL SPEECH ACTS   B7

Unit A7 examines the vocabulary used in describing the relationship among law, power and order. We note there that language can *describe* power (e.g. a textbook may begin, 'Power consists of . . .'); or it can *reflect* power (e.g. the sociolect used by a judge might signify a powerful social class). We can also say that patterns in language use may *correlate* with power (e.g. the status of participants in a legal interaction may match their speaking skills). But can we say that legal discourse actually exercises or *performs* power? In this unit, we look at linguistic approaches based on speech act theory that suggest that it does. In particular, we look at linguistic 'performatives', as enablers of action, before addressing the question of how performative speech acts relate to the wider practice of devising and following legal 'rules'.

How to do things with words: linguistic performatives

First, it is necessary to provide a context for the linguistic concepts we will draw on. Although there were earlier, analogous approaches in rhetoric, the idea that language can be used in a **performative** way is usually associated with a pioneering work by the Oxford philosopher J. L. Austin (1911–1960), *How to Do Things with Words* (1962), compiled from a series of lectures he had delivered at Harvard in the 1950s. Austin noted various utterances that he felt functioned in interesting and unexamined ways, including examples such as: *I name this ship* Queen Elizabeth, *I promise* and *I do* [take this woman to be my lawful wedded wife, as stated in a marriage ceremony]. Such utterances, Austin argued, contrast with statements that describe states of affairs, which are either true or false. These different uses he had identified, Austin felt, form a class that he called **explicit performatives** (having rejected an earlier preference for *operative* rather than *performative* because of the polysemy of *operative*). Austin observed that you can insert *hereby* into first-person performative expressions in a way that is anomalous in statements; and he suggested this was a useful test of whether utterances are functioning as the actions they are talking about, rather than merely describing those actions.

In *How to Do Things with Words*, Austin describes the conditions for what he called 'happy' performance of such verbal actions. He also explores situations in which they fail (**misfire**) and abuses of requirements that surround them. Austin's discussion led to an analysis of three levels within any given utterance: **locutionary acts** (acts of saying something); **illocutionary acts** (use of such acts to convey a particular force); and **perlocutionary acts** (the experience or uptake of such acts by the recipient).

Alongside explicit first-person performatives (which satisfy the 'hereby test'), Austin recognised that performatives can also be realised indirectly. *There is a bull in that field* could be a warning or promise, depending on context. Contractions and ellipses in the verbal form of performatives are also possible; and intonation and use of **deontic modals** such as permissive *may* and directive *shall* or *should* can act as **force-indicating devices**.

There was, however, a twist in Austin's influential work, late in the book: the author concludes that in fact all utterances are performative in one way or another: 'surely to state is every bit as much to perform an illocutionary act as, say, to warn or to pronounce' (Austin 1962: 134).

Speech acts

The name **speech acts** for such verbal acts was not Austin's idea. This general term was introduced by the philosopher John Searle, who has built substantially on Austin's insights. In a series of works, Searle develops Austin's distinction between the illocutionary force of an utterance and its propositional content, a distinction Searle symbolises by the general formula $F(p)$, in which p represents a proposition and F a force-indicating device that signals what the proposition is being used to do.

Much of Searle's work explores conditions under which an utterance can function as a particular speech act; and he produces a taxonomy of criteria for classifying illocutionary acts. Among Searle's 12 criteria, some of the more significant as regards legal uses of language are:

❑ the purpose or point of the type of act (what is the act attempting to get the hearer to do?);
❑ differences in the force or strength with which the illocutionary point is presented (e.g. *suggest* as compared with *insist*);
❑ differences in the status or position of the speaker and hearer; and
❑ differences between acts that require extralinguistic institutions for their performance and ones that do not (as Austin had noted, to *declare* war requires a

speaker of a particular political status; to *excommunicate* someone requires the existence of a church system with associated rules and procedures).

Searle's criteria expose difficulties with Austin's earlier classification into five classes, which had contained several legally suggestive categories: verdictives (containing verdicts, judgments, appraisals and findings); exercitives (involving the exercise of powers, such as appointing and ordering); and commissives (e.g. the act of promising). While acknowledging Austin's achievement, Searle claims that Austin's classification shows confusion between verbs and acts; too much overlap between categories; and too much variation within categories. His own classification proposes the following alternatives:

- ❑ **Assertives** (statements of belief, including verbs such as *conclude* and *deduce*).
- ❑ **Directives** (including verbs such as *order, command, plead* and *permit*).
- ❑ **Commissives** (which commit the speaker to some course of action, e.g. *promise*).
- ❑ **Expressives** (e.g. *congratulate, apologise*).
- ❑ **Declarations** (including verbs such as *resign, fire* and *excommunicate*).

The first of our two extracts in Unit D7, from Brenda Danet, works through Searle's classification offering illustrations that foreground connections with legal categories and events.

Speech acts in law

Speech act theory has been very influential in linguistics (Levinson 1983). Its insights have also been applied in analysing language in law. Tiersma (1990), for instance, uses speech act theory in analysing perjury, as well as the language of defamation (in discussing the latter, he emphasises the act of 'accusing' rather than examining meaning then relating meaning to an effect of falsely tarnishing reputation). Below, we illustrate the use of speech act theory in discussing law through Dennis Kurzon's account of the performative character of statutes, and Sanford Shane's analyses of contracts and hearsay evidence. Other law-related uses of speech act categories have also been made; we consider such work in units where it relates closely to topics under discussion (e.g. Greenawalt's analysis of boundaries to freedom of expression in Unit A8, and Shuy's forensic linguistic analysis of criminal speech acts such as bribes or solicitation in Thread 9).

Kurzon: it is hereby performed

Kurzon's short book *It is Hereby Performed: Explorations in Legal Speech Acts* (1986) pioneered how speech act theory might illuminate the functioning of statutes, private law documents and court judgments.

Kurzon's analysis of statutes examines the role of the **enacting formula** found at the beginning of each statute (see Unit C3). He considers 'enacting' to be performative both in form and function, and to be a member of Austin's category of exercitive acts that indicate a decision that something is to be so, as distinct from a report that something already is so. The consequences of enactment, he states, include that others are compelled, permitted or prohibited to do certain acts.

Enacting formulae appear specific to common-law countries, by comparison with statements of 'having decided to pass a law' contained in many civil law jurisdictions. They also vary between jurisdictions, and have been altered as a result of pressures created by language change as described in Unit A2. In the United States, the enacting formula takes the form:

> Be it enacted by the Senate and House of Representatives of the United States of America in Congress assembled, That

The UK enacting formula shows some similarity, but the present form dates from a modernising statute of 1850 concerned to simplify the language used in legislation at that time. Even in this nineteenth-century, modernised form, however, the language is archaic, including in the use at the beginning of an almost unique form of passive imperative:

> Be it enacted by the Queen's most Excellent Majesty, by and with the advice and consent of the Lords Spiritual and Temporal, and Commons, in this present Parliament assembled, and by the authority of the same, as follows.

In this formulation, apart from the grammatical difficulty presented by the passive imperative, the subject referred to by 'it' is extraposed to the end of the sentence and is effectively the entire text of the statute (i.e. all ensuing provisions). Kurzon's main claim about statutes follows from that extraposition. The enacting formula, he contends, establishes the illocutionary force of the whole text, as a kind of **master speech act** under which all other verbal acts contained in the statute are embedded. A hierarchical relationship therefore exists, he argues, between the speech act of enactment and the many constituent sentences that take the form of speech acts of permitting (*may . . .*), ordering (*shall . . .*) and prohibiting (*shall not . . .*). The master speech act controls those other speech acts: they may permit or forbid specific things, but their authority in doing so derives from a superordinate speech act of enactment that governs them all.

Sanford Schane: speech act explanation of legal data
We have referred elsewhere to Sanford Schane's *Language and the Law* (2006). Two chapters in this book are concerned with speech act analysis, each examining a substantive area of law. In one, Schane tests how far it is possible to elucidate aspects of the law of **contract** by deploying speech act concepts developed to account for general uses of language. A valid legal agreement or contract, Schane informs readers, has three essential requirements: an offer, an acceptance and consideration. He then compares these requirements with the necessity that some speech acts, if they are to take effect, must be performed by particular individuals under appropriate circumstances (e.g. with specific uptake or acceptance). Schane shows that criteria for promising, with minor adjustment, can accommodate the specialised requirements that underpin legal offers. However, although speech act theory can accommodate such details, Schane concludes that this still leaves an underlying question: how precise or even predictive are linguistic accounts of general usage, when invoked to explain specialised legal distinctions or procedures?

This question is explored more directly in Schane's other chapter concerned with speech acts, where he examines the US **hearsay** evidence rule. Extending an insight on the topic expressed much earlier by Austin (1962: 13), Schane initially distinguishes in the American law of hearsay: (a) testimony about events directly perceived through the senses; and (b) testimony based on what a witness heard or read as words spoken or written by someone else. The latter may or may not constitute hearsay, and therefore may or may not be admissible. If the object of the evidence is to establish the truth of what is contained in the statement, then the statement is hearsay; however, the evidence will not be hearsay if its aim is not to establish the truth of what was said but rather to establish the fact that the statement was made. Prominent among four exceptions to the inadmissibility of possible hearsay material are utterances that are verbal acts, or the verbal accompaniments of physical acts that have legal significance in the case.

The theoretical question challenging Schane was this: can a linguistic generalisation capture which statements made by a testifying witness will count as inadmissible hearsay and which ones will not (and so which may be admitted into evidence)? His method for investigating this question was to collect a corpus of legal judgments from a Harvard hearsay exam, and then investigate how successfully speech act theory could account for the 'correct solution' data. His finding was that if a witness offers an out-of-court statement for its illocutionary value, its perlocutionary effects or its locutionary properties (and associated state of mind), it will not be hearsay. However, if offered solely for propositional content, then the statement will be hearsay. Speech act theory on this assessment stood up fairly well, he concludes, to the test of predicting decisions in a given area of law.

How to do things with rules

These short illustrations suggest that law's power is performed at least partly by resources available in general language: speech acts. But Austin and Searle raised other issues surrounding performatives that have received less attention, arguably because the issues in question are less obviously linguistic and more interdisciplinary (some linguists, for example, claim that **institutional speech acts** are not of interest to pragmatics; for them, it is only non-institutional speech acts such as warning, threatening and requesting that are subjects for linguistic analysis; see Sperber and Wilson 1995).

Institutional speech acts

Think of weddings, declarations of war and excommunications. Both Austin and Searle noted that speech acts such as these depend for their success on institutionalised arrangements. A particular role and authorised powers on the part of the speaker may be essential; relevant procedures may be needed; and the lack of a required uptake or compliance by the hearer may make the act void.

In law, such speech acts are complicated theoretically as well as in practice. For example, promulgating a law has both declarational status (the propositional content becomes the law) and directive status (the law is directive in its intent). Other declarations, Searle points out, overlap with assertives; and some institutional procedures, he observes, require facts not only to be ascertained, but also laid down authoritatively following completion of a fact-finding procedure. Argument in tribunals must eventually come to an end with the issuing of a decision; so a judge (like an umpire) asserts factual claims that can be assessed in terms of whether the words accurately represent the facts. But at the same time, the judge's words also have the force of declarations, in that if a judge declares you guilty (assuming this is upheld on any appeal), then for legal purposes you are guilty.

Law is not merely command and control

Often in discussions about law, a distinction is made between narrow and contextually specific commands (with a recognisable addresser, addressee and set of referents) and more generally formulated rules (which are formulated not to be tied to a specific set of circumstances). This topic is addressed in our second extract in Unit D7, where the capability of language to make general statements is argued to be a precondition for formulating legal rules. Part of the challenge in assessing how language performs power is to explain the relationship between speech acts and legal rules.

Legal rules have certainly sometimes been conceived as a sovereign's coercive orders (a **command theory of law** associated with the nineteenth-century legal theorist John Austin (1790–1859), easily confused with the twentieth-century philosopher J. L. Austin discussed above). Influentially, however, in *The Concept of Law* and other works, the legal theorist H. L. A. Hart (1907–1992) rejects that idea, pointing out that individuated, face-to-face directions tend only to be activated in law when general rules are challenged by disobedience. Legal control is usually a matter of broadly formulated rules that apply to everyone and are followed without coercion. Such rules, Hart notes, do not only require, permit or prohibit things; they also enable people to do things (e.g. to make a will, buy a home or get married). Working before detailed publications on speech acts were available, though in informal dialogue with J. L. Austin, Hart compares laws not with commands, but with acts of promising, in that both exercise 'a power conferred by rules'.

In the title of their popular introduction to legal rule-following (a topic that for a period attracted attention especially in response to Wittgenstein's philosophical analysis of rules), it is J. L. Austin (performatives) rather than John Austin (commands) that Twining and Miers (2010) invoke: their book is called *How to Do Things with Rules*. The authors do not discuss speech acts directly, and hardly mention either of the two Austins. But they show through real and hypothetical examples how legal rules must be understood as assertions whose force can only be grasped against a background of institutionally and culturally specific pragmatic inferences. A comprehensive theory of rules, they suggest, needs to account for matters including the validity of rules, the value of adhering to rules, the relationship between rules and the exercise of power and authority, and variations in attitudes towards rules (Twining and Miers 2010: 119).

Issues concerning the relationship between speech acts and legal rules are perhaps stated most clearly, however, in a short chapter by Frederick Schauer in the collection from which our second excerpt in Unit D8 is taken. Schauer argues that in trying to understand language and law, 'the question about rules other than the rules of language, therefore, is not why the rules of language work, but whether the rules of language, which *do* work (whether we can explain why or not), enable *other* rules to work' (Schauer 1993: 316).

DISPUTING 'ORDINARY LANGUAGE'   B8

In this unit, we develop the outline of verbal 'content adjudication' we present in Unit A8. We focus on how the meaning and effect of utterances is decided in fields including media law and the law governing public order, where uses of language may, for example, be alleged to be offensive, threatening, defamatory, an incitement to racial or religious hatred, or a commercial misrepresentation. We examine how courts often rely on a concept of 'ordinary meaning' in these circumstances, and show how this notion offers only an unstable link between two different visions of how language works: one a model of negotiated interaction; the other concerned to regulate communicated effects.

Descriptive and normative accounts of language

To most language users (including lawyers and linguists), it seems self-evident that language use can prompt different interpretations depending on audience and context. Situated inference plays an important part in this process, generating and filtering possible meanings. So does recognition of what speech act is being performed, and what move or transaction an utterance performs in an ongoing interaction. These topics form the subject matter of pragmatics, discourse analysis and conversation analysis. For the purposes of law, by contrast, courts must select among alternative, submitted meanings one single meaning that is found (in the specialised, legal sense of 'found' meaning 'decided', see Thread 7) to be the correct, factual meaning that the relevant law will apply. Sometimes such adjudication is performed in a procedurally detailed manner (e.g. in defamation actions); in some areas, decisions may be arrived at by relying more on the judge's linguistic intuitions (or those of a jury, if there is one).

Similar processes are involved in assessing the effect, rather than the meaning, of a disputed utterance or discourse. Effects in question may range from feeling traumatised through to being deceived into buying or doing something; and those effects may result in further consequences, such as losing money or being injured. In everyday social interaction, it is recognised that discourse can produce very different effects, depending not only on personal beliefs or knowledge, but also on the disposition of the addressee. One person's funny joke may be offensive and demeaning to someone else; an advertising claim may be treated completely seriously by a credulous consumer yet dismissed as an obvious exaggeration by someone more sceptical; and one person's taste in titillation may be another's obscenity. Readers and viewers have different thresholds of tolerance, excitability, suspicion and detachment; and such characteristics are likely to affect how a person views rhetorical exaggeration, irony, intemperate language, invective and potentially manipulative sales discourse.

The 'ordinary' meaning of contested words

Central to the adjudication of meaning and effect by law courts is the concept of **ordinary meaning**: the notion of 'plain' or 'natural' signification rather than strained or opportunistic interpretation. Such 'plain' meaning can be linked to effects that an utterance may be presumed to have on the addressee(s) and others. Courts typically identify such plain or ordinary meanings for non-legal discourse by deciding what an **ordinary, reasonable reader** (as characterised in defamation law) would take the utterance in dispute to have meant or what communicative effect it would have (or would have had). The 'ordinary, reasonable reader', and related **average consumer** (in trademark law), are specialised legal constructs: interpretive variants of the common-law standard of the **reasonable man** [*sic*], also referred to in earlier periods as **the man on the Clapham omnibus** (though these various persons are often narrowed as appropriate by context).

For purposes of litigation, judging requires a standard of interpretation beyond the views of the interactants themselves. In adversarial proceedings, a claimant puts forward one meaning (sometimes several, argued as alternatives); each meaning claimed will be stretched in the direction of his or her overall submission (i.e. paraphrased to accentuate the gravity of defamatory imputation, racially derogatory meaning or false commercial representation). The defendant will submit one or more contrary meanings, stretched in the direction of the defence being made out (i.e. a more innocuous proposition or an ironic or humorous purpose). On what basis can a court decide what the contested discourse means, since the words are not technical legal discourse whose meaning is controlled by law but language in general use in a wider social sphere?

If interpretation starts from the idea that communicated meanings are what a speaker or writer intends, then the defendant will always succeed: the subjective effect that triggered the suit will be found to be unwarranted. Interpretation that prioritises the subjective effect of an utterance on an addressee or other recipient, on the other hand, would mean that the claimant or prosecution will always succeed: the subjective perception will be vindicated, whatever it may have been. Viewed in terms of free speech, granting too much to intended meaning favours free speech but at the risk of condoning potentially serious harms. Granting too much to subjective effect, on the other hand, can have a chilling effect on free speech, by being overly claimant-friendly: increased risk of litigation may discourage socially valuable but controversial viewpoints, which freedom of expression principles seek to protect (Barendt 2005).

In relevant areas of law, these contrasting difficulties are generally overcome by the court acting as a kind of meaning umpire (Durant 2010a). Meaning is typically determined not on the basis of intention or effect, but according to an objective reading of the words constructed by appealing to the (presumed) interpretive judgment of an ordinary, reasonable reader. Description of this interpretive standard as objective can seem strange from an ethnographic point of view (which is likely to emphasise the specificity of and variation in language use, including interpretation); but such description forms part of a framework in law of tests defined as subjective (where they consist of reported experience) and objective (when viewed from an external point of judgment). As regards the public credibility, and ultimately legitimacy, of how law arrives at fixed meaning for everyday discourse, describing a meaning as 'objective' brings an advantage, however: that the word not only carries the meaning 'viewed from outside, as an object', but also the connotation 'unbiased, scientific'.

The adjudicated meaning that is simultaneously ordinary and objective becomes the legal meaning of the contested utterance for the purpose of the litigation. It is then a small step for that meaning to underpin where required a legal standard of **strict liability**, for example in defamation, which holds the communicator liable for the meaning decided by the court with no reference to whether he or she may have intended to communicate that meaning (or whether that was the meaning the addressee or recipient claims to have derived).

Interpreting contested utterances in two areas of law

Now consider briefly how these approaches to identifying meaning take shape in two important but very different areas of law: the civil law of defamation, which we have mentioned already, and criminal prosecution of Internet trolls in English law under s. 127(1) of the Communications Act 2003.

The 'ordinary reader' in defamation

Defamation law protects people (and, slightly less, companies) against untrue statements whose publication has caused or is likely to cause serious harm to their reputation. The effect of 'damage to reputation' has been defined in various ways over the centuries, and has changed substantially along with social values (e.g. in relation to sexuality and sexual behaviour). Centrally, however, reputational damage occurs where the hearer or reader of something published (whether spoken, printed, broadcast or online) will think less well of the individual referred to. (For a detailed account of English libel (defamation) law, with comparative discussion of other jurisdictions, see Barendt *et al.* (2014: 361–453).)

Whether a particular statement produces such an effect, however, depends on what it means. That is established, following a 'judicial filter' in which a judge may throw out claims based on extravagant or implausible meanings, to the strict liability standard described above using the 'ordinary reader' test. Except for a class of exceptions (which we describe briefly below), the legally adopted meaning of the disputed words will be their natural and ordinary meaning, or meaning the words convey to ordinary people. An ordinary person for this purpose has been judicially characterised as 'a person of fair, average intelligence; who is neither perverse, nor morbid or suspicious of mind, nor avid for scandal'. This reader 'does not live in an ivory tower, and is a layman, not a lawyer'; his or her capacity for implication is acknowledged to be possibly greater than that of a lawyer.

The ordinary meaning of 'the words', then, is context-specific **utterance meaning** rather than a literal 'dictionary meaning' of the particular words: it is the meaning of words as tokens (i.e. in a specific use), not types (i.e. in terms of their potential for meaning if used). The ordinary meaning is that of the words as used in a given publication, targeted at a particular type of reader (who is acknowledged to read different kinds of material with different standards of care and attention: newspapers, text messages, headlines, scientific papers, etc.). The meaning arrived at also takes account of inferences prompted by typical use of the words in other contexts, as well as inferences ('indirect meanings') shaped by general knowledge. In some defamation actions, 'ordinary meaning' is extended by a specialised kind of so-called **true innuendo** meaning (Barendt *et al.* 2014: 374–8). Such a meaning is triggered where an inter-pretation significantly different from face-value meaning, with potentially defamatory implications, is implied if the reader of the publication is aware of certain extrinsic facts.

Two key features stand out about the approach to deciding the meaning of an alleged defamatory statement in this way. One is that the resulting meaning is singular: there is one correct meaning. UK defamation law observes an often criticised **single meaning rule**, acknowledged by lawyers as being highly artificial, which requires that from the multiple, different shades of meaning likely to be derived by actual readers, one definitive meaning must be determined. It is on the basis of that one meaning that the gravity of defamatory effect, if any, will be assessed, judgment given, and (potentially) damages awarded. The other feature is that the meaning of a defamatory statement is 'ordinary' only in a highly specialised sense of *ordinary*: 'ordinary' located in a complex network of previous analyses in the relevant case law.

Internet trolls

The approach to determining meaning and effect adopted in defamation law can be usefully contrasted with an approach followed, controversially in some recent cases, to prosecuting Internet trolls for threats, flaming and harassment using s. 127 of the UK Communications Act 2003. Some of the difference between the approach to trolling and to defamation follows from the fact that defamation is a civil matter, whereas prosecutions under s. 127 relate to alleged criminal offences. Another difference concerns the degree of procedural clarity in arriving at meaning. Concerns over the application of s. 127 during a period showing a rapid rise in the number of prosecutions resulted in the then Director of Public Prosecutions (DPP) releasing new guidelines in 2013 in order to establish clearer procedures and a higher threshold triggering prosecution.

s. 127 consists of three subsections. The third states the penalty for being found guilty of an offence: if convicted of 'improper use of a public electronic communications network', someone may be imprisoned for up to six months, or fined. The offence itself is defined in sections 1 and 2. A person is guilty of an offence under s. 127(1a) if he [*sic*] 'sends by means of a public electronic communications network a message or other matter that is grossly offensive or of an indecent, obscene or menacing character'; and guilty under s. 127(2a) if 'for the purpose of causing annoyance, inconvenience or needless anxiety to another, he sends by means of a public electronic communications network a message that he knows to be false'.

As regards interpretation, notice that s. 127(2) specifies an effect that needs to be proved: 'causing annoyance, inconvenience or needless anxiety'. It also specifies a mental state in relation to the falsity of the message: 'knows to be false'. No equivalent purpose or mental state is specified under s. 127(1). In both sections, the scope of the offence can appear problematic because of the challenge in applying the broad terms in which the sections are expressed. 'False', as applied to a message, may have a range of dimensions (which have been examined in detail in other areas of law). More problematic are terms in s. 127(1) including 'grossly offensive' and 'indecent, obscene or menacing character'. The meaning of these terms has also been explored in other legal fields (including in the law of obscenity), but depends significantly on rapidly changing and socially unstable standards in an open and diverse online society.

More immediately problematic, however, is what any particular utterance – a tweet, Web post, blog, etc. – will be judged to convey. Interpreting online messaging, for example, can lead to major challenges created by the rapid evolution of online communication styles and expectations. Interpretation is not difficult in all cases. In some recent trolling cases, a barrage of messages directed towards women who feature either continuously or even briefly in news coverage has contained explicit threats of sexual violence mixed with misogynistic and vituperative comment, traumatising the recipient. It is difficult to see how directly stated threats, including vaginal penetration 'with a 3 foot pole', could not be taken as 'menacing', whatever the channel, manner or context of their expression. But messages in some other cases are not so easily interpreted or judged. In the case *Chambers v. DPP* [2012], one of a number of cases that prompted the new guidelines by the then DPP, the defendant successfully appealed his conviction under s. 127(1) for publishing a message of a 'menacing character': namely, a tweet to his followers after he found that the (Robin Hood) airport he hoped to use to visit a new girlfriend he had met on Twitter was closed by bad weather. The message read: 'Crap! Robin Hood airport is closed. You've got a week and a bit to get your shit together, otherwise I'm blowing the airport sky-high'. No online complaints were made but a security manager routinely monitoring online references to the airport drew attention to the message as a 'non-credible threat'. This resulted in prosecution. Despite the message having been tweeted to the defendant's own contact list rather than the airport (complicating the reference of the pronoun 'you'), his tweet does contain a direct threat, 'If not X, then Y', and that threat is at face value a serious one: to blow up an airport. The interpretive challenge, despite the first instance outcome leading to widespread public ridicule, was hardly negligible: the court was obliged to weigh stylistic markers of an abrasive but ironic online discourse against a directly stated threat that it would have appeared grossly negligent to ignore if anything happened. Interpreting Chambers' tweet raised questions similar to those identified by Greenawalt (which we describe in Unit A7) in his analysis of borderline 'situation-altering' utterances: with respect to indirect expression, at what point does a performative utterance cease to be performative?

In the guidance issued on prosecuting Internet trolls, and with hindsight available following Chambers' successful appeal against conviction, the DPP drew attention to the freedom of expression implications of over-prosecuting the kind of messaging involved in *Chambers*: that a chilling effect might follow from prominent Internet troll prosecutions if they were not evidently 'necessary and proportionate' in accordance with Article 10 of the European Convention on Human Rights. Nevertheless, it was concluded, in some circumstances prosecutions should still be brought. Reflecting the need to weigh up when prosecution would be in the public interest, the DPP's guidance stated that in deciding whether to prosecute, account should be taken of a message's relevant context, including the age of the communicator, the possibility of joking and pastiche, and whether the behaviour was one-off or repeated.

B9   **TECHNIQUES IN FORENSIC LINGUISTICS**

Unit A9 introduces four main ways in which forensic analysis can contribute to the administration of justice. In this unit, we explain how such analysis is performed in a selection of cases and ask some more specific questions: What analytical tools are available? How are those tools used? What are the main challenges associated with forensic linguistic approaches, for instance as regards the reliability of evidence presented?

The language expert

> I do not call myself a forensic linguist. I neither object to the use of the term nor particularly care whether or not I am called one. The fact is, I consider myself a linguist who, in this instance, happens to be carrying out his analysis on data that grows out of a court case. I see no reason to add the word forensic, which is a description of the data and the area in which a language problem resides.
>
> (Shuy 1993: 200)

Implicit in Shuy's view here is that there is no significant difference between a linguist and a forensic linguist; the same linguistic techniques could be applied in either a legal or non-legal setting. An example of analogous investigative techniques being used in legal and non-legal contexts can be found in relation to fiction: it was the forensic linguist Patrick Juola who established that J. K. Rowling was the probable author of the novel *The Cuckoo's Calling* (which had been published under the pseudonym Robert Galbraith), an insight subsequently confirmed (Rothman 2013).

More generally, Shuy's point is that linguistics as a discipline claims truth in its descriptions and scientific rigour in its analyses; the expertise it applies in other fields cannot be bent to the interests of a particular party. It is for the lawyer concerned, Shuy emphasises, to decide whether the evidence a particular linguist would give is helpful to the case being developed. A trained and experienced linguist, Shuy maintains, has the ability to describe language and linguistic processes precisely. Nevertheless, since most cases are problem-based, there will still be creative skill involved in deciding what the most appropriate investigative tool is, or whether to devise a combination of methods that solve a problem more convincingly. Communicating to an audience of legal professionals (especially in a stressful courtroom setting) may be a further challenge, calling for effective presentation of findings (Coulthard and Johnson 2007).

Analytical tools used in forensic analysis of texts

Methods used in forensic linguistic analysis may be quantitative or qualitative. The most commonly applied and recognised forms of analysis, in terms of traditional linguistic sub-disciplines, appear to be phonetic/phonological, followed by corpus-based investigation. The analytical tools described below are organised by sub-discipline. But the reader should bear in mind the following points: the list is not exhaustive; the categories overlap; and more than one method is likely to be used in a given analysis.

Handwriting analysis

Signatures on legal instruments (e.g. on a will, testimony or contractual agreement) have been used as authentication of the identity and intention of the signatory for hundreds of years. To decide whether two samples of handwriting, such as a signature, are written by the same author, it is necessary to study various components of the text: visual similarities, size of words, strength and acceleration of pen movements, etc. Although many linguists are interested in writing systems (historically and comparatively), this kind of handwriting analysis (sometimes known as **graphology**) is a specialised skill rarely if ever taught in linguistics departments.

While most handwriting analyses are performed in order to determine authorship, there has also been some interest in using handwriting analysis to gauge the psychological state of the author. Such interest died down, however, after doubt was cast on whether this method can meet scientific standards of validity (see the collection of essays in Beyerstein and Beyerstein 1992).

Since forgery of signatures is commonly an element in fraud cases, however, some police forces have in-house experts in handwriting analysis and some engage external consultants. But expertise in handwriting analysis now tends to have less relevance because of advances in technology. Fewer people write cheques and many banks and other institutions no longer rely on signatures as a means of identification (e.g. for making withdrawals at counters, verifying a credit card transaction, collecting registered mail, or authorising access to reserved areas).

Forensic phonetics

Forensic phonetic analysis is most commonly used in **speaker identification**. This process typically involves comparison of speakers of two or more speech samples, usually in the form of an audio recording of the speech event type in question (e.g. hoax call or ransom demand) compared against reference samples obtained from suspects. Occasionally, forensic phoneticians also engage in **speaker profiling** when suspects are not known (see Unit C9).

Nolan (2004) warns, however, against relying on the ear alone for speaker recognition. Today, auditory and acoustic methods are often used as a complementary form of analysis. **Auditory analysis** (i.e. perceptual judgment made by phonetically trained experts) can assess voice quality at both the segmental level (pronunciation of consonants and vowels) and at the suprasegmental level (such as intonation and tempo). **Acoustic analysis,** typically automated and digitised in the form of a spectrogram, measures physical quality of sound such as frequency, duration and amplitude (Foulkes and French 2012).

Although forensic phonetics is a highly sophisticated area of linguistic analysis, the reliability of speech evidence cannot be compared to DNA or fingerprints. Since there is no completely unchanging feature of any voice (change takes place over time, and may be triggered by events such as shouting or infection of the larynx), and since no vocal feature appears consistently in all utterances by the same speaker, the forensic phonetician can at best make a probabilistic (as opposed to absolute) statement about speaker identity. Vocal disguise, noise and quality of recording all add to the challenge of accurate assessment.

Apart from speaker attribution and profiling, the forensic phonetician may also contribute to accurate **transcription** of a legally relevant recorded speech event and in designing a voice line-up for earwitnesses (Coulthard and Johnson 2007).

Syntactic analysis

Syntactic analysis may be useful in cases in which communication evidence is presented, in that syntactic complexity, among other linguistic features including vocabulary choice and discourse organisation, offers a proxy indicator of whether a text is comprehensible to the reader.

Levi (1994) reports testifying on how syntactic features such as multiple negatives, complex embeddings, nominalisations, subjectless passive structures and difficult combinations of logical operators (e.g. *and, or, if* and *unless*) are all likely to interfere with understanding. The object of her analysis was a letter sent to inform AFDC (Aid to Families with Dependent Children) claimants of their rights. Part of the letter is reproduced below:

> If your AFDC financial assistance benefits are continued at the present level and the fair hearing decides your AFDC financial assistance reduction was correct, the amount of AFDC assistance received to which you were not entitled will be recouped from future AFDC payments or must be paid back if your AFDC is cancelled.

Levi demonstrated that the letter required substantially higher reading levels than those possessed by welfare clients, who were found on average to have reading skills no higher than eighth-grade literacy. The court ruled that a state agency should communicate in terms comprehensible to the client and ordered a rewrite of the letter (*Doston v. Duffy* 1998).

Semantic and pragmatic analysis

Linguistic meaning is inherently uncertain and is subject as we have seen to divergent interpretations. Evidence as to meaning is also usually interpretive rather than identificatory. It is concerned either with the range of plausible meanings a given word or expression is capable of bearing, or else with the meaning most likely to have been ascribed in a precisely specified context: what, for example, must statement X have meant to readers of document Y on day Z?

Interpretive evidence is only occasionally accepted by courts. Most lawyers and judges see themselves as the appropriate experts and adjudicators on meaning (Coulthard and Johnson 2007); legal professionals are sometimes also sceptical whether expertise in meaning can extend far beyond articulate presentation of ordinary language competence. When there is doubt as to meaning, they are more likely to appeal to a dictionary than a linguist, notwithstanding the fact that linguists do not focus only on denotational (dictionary) meaning but also research common usage, etymology, collocation, and social and contextual meaning.

Meaning evidence can nevertheless occasionally form the basis for argument as to the adequacy or otherwise of product warnings (e.g. the commonly used 'For external use only' warning label; see Tiersma 2002), or regarding similarities between two trade marks (e.g. whether the prefix *Mc* carried a purely patronymic or more general meaning in *McSleep v. McDonald's*; Shuy 2003) Meaning evidence has also been submitted where the question for the court was one of comprehensibility, for example regarding the difficulty of words in jury instructions (see *reasonable doubt* in Dumas 2002).

To the extent that the meanings of utterances are commonly underdetermined by their semantics, pragmatic dimensions of meaning can also become objects of analysis in a legal context; we look in more detail at how Gricean maxims have been invoked in 'language crime' cases in Unit C9.

Corpus analysis

Corpus tools provide a useful resource in **authorship attribution** if a sufficient sample is available for comparison between the text or texts in question and other relevant texts of known authorship. It is possible to compare texts in order to see how similar they are in terms of stylistic markers such as relative frequency of particular words and their patterns of co-occurrence or collocation. Such techniques could in principle also be helpful in copyright infringement cases in establishing the extent of discontinuous direct copying embedded in a publication allegedly derived from a prior published work (Durant 2010b).

Relatedly, corpus analysis has been used in textual disputes concerned with unauthorised appropriation of words and ideas: **plagiarism.** A corpus linguist (offering a different kind of authority from automated plagiarism software) can identify textual features showing (or appearing to rule out) evidence of direct borrowing. Detecting paraphrased or translated plagiarised texts is more challenging. But recently, forensic linguists have started to develop relevant techniques for this (Turell 2008). Advanced plagiarism software works very differently from Web search engines; for example, it allows **segment-by-segment comparison** (improving precision), and can be set to register different word forms as still constituting a match (e.g. *detecting* and *detection*; see Woolls 2012).

Problems associated with plagiarism have escalated in many walks of life, including education, because of the availability of texts on the Internet. Many universities and professional bodies now use automated plagiarism detection software to screen submitted material. The Internet has, however, simultaneously proved to be a very helpful corpus for use in detecting plagiarism as well as in committing it.

Discourse analysis

Forensic discourse analysis typically examines conversational features (e.g. back-channel behaviour, topic initiation, topic recycling, response and interruption strategies, intonation markers, pause lengths and local strategies of ambiguity resolution) in order to ascertain what is going on not only at the surface level of discourse, but also at the level of intention and motivation.

Bribery, which Shuy (1993: 20) describes as 'one of the more common "white-collar" crimes', provides a clear instance of a complex but analysable discourse event: a bribe can be clearly described in terms of a 'completed and felicitous' bribe structure; so alleged bribery events can be analysed into a series of necessary, component elements: problem, proposal, completion and extension. Each phase in a bribe, according to Shuy, involves typical tasks and roles for the bribe offerer and for the bribe receiver, as well as typical forms of talk that realise that phase. Through analysis of the speech-event structure of bribery, a bribe can be distinguished from other, cognate (but in legal terms non-equivalent) speech events such as an offer: 'The difference between an offer and a bribe', Shuy (1993: 43) suggests, is simply this: 'in the quid pro quo of a bribe, one of the elements is illegal'.

Ethnography and social scientific tools

Linguists have also adopted methods of data collection traditionally used in other social science disciplines that can also be useful in legal investigations and proceedings. Such methods seek to demonstrate, for example, how an average person or a certain population understands or reacts to a given text. Methods used include suitably structured questionnaires and surveys (though these kinds of study may be undertaken by survey experts instead), ethnography, computational and statistical tools, or controlled experiments (e.g. Remez *et al.* 1997; Charrow and Charrow 1979). In a controlled study, Stephan and Stephan (1986) show how mock jurors judged the defendant to be more guilty if his or her testimony was presented in a foreign language before it was presented in English by an interpreter. Similarly, Frumkin (2007) showed that accent and ethnic background affect mock jurors' perceived but unjustified preferences in eyewitness testimony.

Ethnography offers useful ways for revealing problems in **cross-cultural communication**. Distinctive language habits formed by social groups may be misunderstood by an out-group. Eades (2002), for example, found that Aboriginal people in Australia have a tendency to say 'yes' in answer to a question even when they do not understand that question or may disagree with the proposition put to them. Such a convention can lead to disastrous consequences in a legal setting, for instance if a police officer takes an apparently positive response as an admission of guilt. Even not saying anything can be problematic in this context. Silence, for Aboriginal people, is considered acceptable etiquette before answering a question but may be interpreted as evasion in court. Based on long-term analysis of cross-cultural communication breakdowns, Eades has drawn attention to numerous instances of how the Australian justice system has failed its Aboriginal population in relation to language issues.

The forensic linguist as expert witness

While recognising how far forensic linguistics has grown as a professional specialism over the last two decades, we conclude this unit with brief comment on the process that leads from recognition of a language issue in a legal setting through to the admissibility and submission of expert evidence in a courtroom.

Problems commonly arise surrounding the particular language used in a situation associated with a crime or legal dispute. Some kind of analysis of and speculation about that language – at varying levels of linguistic awareness and formality or informality – very often takes place during investigation of an alleged crime or dispute. Mostly detectives and/or lawyers examine the language-related problem themselves, based on their own skills and professional experience. They may also express their observations (including in court) using words and concepts that reflect their investigative or legal approach and expectations; but usually such **folk linguistic** commentary takes place 'behind the scenes', during whatever investigation takes place.

Where legal procedures allow, however, investigators or lawyers have increasingly seen value in deepening or extending such understanding by commissioning specialist examination of the data and incorporating resulting insights into the ongoing investigative and possibly trial process. Where one or more linguistic experts are engaged, occasionally (but increasingly frequently) the linguist goes to court and participates as a consultant, or **expert witness** (Coulthard and Johnson 2007). The resulting expert evidence may or may not be admitted by the court, usually after legal argument and in the context of widespread reluctance in some legal systems to allow expert opinion where the possibility exists of doing without it. In particular, some judges are sceptical whether understanding language calls for anything more than a competent speaker's common sense. At present, submission of expert linguistic evidence also takes place very unevenly in different jurisdictions, with the greatest reported frequency in the USA and Australia. It remains to be seen, therefore, depending not only on linguistic but also legal factors, whether the recent development of this linguistic specialism continues its presently upward trajectory.

BILINGUAL AND MULTILINGUAL LEGAL SYSTEMS   B10

In this unit, we examine a number of specific linguistic challenges involved in bilingual and multilingual legal systems. We consider, for example, what makes translation of legal texts particularly difficult, describe cross-cultural communication barriers that exist in the courtroom, and examine how legal meaning is decided for divergent language texts of the same law. Much of the research (and related policy thinking) on which our discussion in this unit is based comes from Canada and the European Union, two of the world's most developed bilingual and multilingual jurisdictions, as well as from international law. But we also show how researchers have become engaged with these topics in other bilingual postcolonial territories, including Malaysia and Hong Kong.

Overcoming obstacles in legal translation

Unit A10 notes the significance of legal translation in multilingual jurisdictions. Here, we analyse why legal translation is a particularly difficult, specialised subfield within translation.

The most widely discussed problem in **legal translation** is that of terminology: lack of equivalent terms and concepts in the target language and culture. As well as situations where concepts (e.g. common-law concepts such as *consideration* or *equity*) are not represented in the target language vocabulary, there are situations where seemingly equivalent terms do exist but have different meanings, leading to the phenomenon lexicographers call **false friends** (i.e. words that look deceptively similar but differ in meaning). The word *law*, for example, has complex historically developing and synchronically available meanings in English (clearly shown in the *OED* entry for the word). But closest equivalent words in other languages can carry a different mix of denotations and connotations. The French word for law, *droit*, also conveys the meaning of 'right' (especially in the plural; cf. 'les droits de l'homme'), whereas the Chinese word for law, *fa*, has a more punitive connotation (Liang 1989). To bridge such cross-cultural semantic gaps, techniques including paraphrase, borrowing or even coining new terms are sometimes needed if a foreign legal concept is to be represented in a way that avoids confusion. When such techniques are used, until the adopted or new term or terms gain currency, texts in the target language cannot be fully understood without reference to the source text, potentially reducing access to justice for monolingual speakers of the target language.

The dominant legal traditions in the world today have long histories. When common-law English is used as a source language for translation, accordingly, the translator is forced to address consequences of its history in three major source languages: Latin, Norman French and Anglo-Saxon. Many frequently used **doublets**, or word-pairs, in legal English (as described in Unit B2) are formed by juxtaposition of Anglo-Norman and Anglo-Saxon words, as in *fair and equitable* and *full and complete* (Varó 2008). Translation of such combined terms into a target language that does not share the same history is a challenge. Most importantly, there is the question of whether the two etymologically different synonyms or near-synonyms have to any significant extent diverged in meaning (as happened in some semantic fields, e.g. philosophy). Such semantic divergence would require translation of each word, but two words would not normally be required otherwise.

In terms of syntax, **ambiguity** and other effects created by complex structures, embedding, agentless passives, qualifiers and insertions pose further obstacles. Since legal certainty is of paramount importance, legal translators need to develop sensitivity to ambiguities in the original text, for example ambiguity between the technical and ordinary meaning of a word, and seek clarification where necessary. At the same time, **vagueness**, as we have seen, is sometimes retained in drafting in order to allow for development of a particular law in response to unforeseen fact-situations. Even apart from meaning, there is the question of whether translation should attempt to find equivalents for the distinctiveness of register, archaism, redundancy, and other features of legal English discussed in Unit B1 that play a part in law's symbolism. Finally, in practical terms, another feature of common-law systems that makes localisation difficult is their reliance on precedent, since the task of translating the whole body of case law is formidable and hugely expensive.

Overall, it is sensible to think of legal translation as a distinct practice (e.g. by comparison with translation of literary texts, scientific journals, meeting notes and instruction manuals). A systematic framework for legal translation is presented in Šarčević (1997); she emphasises that translators must pay attention both to different types of legal texts and to their respective communicative functions (e.g. are they intended to be prescriptive, descriptive or some combination of the two?), and notes that source and target legal texts may perform different functions and carry different statuses. Arguing that translators must choose translation strategies based on legal criteria that will be used to interpret the translated legal text, Šarčević advocates a receiver-oriented approach.

Cross-cultural communication in the courtroom

Cross-cultural aspects of communication in the courtroom are mediated by court interpreters. However, in many jurisdictions access to an interpreter is not an unconditional right, but depends on whether the person who requests assistance can understand and speak the language of the court. In assessing need for an interpreter, the court decides whether a person can understand and speak the language used in court adequately; but as Eades (2003) shows, courts are generally not conversant with ways of assessing second-language proficiency or with the specificity of the competence required in a courtroom context. Even in a bilingual or multilingual jurisdiction, litigants or defendants do not usually have the right to choose which official language the trial will take place in (see Leung 2016).

Internationally, very many people assume that the United States is a monolingual, English-speaking country. But the country's linguistically diverse population means that the US legal system deals with large numbers of multilingual speakers on an everyday basis. Berk-Seligson (2002 [1990]) reports ethnographic work she conducted in bilingual American courtrooms involving English and Spanish (the most frequently used languages in US court-interpreted proceedings). She argues that the presence of a court interpreter transforms normal courtroom proceedings into bilingual events, and shows how the courtroom interpreter can alter a speaker's meaning even without misunderstanding the original testimony, especially at the pragmatic level. She challenges a common misperception on the part of courtroom personnel that court interpreters are like machines, converting speech from one language into another, and calls for deeper understanding of the multidimensional nature of the interpreter's role.

The highly distinctive situation of the bilingual jurisdiction of Hong Kong is examined in Leung (2008). In Hong Kong, courtroom interpretation is a service provided not, as is the case in most other jurisdictions, for linguistic minorities, but for the linguistic majority (i.e. Cantonese speakers). This situation, and the superior status of English, is a colonial legacy that arguably cannot provide optimal access to justice for the majority population. Examining data collected on rape trials in Hong Kong, Leung (2008: 203) argues that even 'high quality interpreters with the best intentions' face problems created by inherent linguistic differences between the languages involved. Her examples include not only legally relevant conceptual incongruity between source and target language words, but also grammatical categories that do not exist in English (such as **utterance finite particles** in Chinese, which can only be realised in English by intonation).

Finding legal meaning in multilingual law

Legal communication between nations and in international institutions is described in detail in Tabory (1980). This classic work surveys linguistic practices in diplomatic affairs historically, discusses current problems in the preparation and interpretation of multilingual documents, and makes recommendations as regards how problems may be overcome. In the historical survey presented in the book, Tabory reminds us that for many centuries of human civilisation, international affairs were conducted in a small number of languages each functioning for a region or period as a lingua franca. Thanks to the doctrine of equality of nations popularised after World War I, many countries have more recently sought to have their languages accepted on an equal status with others, giving rise to now commonplace kinds of bilingual and multilingual treaty. Tabory also offers detailed analysis of the provisions of the 1969 Vienna Convention on the Law of Treaties, which embodies rules and principles regarding how multilingual treaties should be read.

Two important book-length publications exist in Canadian jurisprudence on how bilingual laws are interpreted at national level: Beaupré (1986) and Bastarache *et al.* (2008). Beaupré's *Interpreting Bilingual Legislation* was the first monograph to deal systematically with problems of interpreting equally authentic Canadian bilingual statutes. He describes the development of the rule of legal equality between French and English legislative texts, and traces how federal legislation has been interpreted in Canada, summarising methods adopted to resolve language versions in conflict. Based on his documentation of substantial differences between how legal meaning is constructed in unilingual and in bilingual jurisdictions, Beaupré (1986: 4) concludes that 'there is such a thing as a bilingual approach to the interpretation of legislation' and argues that classic canons of construction are not well-suited to the task of construing a bilingual statute. (We discuss specific strategies used in interpreting bilingual and multilingual law in Unit C10.) Bastarache *et al.*'s *The Law of Bilingual Interpretation* extends Beaupré's research, probing the legal tradition and legislative thinking behind the interpretation of bilingual laws in Canada. The authors have opened up new questions (e.g. whether a legislature has a mother tongue), and they assess theoretical implications of alternative answers to the questions they raise. Since Canada is not only bilingual (English and French), but also **bijural** (common law and civil law), Bastarache *et al.* are well placed to offer insights into how two legal cultures, as well as two legal languages, can function together.

Another region where multiplicity of languages has been a major concern is the European Union; and a substantial research literature has also been produced on the topic of multilingual law in Europe. In his quantitative analysis, for example, Baaij (2012) reports that between 1960 and 2010, the European Court of Justice (ECJ) delivered 246 judgments that involved comparison of language versions. Of these, 170 reported discrepancies between language versions of the provision in question. Baaij's data analysis suggests that combined teleological and literal interpretive methods are needed to ensure uniform interpretation and application of EU law. Presenting a qualitative analysis, Solan (2009) lists three goals that need to be met in the linguistic practices of a supranational legal regime: equality, fidelity and efficiency. Showing how equality and efficiency are often in tension with each other, Solan focuses on the issue of fidelity. He develops an argument that proliferation of languages has assisted rather than harmed statutory interpretation by the ECJ. He describes the approach adopted as 'Augustinian' (i.e. analogous to how St Augustine sought to understand biblical scriptures by comparing the Latin version with Hebrew and Greek originals), and claims the approach is able to take advantage of multiple versions of the same law in discovering its intended meaning. Since the best evidence of legislative intent comes from the language in which law is expressed, additional language versions according to Solan provide a resource of unique cues that make it possible to triangulate legal meaning that are not available in a monolingual jurisdiction.

Section C
EXPLORATION
ANALYSES AND EXAMPLES

C1   **PERCEPTION OF LEGAL LANGUAGE**

From a linguist's descriptive point of view, all language varieties are equal; value judgements are irrelevant. In wider society, however, some varieties are commonly associated with strong expressions of attitude, either of liking or dislike. This phenomenon is perhaps most focused linguistically on accents, especially contrasts between urban and rural accents (since either may be perceived as harsh, mellifluous, grating, etc.). Such attitudes may also be directed towards whole dialects and gen-erational language styles. The rush to linguistic judgement or prejudice merges into wider social attitudes directed towards other semiotic phenomena, including clothing styles, behaviour and cultural tastes. Attitudes towards language variation can also contribute to the relative social prestige of a variety, even if perceptions underpinning the attitude in question are based on stereotypes of speakers, places or professions rather than linguistic facts.

Expressions of feeling are especially animated in relation to the variety we have described as legal language. Around this variety – for all its internal variation and substantial change over time – circulates a great deal of criticism, scorn and campaigning for reform. There is also a substantial literature of parody and wider satire. In this unit, we examine such critical representations of legal language. What features, we ask, have become so conventionalised that, even used selectively and transferred to other subject matter, they still give rise to particular respect, dissatisfaction or amusement? Discussion of these aspects of legal language will connect our description of the variety's characteristics, history and functions to a wider social context of beliefs, attitudes and continuing controversies.

Attitudes and perceptions

Attitudes towards different accents have been studied in fields cutting across linguistics and psychology (Giles 1970; Giles and Coupland 1991). Few scholarly studies have been published of attitudes towards professional varieties in particular, however. Criticism of legal language is nevertheless common not only among laypeople, but even among legal scholars and legal professionals, who in some cases are also authors of parodies and satire of the language they themselves use professionally.

As regards English in particular, here is Tiersma:

> One of the great paradoxes about the legal profession is that lawyers are, on the one hand, among the most eloquent users of the English language while, on the other, they are perhaps its most notorious abusers. Why is it that lawyers, who may excel in com-municating with a jury, seem incapable of writing an ordinary, comprehensible English sentence in a contract, deed, or will?
>
> (Tiersma 1999)

Note Tiersma's strong polemical terms, including 'notorious abusers' and 'incapable'.

> ❏ Sometimes it is difficult to decide whether, in a given context, the widely used phrase 'talking like a lawyer' is a compliment or an insult. Keeping Tiersma's comments above in mind, can you see reasons why these two apparently opposite perceptions should be so closely connected with one another?

Linguistic perception and social comment

As with accent perception, linguistic value judgements often get confused with social judgements in which references made to language are merely symptomatic: the opinion is about professional practice, rather than about the language used by that profession. Among the most widely quoted polemical descriptions of legal language are the following:

Swift, Gulliver's Travels

Here is Jonathan Swift (1667–1745), satirising lawyers in his reversal of social roles between humans (presented as 'Yahoos') and horses ('Houyhnhnms') in the fourth part of *Gulliver's Travels* (1726):

> There was a Society of Men among us, bred up from the Youth in the Art of proving by Words multiplied for the purpose, that *White* is *Black* and *Black* is *White*, according as they are paid. To this Society all the rest of the People are Slaves.

This society of men (the legal profession):

> hath a peculiar Cant and Jargon of their own, that no other Mortal can Understand, and wherein all their Laws are written.

Bentham, Works

Writing in an idiom that combines analysis and satire, here is the philosopher Jeremy Bentham (1748–1832) assessing lawyers' claims regarding the degree of precision they achieve through their use of language:

> For this redundancy – for the accumulation of excrementitious matter in all its various shapes . . . for all the pestilential effects that cannot but be produced by this so enormous a load of literary garbage, – the plea commonly pleaded [is] . . . that it is necessary to *precision* – or, to use the word which on similar occasions they [lawyers] themselves are in the habit of using, *certainty*.
>
> (Bentham, *Works*, Bowring edition, 1843: 260; for discussion, see Mellinkoff 1963: 261–6)

Dickens, Bleak House

Here, in his celebrated indictment of the ineffectiveness of mid-nineteenth-century English law as embodied in the Court of Chancery, is a description of members of the High Court by Charles Dickens (1812–1870) as:

tripping one another up on slippery precedents, groping knee-deep in technicalities, running their goat-hair and horse-hair warded heads against walls of words.

(*Bleak House*, 1852–1853: Chapter 1)

> ❏   In these brief quotations (inevitably presented here out of context), what aspects of legal language seem most to incite the author's dislike? How closely interwoven are those features with supposed non-linguistic characteristics of the legal profession?

Equally polemical literary comment against alleged excesses of legal language can be found throughout dictionaries of quotations (including specialised dictionaries of legal quotations), as well as in anthologies such as Brian Harris's *The Literature of the Law* (1998) or Daniel White's *Trials and Tribulations: An Appealing Anthology of Legal Humour* (1989).

Judicial comment

As suggested above, lawyers themselves make (and choose to publish) withering criticisms of inappropriate or excessive drafting of documents, incomprehensible legislation, and over-oratorical courtroom speeches.

Here are two widely quoted examples:

❏   In a speech in Washington, DC (11 May 1929), the eminent and influential US judge Learned Hand suggested that 'There is something monstrous in commands couched in invented and unfamiliar language; an alien master is the worst of all. The language of the law must not be foreign to the ears of those who are to obey it.'

❏   In a case concerned with terms of a lease, leading UK judge Mr Justice Hoffmann (now Lord Hoffmann) found the flood of words in the lease so 'torrential' that he felt there might be some justification in a submission that he should set aside the normal principle of legal interpretation that requires account be taken of every word.

> ❏   How important is it, in reading such criticisms of legal language (whether by legal professionals or others), to distinguish not only the targets of satire or polemic, but also the aims? For example, is it possible to tell whether criticisms are motivated by linguistic conservatism (e.g. as a critique of falling standards in legal drafting) or by appetite for reform?

Parody and stereotype

One (potentially risky) way into exploring a controversial linguistic variety is to examine exaggerated versions of it found in caricature. Often such representations accentuate characteristics used by writers as a kind of shorthand, because those characteristics are assumed to be perceptually salient among likely readers. Such characteristics can be tested against naturally occurring data; comparing such stereotypes with actual data often suggests that the conventional perceptions are highly inaccurate.

The two types of data are not incompatible if used *as starting points* in analysis. Taking account of caricature may even help clarify the relationship between features of a variety that are believed sufficient to prompt a predictable response from readers or listeners and other features that are scarcely noticed or not noticed at all. In the following extract, we consider the power and effects of caricature and myths about language by considering two well-known parodies of legal discourse.

'I give you my orange'

Our first parody is a celebrated humorous imitation of legal language written in 1835 by Arthur Symonds, in a book called *The Mechanics of Law-Making*. Symonds' caricature of the language of conveyancing documents develops the idea that legal language could not tolerate someone making a simple gift by just saying or writing five words: 'I give you my orange'.

If expressed in legal language, the speaker in Symonds' parody is presented as needing to say or write this:

> I hereby give you all and singular, my estate and interest, right, title, claim and advantage of and in my orange, with all its rind, skin, juice, pulp and pips, and all right and advantages therein, with full power to bite, cut, suck and otherwise eat the same, or give the same away as fully and effectually as I am now entitled to bite, cut, suck or otherwise eat the same orange, or give the same way, with or without its rind, skin, juice, pulp, and pips, anything hereinbefore, or hereinafter, or in any other deed, or deeds, instrument or instruments of what nature or kind soever, to the contrary in any wise, notwithstanding.
>
> (Symonds 1835: 75)

Note that this 114-word extract consists of just one sentence. Write a paraphrase, dividing that sentence into as many shorter sentences as you need to express the meaning. As you do this, note which expressions or ideas are difficult – or even impossible – to restate.

 Activity

❑ Make a list of features that are prominent in this caricature that you associate with legal style. The overall performative speech act is clear: 'I (hereby) give'. Beyond that, you will find it difficult to categorise and restate exactly what is going on.

❑ Think first in terms of vocabulary (including length of words, mix of word classes such as adjectives, nouns and verbs, as well as differences between apparently ordinary or everyday words and terms confined to a restricted, legal circulation).

❑ Now look at word order, and choice of grammatical constructions (which you will see more clearly when you try to rewrite).

❑ What about rhetorical devices (e.g. reinforcing repetition, use of lists)?

❑ Now ask yourself: how does difficulty in understanding exactly what is being said contribute to the overall satirical effect?

This famous passage is discussed in many works; a useful description of its jargon features can be found in Butt (2013: 250–1).

'The sky is blue'

Our second parody of legal language is by Daniel R. White, who worked as a corporate lawyer in Washington, DC before turning to creative writing; it can be found in his anthology *Trials and Tribulations: An Appealing Anthology of Legal Humour* (1989). In a short essay 'The sky is blue', White creates a scenario in which a junior associate in a law firm is taken to task by a senior colleague for saying 'The sky is blue'.

The theme is basically the same as with 'I give you my orange': a simple proposition judged to be inadequate as a legal statement. This time, however, we will not quote the passage. Instead, you are presented with a paraphrase. So now you have to concentrate not on choice of particular words or grammatical forms, which have been changed, but on the effect created by more abstract rhetorical strategies:

> For a lawyer, the senior colleague explains, 'The sky is blue' is not an adequate proposition. The first qualification needed is that the sky must be described only as 'generally' blue, since it may not always be blue. Also, it can only 'appear' rather than categorically be that colour. The proposition must also be defended against possible challenges, including that the sky might not be blue in other parts of the world. So: particular places must be specified, for instance in a list. And what about the meaning of 'sky'? 'Sky', the older colleague explains, cannot be simply assumed as something you see when you look up, since there may be other things you see that are *not* sky. In any case, the sky will only be visible if you are outside. So those aspects need to be incorporated into the statement, as well as the times at which the perception is possible (presumably during the day, since for instance stars, the colleague points out, are not blue). The senior partner complains that the proposition 'has more holes in it than Swiss cheese'.

 Activity

❑ Describe the main characteristics of legal discourse that White draws attention to in the story (at least as you have experienced it in this paraphrased treatment).

❑ What characteristics of 'lawyerly' thought, speech patterns and rhetorical moves does White emphasise?

❑ How separable, or interwoven, do the following aspects appear to be in this passage: (i) ways of using language; and (ii) the purposes for which particular uses of language have developed or been designed?

❑ The passage is clearly intended to be humorous. But are there characteristics attributed to legal language that you would want to defend – as being desirable or even essential in particular contexts of use?

Finally, consider White's way of ending his short essay. He appends '10 principles of legal writing', which include the following:

never to use one word where ten will do; never to use a small word where a big one will suffice; never to use a simple statement where it appears that one of substantially greater complexity will achieve comparable goals; never to use English where Latin, mutatis mutandis, will do; and always to qualify virtually everything . . .

(White 1989: 246)

Extrapolating from features of style to overall effect, White concludes, 'If a layperson can read a document from beginning to end without falling asleep, it needs work'. What point do you think White is making in this concluding comment, given the seriousness of legal language in its social effects?

Finally, compare the two parodies of legal language we have presented. Keep in mind that you are engaged in a thought-priming activity here, rather than searching for correct answers. Fuller description of legal language varieties is presented elsewhere in Thread 1 and in Threads 2 and 3.

❏   How far do the two passages point towards similar idiosyncrasies or excesses? Do any major differences between the targeted characteristics stand out?

❏   The two passages were published over 100 years apart. Is the degree of similarity or difference you see between the two passages surprising?

REFORMING LEGAL LANGUAGE

C2

In this unit, we discuss claims and counterclaims that surround proposed reforms of legal language. We show why making changes to legal language is difficult by presenting a practical task based on an early English statute, and conclude with observations about current 'plain language reform' proposals.

Legal language and its critics

Units A2 and B2 trace the formation of legal English through complicated contact between French, Latin and English, and links processes of language change not only to political developments, but also to the formation of a community of practice – lawyers – who subscribe to a number of principles about their professional language use:

❏   standardisation and consistency of documents in the face of contextual variability;

❏   resilience of legal documents in the face of challenge by other lawyers involved in adversarial proceedings; and

❏   decontextualisation in document drafting, so that legal documents can be interpreted in different situations arising in later periods (see Butt 2013 for discussion of drafting principles based on these linguistic norms).

Despite presumed good intentions behind these professional principles, criticisms of legal English have been expressed almost throughout the historical period in which legal English has been recognised as a variety. In recognition of difficulties surrounding legal language and response to such criticism, many efforts have been made within the legal profession towards reform, including in the UK by the 1975 *Renton Committee Report on Legislation* which was established to achieve 'greater simplicity and clarity in statute law', as well as by frequent updating of the Civil Procedure Rules (CPR), most recently based on Lord Woolf's recommendations for user-friendly language in his *Access to Justice* report (1996), which replaced expressions such as the historical term *plaintiff* with *complainant*, *inter partes* with *between parties, Anton Pillar order* with *search order*, and *pleading* with *statement of case*. From 1979 onwards, despite such reforms, the Campaign for Plain English (www.plainenglish.co.uk), with parallel organisations in other countries, has tried to bring about more radical rewriting of legislation and related documents, not to change what is said but so that whatever is said is expressed in an accessible, contemporary style.

Tensions between 'change' and 'no change'

Engaging with issues surrounding reform of legal language, either theoretically or practically, calls for more precise formulation of what the problems are. In his brief overview of legal English, Crystal (2010: 374) likens critiques of established legal usage to criticism of the language of science for its impenetrability and the language of religion for its mystique. His view of reform remains a cautious one:

> The goal of a simplified, universally intelligible legal English has an undeniable appeal, but it has to be pursued wisely if the results are not to raise more problems than they solve. A blanket condemnation of legal language is naive, in that it fails to appreciate what such language has to do if it is to function efficiently in the service of the community. Equally, there are no grounds for blanket acceptance.

How justified is this view? There is a tension, Crystal insists, between achieving relative accessibility of documents by accommodating to current usage conventions (which will then continue to change following any particular reform), and maintaining the authority of documents on the questionable basis that they were fixed definitively when first produced. That tension lies at the heart of the practical issues we now consider.

Reading a chapter of thirteenth-century English law

Reform of legal language is felt to be most urgent in how it affects us now. But fundamental challenges in rewriting law can be exposed more clearly if we look at a historical example. Below, we reproduce Chapter 1 from CHARTA FORESTAE, or the 'Charter of the Forest' (a charter consisting of 16 such chapters). The charter was enacted at Westminster in 'Anno 9 Henry III *and* A.D. 1225', shortly after the foundational English legal document Magna Carta (1215, now 800 years old).

In primis omnes forefte quas HENRICUS EX Avus nofter afforeftavit videantur per bonos & legales homines & fi bofcum aliquem alium quam fuum diominicum afforeftaverit ad dampnum illius cujus bofcus ille fuerit deafforeftetur & si bofcum fuum proprium afforeftaverit remaneat forefta falva communa de herbagio & aliis in eadem forefta illis qui prius eam habere confueverunt.	'FIRST, We will that all Forefts, which King HENRY our Grandfather afforefted, fhall be viewed by good and lawful men; (2) and if he have made Foreft of any other Wood more than of his own demefne, whereby the Owner of the Wood have hurt, forthwith it fhall be difafforefted; (3) and if he have made Foreft of his own Wood, then it fhall remain Foreft; (4) faving the Common of Herbage, and of other things in the fame Forests, to them which before were accuftomed to have the fame.

Your initial reaction to this piece of text will probably be that this source of law is antiquated, and possibly impenetrable, and that it cries out for rewriting into contemporary English.

1   List your grounds for this impression (be as precise as you can).
2   Now rewrite the chapter as well as you can into modern English.
3   When you have done this, consider the following points:

3.1 Among features you are likely to have noticed in rewriting are:

❏   the existence of parallel texts (Should you have rewritten the Latin or the English version? Which one states the law? Or are both versions statements of law, which you needed somehow to synthesise if there are differences between them?);

❏   use of 'f' (our simplified font representation) in place of modern 's'; and

❏   capitalisation in the English text of most, but not all, nouns and selective use of upper case both for the first word of the chapter and for the name of the monarch, King Henry.

3.2 You might also have wondered about other features, including:

❏   words whose meaning may no longer be clear, such as unusual 'demefne' and unusual-in-this-context 'hurt' (you can find detailed discussion of such terms, and the legal concepts they signify, in histories of English law such as Pollock and Maitland 1895 or Baker 2002); and

❏   coreferring use of 'the fame'.

3.3 Now step back from this venerable/antiquated source of English law that you have been working on. Ask yourself: what version of the source text are you reading, exactly?

In order to work on a facsimile of *Charta Foreftae*, you have to look elsewhere. The version reproduced above comes from:

Statutes at Large: from MAGNA Charta to the END of the REIGN of KING HENRY the SIXTH, To which is prefixed, a TABLE of the TITLES of all the Publick and Private Statutes during that Time. VOLUME the FIRST, LONDON MDCCLXIX.

3.4 The edition of the thirteenth-century source of law we are looking at dates, then, from 1769 (= MDCCLXIX). It comes from an edition with a brief Preface by the editor, Owen Ruffhead, in which he feels obliged to 'fay fomething with regard to the Tranflation'. Reference to 'translation' reminds us that a thirteenth-century English law would not have been enacted in English, but in Latin (see Unit B2). The English version you have just rewritten – presuming you didn't work from the Latin – is not the original, but an eighteenth-century modernisation (i.e. you have just rewritten a rewriting).

3.5 You may conclude that this fact would make an updated, twenty-first-century translation all the more urgent, if this piece of legislation on forests and forestation continued to be in force. But notice something else in the eighteenth-century modernisation: Ruffhead comments in his Preface (using the verb form 'hath' alongside 'has', despite the former having been virtually obsolete in general English for nearly a century by the time he was writing) that:

it has been observed by Mr Serjeant *Hawkins*, that the old Tranflation hath obtained a kind of prefcriptive Authority.

Ruffhead anticipated criticism of his 1769 update even by comparison with earlier renderings (let alone with the original) if he introduced changes into the language. His defence of such changes, however, is that although 'it might juftly be deemed Prefumption to alter the old Tranflation', his purpose is exactly to extend access to law by means of the modernisation: 'the Tranflation is intended for the Benefit of thofe who are not qualified to refort to the Original'.

3.6 Ruffhead's strategy raises an editorial dilemma:

In the early Statutes, the Errors of the Verfion are exceedingly numerous . . . The Reader will perceive frequent, and very material Miftakes.

And his response to those mistakes is that since the old translation:

by long Ufe, hath acquired a kind of prefcriptive Authority, it hath been judged proper to leave the Text, as it ftands in former Editions, and to infert the propofed Amendment in the Margin'.

3.7 Consider these points together. Even *mistakes* in a translation that serves as a proxy for a legal original have taken on legal authority that needs to be preserved. If Ruffhead is to avoid simply reproducing errors that have now become 'authoritative', he must proliferate legal variants that risk undermining the text's authority and may create inconsistency of interpretation and application. He will also have to add notes that can themselves be challenged, and which in any case will add to, rather than decrease, the barrier of legal style – and the specialised education necessary to deal with such style – that stands between citizen and law.

❏ Consider Ruffhead's editorial dilemma as a hypothetical case study that has similarities with, as well as differences from, contemporary challenges in rewriting law *without changing it*. Work through his challenges, as you see them, identifying benefits and problems associated with different strategies that a modern legal editor (or legislator involved in 'codifying', or consolidating, previous law) might adopt.

❏ Does this activity suggest anything about what consequences might follow from adopting a strategy of leaving existing laws as currently written but introducing new laws in a more accessible, plainer English style?

A case for reforming legal language?

As we saw in a quotation above, Crystal urges caution in advocating wholesale reform of legal language. The practical question arises, for instance, whether reforms should be applied only to new legislation and related documents, or whether one implication of opting for such reforms is a need to review all earlier legal sources (especially as these are likely to present the most acute problems of understanding). Given the daunting scale of redrafting all earlier legislation, another issue arises: whether, if modified legal style is only introduced gradually, inconsistency between legal documents dealing with the same matters but written in different periods will be increased. Such issues have been extensively discussed, and appear to call for pragmatic responses that may vary between different legal settings and purposes.

READING A STATUTE   C3

In Unit B3, we have explored how understanding the concept of genre can illuminate both the historical development and current functioning of legal text types. In this unit, we look at an extract from perhaps the most recognisable legal genre: the statute. Statutes state what the law is. But the present division of labour between legal professionals and the general public is reflected in the fact that statutes are rarely read outside the legal profession. Reading a statute, we show, calls for familiarity with basic genre features even in order to find information let alone understand legal import and consequences. In particular, we explore the statute's text-mapping features and strategies adopted for directing readers towards information they will need.

Reading an extract

Using one text – in fact, only part of one text – to illustrate a genre consisting of many different pieces of legislation, produced in different areas of law (criminal law, maritime law, family law, etc.) and over a number of centuries, calls for comment.

We have chosen to present one particular piece of legislation (otherwise referred to as a law, enactment, statute or Act of Parliament): a relatively minor piece of legislation called the Riding Establishments Act 1964 from the UK. For additional comment, we refer to an amending act that changed some provisions of that Act six years later: the Riding Establishments Act 1970. These two pieces of legislation were no doubt highly important to interested parties, but they have been chosen here because their content is unlikely to distract readers from questions to do with 'reading' onto issues of law and policy that many pieces of legislation quickly raise (e.g. Acts of Parliament concerned with official secrets, assisted suicide, terrorism, education or public health).

For presentational reasons, we have also chosen a statute considerably shorter than most. Length and degree of detail of provisions are two historically varying characteristics of the statute as a text type. In the UK, so is the number of statutes enacted each year (an upward trend). Because of such variation, choosing which period to take an illustrative statute from is a further consideration. It is potentially interesting, for example, to compare statutes from successive periods, as well as between different common-law jurisdictions. In looking at the extracts below, keep in mind that our aim is to illustrate features of legislation as a text type: what Finch and Fafinski, in their skills training for law students, call 'the anatomy' of a statute (Finch and Fafinski 2011: 65–73); other aspects, including many legal specifics, would call for a more detailed and different kind of discussion.

We cannot reproduce a whole Act here. Instead, we present preliminary material in REA 1964, followed by an abbreviated Section 1 (abbreviated from now on as s. 1). With brief comment, we then omit ss. 2–5 (because in formal terms they resemble s. 1), and resume at s. 6 (which carries the added sidebar heading 'Interpretation'). We indicate omitted material by ellipses, and continue from s. 6 through to s. 9. We then omit the final, appended 'Table of Statutes referred to in this Act', which lists (by 'Session and Chapter') the short titles of nine pieces of legislation referred to in the Act. With REA 1970, we reproduce only preliminary material that differs from REA 1964, plus selected and abbreviated material from ss. 5–8.

To strengthen your sense of the two statutes as whole documents, we urge you to look at PDFs of them freely available online (for layout, typography, etc.). You can do this through a portal such as Westlaw, Lexis Library or JustCite, or at www.legislation. gov.uk (where for other UK statutes, since 1998, you can also find 'Explanatory Notes').

Read through the first extract and consider the questions and tasks that follow.

The Riding Establishments Act 1964

An Act to regulate the keeping of riding establishments; and for purposes connected therewith. [31st July 1964]

BE IT ENACTED by the Queen's most Excellent Majesty, by and with the advice and consent of the Lords Spiritual and Temporal, and Commons, in this present Parliament assembled, and by the authority of the same, as follows:-

1.-(1) No person shall keep a riding establishment except under the authority of a licence granted in accordance with the provisions of this Act.

(2) Every local authority may, on application being made to them for that purpose by a person who is an individual over the age of eighteen years or a body corporate, being a person who is not for the time being disqualified,-

(a) under this Act from keeping a riding establishment; or

(b) under the Protection of Animals (Cruelty to Dogs) Act 1933, from keeping a dog; or

(c) under the protection of Animals (Cruelty to Dogs) (Scotland) Act 1934, from keeping a dog; or

(d) under the Pet Animals Act 1951. from keeping a pet shop; or

(e) under the Protection of Animals (Amendment) Act 1954, from having the custody of animals; or

(j) under the Animal Boarding Establishments Act 1963, from keeping a boarding establishment for animals;

and on payment of a fee of ten shillings, grant a licence to that person to keep a riding establishment at such premises in their area as may be specified in the application and subject to compliance with such conditions as may be specified in the licence.

(3) Where an application for the grant of a licence for the keeping of a riding establishment at any premises is made to a [. . .]

[. . .]

6.-(1) References in this Act to the keeping of a riding establishment shall, subject to the provisions of this section, be construed as references to the carrying on of a business of keeping horses [. . .], but as not including a reference to the carrying on of such a business –

(a) in a case where [. . .]; or

(b) solely for [. . .]; or

(c) by [. . .]; or

(d) by [. . .].

(2) [. . .]

(3) [. . .]

(4) In this Act the following expressions have the meanings respectively assigned to them, that is to say-

"horse" includes any mare, gelding, pony, foal, colt, filly or stallion and also any ass, mule or jennet;

"local authority" means the council of [. . .];

"premises" includes land;

"veterinary practitioner" means a person who is for the time being registered in the Supplementary Veterinary Register in pursuance of the Veterinary Surgeons Act 1948;

[. . .].

7. Notwithstanding anything in this Act, a person who, immediately before the date of commencement of this Act, was keeping a riding establishment at any premises, and who is not disqualified as mentioned in section 1 (2) of this Act, shall be entitled to keep such an establishment at those premises without a licence under this Act –

(a) for the period of one month beginning with that date; and

(b) if before the expiration of that period he applies for a licence under this Act in respect of those premises, until the licence is granted or finally refused or the application is withdrawn

8. The Riding Establishments Act 1939 is hereby repealed.

9.-(1) This Act may be cited as the Riding Establishments Act 1964.

(2.) This Act shall not extend to Northern Ireland.

(3) This Act shall come into operation on 1st April 1965.

Table of Statutes referred to in this Act

[list]

Questions and tasks 1: on REA 1964

A statute, or (in the UK) an Act of Parliament, 'enacts' law. It is performative in bringing law into being after parliamentary debate, being passed by the legislature, and legal drafting. The statute's 'preliminary' materials, before anything about riding establishments is mentioned, bootstrap the document into being as a piece of law. Each Act has two titles: a short title and a long title (the first two blocks of text in the abstract above).

1   Titles are generally used to refer to a document you are not at the time looking at. No one tells you how you should refer to a novel or film; you choose, for instance, whether to abbreviate or use a personalised shorthand. Now read s. 9(1).

Why should a section of this kind be needed for a legal text, but not with non-legal text types?

2 The long title of REA 1964 (ask yourself why it seems permissible here to use an abbreviation rather than referring to the Act in accordance with the instruction in s. 9(1)) begins 'An Act to regulate . . .'. Is this wording the same as the long title of the Riding Establishments Act 1970 (below)? If not, what is the difference between the two?

3 The year of the Act is clear: 1964. With books, year means year of publication. With a statute, however, there are at least two important dates; and s. 9(3) refers to 1965 rather than 1964. What in the preliminary material tells us what 31 July 1964 refers to? (*Answer at the end of the unit.*)

4 What does 'Chapter 70' mean? UK statutes are divided into 'sections' (sometimes grouped as 'Parts'); and 'sections' are divided into 'subsections'. But 'chapter' is a less self-evident term, especially for people used to books. (*Answer at the end of the unit.*)

5 Now read what is called the 'enacting formula' closely: 'Be it enacted . . .'. Note a range of register features described in Threads 1 and 2. But remember that genre is performative rather than textural: the enacting words do a job. Who are the bodies who give 'advice and consent'? And advice and consent to whom? (*Answer at the end of the unit.*)

6 In the published layout of the statute, there is a rolling sidebar of abbreviated headings: s. 1 is called 'Licensing of riding establishments'; s. 6 is 'Interpretation'; s. 7 is 'Transitional provision'; s. 8 is 'Repeal'; and s. 9 'Short title, commencement and extent'. How similar do you think these short titles or headings are to entries in the sidebar used in other Acts? Look online to compare. What does the extent of similarity or difference suggest about the genre structure of statutes?

7 The long sentences that make up the provisions of any Act combine register (e.g. we can comment on grammatical and vocabulary choices) and genre (the sentences serve purposes within an unfolding logical construction). In order to make sense of each sentence, practice is generally needed in looking for underlying grammatical and logical structure. Once you have grasped the main structure, however, you can add in each dependent clause and phrases that specify additional detail, qualifications and exemptions.

Note the following patterns in s. 1, for example:

s. 1(1) No person shall A except B.

s. 1(2) Every A may B, so long as a, b, c, d, e, f and may also C, subject to g.

Read s. 1 and s. 2 closely. Divide them into chunks using whatever grammatical categories and basic logical relations you know. Restate what the legislation is saying, keeping as close to the original as possible without simply repeating it. Now elaborate on your version, as if you are explaining what the section says to someone who wants to know what it 'means' in a wider sense. It can be helpful to write more than one version and compare the alternative versions you produce. The challenges you face in doing this can offer important insights into the relationship between language style and using language to think with.

8 Now read s. 6(4). 'Horse' is not defined exactly (check one or more dictionary definitions to see differences). Rather the scope, or extension, of the category that the word 'horse' can refer to is prescribed. Do you find it odd that we need interpretive help in understanding 'horse', but not with the much rarer word 'jennet', also in s. 6(4)?

9 In common parlance, 'premises' (typically buildings) contrast with 'land' (much of which is not built on). Given the subject matter of this Act, any vagueness in that relationship seems likely to be important. But what about 'veterinary practitioner'? A basic dictionary definition might start 'person who treats animal health; animal doctor', or something like that. Here, however, the subsection focuses on professional registration. How would you characterise the approach adopted in the statute to definition and interpretation?

10 Why are ss. 8–9 important in the genre of the statute?

'Further powers': the Riding Establishments Act 1970

Now read the following extract:

1970 CHAPTER 32

An Act to confer further powers on local authorities with respect to the licensing of riding establishments and to amend the Riding Establishments Act 1964.

[29th May 1970]

[. . .]

5. Section 6 (Interpretation) of the principal Act shall be read and have effect as if in subsection (4) thereof after the words "that is to say" there were inserted the following definitions (namely)-

"approved certificate" means-

(a) any one of the following certificates issued by the British Horse Society, namely, Assistant Instructor's Certificate, Instructor's Certificate and Fellowship;

(b) Fellowship of the Institute of the Horse; or

(c) any other certificate for the time being prescribed by order by the Secretary of State;

"authorised officer" means a person authorised by a local authority in pursuance of section 2 of this Act;

6. The principal Act shall be read and have effect as if after section 6 thereof there were inserted the following section-

"6A. Any order made under this Act shall be made by statutory instrument and may be varied or revoked by a subsequent order made in the like manner."

7. In this Act the "principal Act" means the Riding Establishments Act 1964.

8.-(1) This Act may be cited as the Riding Establishments Act 1970 and the principal Act and this Act may be cited together as the Riding Establishments Acts 1964 and 1970.

(2) This Act shall not extend to Northern Ireland.

(3) This Act shall come into operation on 1st January 1971.

Questions and tasks 2: on REA 1970

11 ss. 5–6 ('Interpretation') differ from the 1964 Act. The 1970 sections do not explain the scope of terms. Instead, they do something different that nevertheless also affects interpretation. Describe how these sections, and their use of the words 'as if', bring about a correction to or alteration of the law.

12 s. 8 of REA 1964 repealed an earlier Act: the Riding Establishments Act 1939. By contrast, ss. 7–8 of REA 1970 do *not* repeal REA 1964 in order to introduce the changes stated in ss. 5–6. Rather, ss. 7–8 are concerned with preserving a clear distinction between the 1964 and 1970 Acts. Readers unfamiliar with the statute as a text type are often surprised that a specific section is needed to instruct users how to refer to the statute they are reading. But notice that the phrase used in the statute is not 'referred to', but 'cited as'. Why do you think arrangements such as specifying citation forms should be important in relation to legal documents when such arrangements are not usually needed for other text types?

13 Sometimes when amendments and case law become complicated, a drafting solution is sought in the form of 'codifying legislation' (Bennion 2001; Butt 2013). Such legislation brings together cumulative developments and replaces the existing law. Based on your reading of these statute extracts, how easy or difficult do you think it is to use language to formulate a precise and detailed system of rules? (For further discussion, see Thread 7; and for general discussion, see Twining and Miers 2010.)

Further information related to questions above

Q2 The long title matters in some circumstances because a court may refer to it as contextual indication of what parliament intended, since it clarifies the purpose of what the Act says.

Q3 Date of royal assent; and date of commencement (i.e. coming into force).

Q4 'Chapter' is an archaic name assigning a number to each statute enacted in a given calendar year: so, 70th during 1964.

Q5 See Unit B7 for discussion of the grammar and performative effect of the enacting formula. The authority of the UK legislature (effectively here, the authority to enact laws) is known as 'the Queen in Parliament', and is composed of the Monarch, the House of Lords and House of Commons. The enacting formula is standard on UK legislation (except where reference to the 'advice and consent of the Lords Spiritual and Temporal' is removed because parliamentary measures have been used to force legislation through parliament against the wishes of the House of Lords).

RESTRICTED VERBAL INTERACTION IN COURT

In this unit we look at some examples of constraints on interaction in courtroom discourse, especially examples involving question-and-answer routines between lawyers and witnesses and the funnelling of witness narratives towards legally relevant points.

Identifying presuppositions in legal questions

Given the structure of an adversarial trial (see Unit A4), the most frequent direct speech act lawyers routinely perform is asking questions. Central to advocacy training, accordingly, is how to use question forms, both individually and in strategic combinations, in order to achieve persuasive effects as well as elicit answers.

To understand questioning in courtroom evidence, it is necessary first to see the difference between different types of questions, especially loaded and leading questions.

❏ **Loaded questions** are questions that contain **presuppositions** that have not been established (e.g. 'Do you *still* beat your wife?' presupposes previous beatings).

❏ **Leading questions** are questions that predispose the addressee towards giving a certain answer. Such questions may directly suggest the answer the examiner wants, making the addressee feel that words are being put into their mouth (e.g. 'You rushed towards him, didn't you?').

The same question may be both loaded and leading. While loaded questions can be objected to by either side in an adversarial trial, this is not the case with leading questions. In evidence-in-chief, such questions are not permitted except in a small number of circumstances: on preliminary matters that precede questions about the facts in issue (e.g. the witness's name and address); on matters not in dispute; when dealing with a fact already in evidence; and where leave has been granted to treat the witness as hostile. In cross-examination, on the other hand, leading questions are permitted as a standard type of question, because of the different purpose of the examination (see further discussion on this in Unit B5).

Even though it is the witness who is seemingly in the spotlight during examination and cross-examination, it can be the questions posed to that witness which influence jurors' impression most. This is why questioning, which appears to be a form of elicitation entirely dependent on the answers it extracts, can also function as a form of persuasion. As described by Matoesian (1993: 151), 'loaded or leading questions may register strong impressions about evidence, regardless of the answer, because they frame expectations about both the forthcoming answer and the question's truth content'.

Consider each of the following questions:

1 What has your husband done to you to make you want to kill him?
2 You immediately left the scene after the collision, correct?
3 Are you sorry you caused such a terrible tragedy?

4 Was he drunk when you stabbed him?
5 As a matter of fact, you shared the information with him, didn't you?
6 You left work at eleven?
7 Was it a hot day?
8 Is it not true that you read and deleted that email?
9 Did you realise that your gun was loaded?
10 You didn't actually see anything, did you?

<table>
<tr><td>

❏ Using the brief definitions given above, identify loaded and leading questions in this list, and describe why you consider each to be loaded or leading. Keep a note of difficulties you encounter in deciding; you can use the difficulties you observe in refining the informal tests you develop for distinguishing between the two.

❏ To what extent is context important in deciding whether a question is loaded, leading, or neither? Illustrate by looking more closely at one or two of the examples.

❏ What sort of presupposition or blame attribution might jurors register in their minds simply after listening to each of these questions, even without hearing any kind of answer?

❏ What kinds of expectation, prejudice or imagined scenario are such impressions based on?

</td></tr>
</table>

Activity ★

Understanding narrative restrictions in courts

In Unit B4, we explore how although witnesses are expected to give their testimony in their own words, often they do not get to narrate their story freely. There are two reasons for this. First, their turns are limited to responding to questions. Second, further restrictions are imposed on what they can say in the answers they give. Some of those restrictions are outlined in a widely cited legal and anthropological field study by William O'Barr and John Conley, which has been revisited in a number of influential later publications and commentaries:

> Our analysis of our earlier data repeatedly confirmed the intuition that lay witnesses come to formal courts with a repertoire of narrative customs and strategies that are often frustrated, directly or indirectly, by the operation of the law of evidence.
>
> (O'Barr and Conley 1990: 101)

The O'Barr and Conley list describes a number of legal restrictions imposed on witnesses in most American courts. These include:

1 A witness may not ordinarily repeat what other persons have said about the events being reported.

2   A witness may not speculate about how the situations or events being reported may have appeared to other people or from other perspectives.

3   A witness may not ordinarily comment on his or her reactions to, or feelings and beliefs about, events being reported.

4   In responding to a question, a witness is ordinarily restricted in digressing from the subject of the question to introduce information about something he or she believes critical as a preface or qualification.

5   A witness may not normally incorporate into his or her account any suppositions about the state of mind of the persons involved in the events being reported.

6   Value judgements and opinions by lay witnesses are generally disfavored.

7   Emphasis through repetition of information is restricted.

8   Substantive information may not be conveyed through gestures alone.

9   A witness is generally forbidden to make observations about the questions asked or to comment on the process of testifying itself.

These restrictions, O'Barr and Conley argue, are required by the statutory or common law of evidence or by unwritten custom followed in formal courts. But they query (O'Barr and Conley 1990: 102) how appropriate such restrictions are, because our ordinary ways of speaking suggest that each forbidden practice is common, if not essential, in everyday narration:

> It appears that frustration and dissatisfaction are inevitable results of such constraints. One federal judge has commented at some length on the fact that litigants frequently feel dissatisfied because the trial process does not afford them a fair chance to tell their stories (Weinstein 1977). He reports that greater satisfaction for litigants in small claims procedures seems to be related to the absence of formal rules of evidence. On the basis of his experience, Weinstein believes that
>
> > allowing litigants to introduce evidence relatively freely and to rely on hearsay, provided the opponent can call the declarant and otherwise attack him with a minimum of barriers, tends to tranquilize him. This truism is demonstrated repeatedly in magistrates' courts where a complaining witness pours out his heart to an attentive judge and then, having had his day in court, withdraws the complaint (1977: 521).

★ **Activity**

❏   Do you agree that the listed prohibitive acts seem common in everyday speech? Illustrate each in one or two likely contexts. What functions do they serve in such contexts?

❏   Now consider each restriction in the specific context of giving evidence. What do you think the rationale is behind each restriction?

❏   Might it be better if adversarial legal systems allowed more 'storytelling' by witnesses, then filtered what was said in terms of **probative value**, rather than preventing material being introduced in the first place?

> ❏ Is the answer to the previous question purely a matter for the law of evidence? Or does it also depend on how important litigant satisfaction is for a legal system (i.e. an aspect of the wider legitimacy of proceedings rather than specifically of law)?

Cooperation in cross-examination?

Implied meanings researched under the heading of **implicature** in pragmatics help to explain how we mean more than we actually say (see Levinson 1983: Chapter 3). For example, A asks B: 'Did you see my email?' and B responds: 'I've just finished work'. Even though A and B appear to be talking about completely different topics, A may have no difficulty understanding B's reply as suggesting she has not had time to read her emails yet, having been at work.

The philosopher Paul Grice, whose work has given rise to a great deal of research in pragmatics (Grice 1989), suggested that conversation is guided by an implicit principle, the cooperative principle (CP), which operates on the basis of four maxims: quality, quantity, manner and relation (the last of these sometimes referred to, and later developed into a specific theory, as relevance; Sperber and Wilson 1995). Put simply, for efficient communication to take place, Grice argues that speakers will be presumed to 'speak sincerely, relevantly, and clearly, while providing sufficient information' (Levinson 1983: 102; see the rest of that chapter for further explanation and examples). Grice did not assume that people follow these maxims all the time, though he suggests that much that passes unnoticed in everyday conversation can only be explained on the basis that the CP is widely followed. It is when maxims are apparently not followed that implied meanings are retrieved, as the hearer infers an intended meaning by assuming that the CP *is* still being adhered to at a deeper level. B's apparently irrelevant response in the example above prompts A to draw the inference that B's work prevented her from checking her email (an inference that may depend on other surrounding assumptions such as that B either does not have email on her phone or is not able to look at her phone during work, etc.). The overall coherence of A and B's conversation is maintained by suitable inferences.

The question arises, however, how far a presumption such as that of the CP can apply in an adversarial setting such as a courtroom, whose structure and purpose might appear to discourage cooperative effort among speakers. This question has been addressed at two different levels: in legal theory (jurisprudence), for example by legal philosophers such as Andrei Marmor (see Unit D7 for discussion); and through observation and analysis of courtroom examination of witnesses and cross-examination in trials (Penman 1987).

Penman reports that all the interactions he observed could be construed as being congruent with Grice's CP. However, the author argues that the data nevertheless do not provide support for the assumptions underpinning Grice's model, since whatever cooperation was observed did not occur naturally but was coerced by the court through rules of allocated turn-taking. Equally important, Grice's account of conversational inference does not explore the purposes of verbal interaction other than information exchange, or relationships between conversation participants other than those involved in a slightly idealised model of conversation.

An example of courtroom interaction can illustrate this point. The extract below is taken from a negligence case in Hong Kong, reported in Ng (2009: 112–13). A former ballerina (W) sought damages from her previous employer for a career-ending injury resulting from a slippery floor. C is the defence counsel.

C: Do you agree that people who remain as corps de ballet dancers for up to five years or more may remain at that level of corps de ballet dancers for five years or more?

W: Yes.

C: And they come to a point where there is no progress to a higher level at coryphée and they just leave the company. Do you agree?

W: Yes.

C: And do you also agree that people offered solo spots, as you say you were in *Pakita*, might sometimes not be promoted?

W: Yes.

C: Now, Ms Charles (ballet instructor) has also said that, although you have a good physique, you have little stage personality. Again, is it your evidence that she is being dishonest when she expresses that view, or are you prepared to accept that that is a view she expresses in good faith?

W: Yes.

C: You agreed that view is expressed in good faith.

W: Yes, on this point.

C: And do you not agree that this aspect of little stage personality is in other words talking about a dancer's charisma, which is that intangible thing beyond technique?

W: That would depend on the number of times of performance a dancer has got. A dancer would be able to acquire such stage personality through the performances.

C: That's not correct. As a matter of common sense, that's not correct, isn't it? In reality, some people have charisma and some don't. Some don't and some acquire it; some don't and some never acquire it. That's the reality, isn't it?

[W tries to say something]

C: Madam Chan, please wait for the question before you answer.

C: Do you agree that's the reality of the situation?

W: Yes.

C: I'd like to move to another area if I may.

 Activity

❏ Why do you think many of C's questions are hypothetical, or about ballet dancers in general, rather than about W herself? What is established by the technique of starting with general statements in question form?

❏ Express as a single proposition the overall argument that C's chain of questions builds up to.

C4

❑ Does W show signs of awareness of what C is trying to suggest? If so, identify where and how her words show this. Does she have any opportunity to defend herself against such implications?

❑ Why do you think C interrupts W?

❑ Towards the end of the excerpt, why does C intervene to move on to another area so quickly?

❑ Now consider the excerpt in terms of Grice's CP. Do this by looking at each turn. How far can a Gricean framework account for the interaction between C and W?

Making your own case: the experience of unrepresented litigants

For reasons of legal consistency (but with further consequences), an unrepresented litigant is held to the same evidentiary standards as a lawyer in a trial. The verbal behaviour of such a litigant, however, will deviate from the lawyer's professional norm. To take a minor example, such a litigant may mistakenly address the judge directly, using 'you', a style of address common in most social settings but highly unusual in a courtroom. Such an error is a breach of etiquette but may not have serious consequences.

But there are other kinds of error that may have serious consequences. At trial, **objections** are properly initiated only for evidential or procedural reasons. However, Leung (2015) provides examples, also from Hong Kong, where unrepresented litigants have attempted to use 'objection' as a means to express disagreement:

Example 1

D: Mr. X (plaintiff) never gave me the document –

P: (stands up; interruption) I object!

J: Don't fight for a turn! You sit down. He was talking!

The problem here concerns the plaintiff P's transgression of the court's turn-taking system. In another example, the plaintiff also transgresses, but by an almost opposite strategy: seeking a turn by politely asking for one.

Example 2

P: Your Honour, can I talk now?

J: Ask all your questions in one go later. Take notes so that you won't forget!

Faced with this remonstration, P could only explain that he was old, forgetful and illiterate and so could not take notes.

> ❏ Discuss P's verbal behaviour in example 1. Where do you think he got the idea of saying 'I object!' from, as a way of intervening?
> ❏ The principle of orality, or primacy of speech, has traditionally been cherished in common-law systems. But to what extent does this example suggest a modern adversarial courtroom is suited to the needs of an illiterate advocate?

The following exchange shows how unrepresented litigants often see procedural requirements mainly as obstacles to their narration.

Example 3

J: You are going to testify in a moment. Will you use the witness statement you submitted to the court?

R: What?

J: The witness statement you handed to court – will you be making use of it?

R: What?

J: You handed the court a witness statement – will you use it?

R: Statement?

J: Use the witness statement or not?

R: He does not want it. (Switches to start narrating his story)

J: Wait, Mr. X, don't start yet . . .

Lay advocates are also responsible for cross-examining witnesses. Cross-examination is a highly specialised genre, however, and unrepresented litigants often fail to see the point of allowing their opponent to speak.

Example 4

J: You can now cross-examine, Mr. X.

R: (respondent): What?

J: Ask him questions!

R: (to applicant): Eh then, you say you don't rent it (a property) to me, you say it!

Our final example is also taken from cross-examination. The plaintiff seemed to have difficulty keeping his questions legally relevant.

Example 5

P (to D): Do you sometimes look for part-time jobs?

J: How is that related to our case?

P: He said he is poor!

J: Whether he is poor or not has nothing do with this case.

❏ Describe the unrepresented litigant's verbal behaviour in examples 3, 4 and 5. Characterise as precisely as you can the misunderstandings involved.

❏ Consider differences between courtroom procedures and everyday communication. Are such difficulties on the part of litigants to be expected?

Activity ⭐

TECHNIQUES IN LEGAL ADVOCACY

C5

This unit explores a number of questions about the rhetorical strategies employed by lawyers in developing their case. We describe discourse strategies used at different stages in court proceedings: making an **opening statement**; presenting an account of the facts in issue by taking witnesses through **examination-in-chief**; **cross-examining** witnesses whose evidence appears to conflict with the account presented; and delivering a **closing argument**.

Gaining attention in an opening statement

In Unit A5, we present a short extract from a famous nineteenth-century opening speech by Edmund Burke in impeachment proceedings against Warren Hastings. In doing so, we contrast Burke's high oratory with the simpler style encouraged in modern advocacy manuals as the best way to open, by summarising the facts and introducing the main issue(s) in dispute. We now juxtapose the opening speeches made by the two sides in a single trial, taken from the transcript of a widely reported American case. The speeches show how the prosecution and defence opened their respective arguments in the 1997 trial of Timothy McVeigh, following the Oklahoma City terrorist bombing in 1995 that killed 168 people.

Prosecution

HARTZLER: Ladies and gentlemen of the jury, April 19th, 1995, was a beautiful day in Oklahoma City – at least it started out as a beautiful day. The sun was shining. Flowers were blooming. It was springtime in Oklahoma City. Sometime after six o'clock that morning, Tevin Garrett's mother woke him up to get him ready for the day. He was only 16 months old. He was a toddler; and as some of you know that have experience with toddlers, he had a keen eye for mischief. He would often pull on the cord of her curling iron in the morning, pull it off the counter top until it fell down, often till it fell down on him.

That morning, she picked him up and wrestled with him on her bed before she got him dressed. She remembers this morning because that was the last morning of his life.

That morning, Mrs. Garrett got Tevin and her daughter ready for school and they left the house at about 7:15 to go downtown to Oklahoma City. She had to be at work at eight o'clock. Tevin's sister went to kindergarten, and they dropped the little girl off at kindergarten first; and Helena Garrett and Tevin proceeded to downtown Oklahoma City.

Usually she parked a little bit distant from her building; but this day, she was running a little bit late, so she decided that she would park in the Murrah Federal Building. [. . .]

Defence

JONES: Special attorney to the United States Attorney General, Mr. Hartzler, and to Mr. Ryan, the United States Attorney for the Western Judicial District of Oklahoma and to Mr. Timothy McVeigh, my client, I have waited two years for this moment to outline the evidence to you that the Government will produce, that I will produce, both by direct and cross-examination, by exhibits, photographs, transcripts of telephone conversations, transcripts of conversations inside houses, videotapes, that will establish not a reasonable doubt but that my client is innocent of the crime that Mr. Hartzler has outlined to you.

And like Mr. Hartzler, I begin where he began. As he said, it was a spring day in Oklahoma City. And inside the office of the Social Security Administration located in the Alfred P. Murrah Building, named after a distinguished chief judge of the United States Court of Appeals for the Tenth Circuit, a young black woman named Dana Bradley was feeling the atmosphere a little stuffy and warm; so she left her mother, her two children, and her sister in line and she wandered out into the lobby of the Alfred P. Murrah Building. And as she was looking out the plate glass window, a Ryder truck slowly pulled into a parking place and stopped. She didn't give it any particular attention until the door opened on the passenger side, and she saw a man get out.

Approximately three weeks later, she described the man to the Federal Bureau of Investigation agents, as indeed she did to us and to others, as short, stocky, olive-complected, wearing a puffy jacket, with black hair, a description that does not match my client. She did not see anyone else. [. . .]

 Activity

- ❏ Describe the main strategies each advocate adopts in order to gain the jurors' attention.
- ❏ Why do you think the prosecution focuses so precisely on minute details of the last morning of one person among the 168 victims?
- ❏ How does the prosecution's opening resemble storytelling? How, for example, does it encourage you to form a mental image of the scene?
- ❏ What effect is created by the defence lawyer going through steps in the trial and types of evidence in the form of a list?
- ❏ How (and how far) is the effect of the opening by the defence affected by the fact that it comes after the prosecution's opening?

Constructing a story during examination-in-chief

Advocates aim to lead witnesses through a process of telling a story during examination-in-chief, by carefully constructing suitable questions. Evans (1998) encourages initially asking a question that lays a foundation to show *how* a witness learnt about something (e.g. establishing the location of the witness, or in what capacity he or she was there) before asking what the witness actually saw. He also suggests asking a closed question (e.g. 'Did you hear something?') followed by an open question ('What did you hear?') to add to 'the story-telling energy' of the examination (Evans 1998: 87). Such techniques arguably apply psychological insights gained as much through professional experience as from study or research.

Requests put to the witness fall into three activity types: narrate, specify and confirm. Here are some examples adapted from Heffer (2005: 112).

Narrate	What happened around noon?
	Did anything happen when he came?
	Tell us what he did next.
	Did he say anything to you?
Specify	Where were you when you noticed the car?
	Who was in front?
	Do you mean this side or the far side?
	Did you agree to go with him?
Confirm	Is that a Horeston?
	You had the horse on the beach.
	You admitted that you had sexual intercourse.
	The knife just found itself in your hand, did it?

The further down the table you progress, the more control the examining lawyer exerts over permissible answers. Notice, incidentally, that some of the questions are not constructed directly as interrogatives.

During examination-in-chief (direct examination), simple **polar questions** can elicit answers that involve considerably more than a yes/no answer:

Q: Is demolition work at height dangerous?

A: Yes. It is a very hazardous activity. Over half of all fatal accidents in the construction industry every year are due to falls from a height. Up to about 10 per cent . . . (*plus a further 50 words*)

Q: Is this known within the industry?

A: In my experience, it is widely known within the industry. There are a number of guidance documents . . . (*plus a further 30 words*)

(Heffer 2005: 115)

Activity

❏   Polar questions asked during cross-examination, rather than during examination-in-chief, usually only generate a yes/no response, with no follow-up comment. Why should apparently identical question types be answered so differently in different sections of a trial?

❏   How far do you think Grice's theory of cooperative exchanges in communication could be used to explain this difference?

Controlling a witness during cross-examination

Consider the following, often discussed example of a cross-examination question put to William Cadbury, a senior member of the Cadbury's chocolate company when the company sued the *Evening Standard* for defamation in 1909 in respect of statements concerning Cadbury's exploitation of slaves. Edward Carson KC posed a question constructed so that a reply, whether in the positive or negative, would be seriously damaging:

> Have you formed any estimate of the number of slaves who lost their lives in preparing your cocoa from 1901 to 1908?

 Activity

❑ What would the effect be of either of the direct answers to this question?
❑ If you were William Cadbury, how might you have answered the question to avoid problems associated with either of the two alternative direct answers?

In fact, Cadbury reportedly answered, 'No, no, no'. The force of the question, it appears, was not in the speech act of asking, or the response of estimating, but in an embedded presupposition: that slaves lost their lives preparing cocoa during the years referred to. Such presuppositions cannot be negated or overridden by a yes or no answer. While the way in which such a question is constructed may be dependent on the facts of a case, such examples illustrate how a cross-examination question can be used to control a witness by eliminating options otherwise available in answering.

Silence as control

Now consider an example taken from research into courtroom interaction by Gregory Matoesian (1993). The extract shows how a cross-examining lawyer (DA) strategically delays the start of their next turn in order to convey a silent comment on an answer given by an alleged rape victim (V). In Matoesian's transcription (a linguistic transcription, rather than the very different format of an official court transcript; for discussion, see Gibbons 2003; Eades 2010), underlining indicates stress or emphasis in a word; a colon marks a prolonged sound; and capital letters indicate sounds uttered with increased volume. The number in brackets indicates the duration of a silence, measured in seconds.

> DA: Is it your testimony:::? (1.0) under swor:::n(.)
> >SWORN< oath (0.8) that in four hours at the Grainary
> (.) you only had two drinks?
> (1.2)
> V: Yes
> (45.0)
> DA: Linda . . .

(Matoesian 1993: 145)

❑ What effect do you think is created by such an extremely extended period of silence (45 seconds)?

❑ Matoesian (1993: 147) argues that 'access to linguistic resources by the cross-examiner and witness is asymmetrical'. Silence is not usually considered a 'linguistic resource', although conversation analysis has shown that in some circumstances it is. How far is silence here an example of a linguistic resource being strategically used?

Reformulation

As described in Unit B5, lawyers may rephrase a witness's words in favour of their own position during questioning. Consider the following two examples.

EXAMPLE 1

C: Good, but I am also . . .
W: (interrupts) I did not tell them everything.
C: Yes we shall get to that. You did not tell them everything, did you, so you *concealed* certain things did you not?
W: I know I only told them, I don't know, I did not. . . . I don't know.

(Lerm 1997: 172)

EXAMPLE 2

C: Were they in fact *a Protestant mob* that was attempting to burst out into Divis Street?
W: Prior to sending this message I must have known there was *a crowd of people* there.

(Atkinson and Drew 1979: 111)

Activity

❑ Comment on the **reformulation** by the lawyer in example 1 and by the witness in example 2. What appears to have been the intended effect in each case?

❑ Do lawyers and witnesses have equal opportunities in using reformulation as a persuasive device?

Pre-ruling withdrawal

In our next example, the cross-examining lawyer asks a series of questions, including one susceptible to objection that he readily withdraws himself even before the judge rules on the objection. Double brackets '[[' in the transcript indicate utterances that begin simultaneously; single brackets '[ ]' denote a period of overlapping talk. Parentheses '( )', when blank, indicate speech that is inaudible; when the brackets enclose words, there is doubt in the transcription.

DA: Did you have any marijuana?

(.)

V: No.

(.)

DA: You have used marijuana have you not?

(.)

V: Yes I have.

(1.8)

DA: You enjoy its use do you not?

PA: Objection yer honor (that isn't relevant)

[[

V: ( )

DA: I'll withdraw that ( ) yer honor

[ ]

J: Sustained

(Matoesian 1993: 114)

❖ **Activity**

❑   Why do you think DA withdrew his question so readily? What strategy might underpin a decision to do so?

❑   We have discussed how cross-examination questions typically do not seek new information, but are used for other purposes. Even though the question above does not solicit an answer, do you think the question objected to here still served a purpose in DA's construction of his case?

Leading jurors to a conclusion

The closing argument is the final opportunity for lawyers to engage in persuasion. It is also important because of its **recency effect**: it will remain more vivid than previous material. Below is an excerpt taken from a closing argument delivered by defence counsel Clarence Darrow in a famous 1924 American case, *State of Illinois v. Nathan Leopold & Richard Loeb*. Leopold and Loeb were prosecuted for murdering a 14-year-old boy, Robert Franks, in Chicago. They both confessed to the crime. The trial was therefore not a jury trial; and the closing argument was accordingly a plea to convince Judge Caverly to impose life imprisonment rather than capital punishment. The original speech was 12 hours long; we only look at a very small fragment from it here (a full transcript is available online; see the further reading and resources section for details).

Many may say now that they want to hang these boys. But I know that giving the people blood is something like giving them their dinner: when they get it they go to sleep. They may for the time being have an emotion, but they will bitterly regret it. And I undertake to say that if these two boys are sentenced to death, and are hanged on that day, there will be a pall settle over the people of this land that will be dark and deep, and at least cover every humane and intelligent person with its gloom. I wonder if it will do good. I marveled when I heard Mr. Savage talk. Mr. Savage tells this court that if these boys are hanged, there will be no more murder. Mr. Savage is an optimist. He says that if the defendants are hanged there will be no more boys like these. I could give him a sketch of punishment, punishment beginning with the brute which killed something because something hurt it; the punishment of the savage; if a person is injured in the tribe, they must injure somebody in the other tribe; it makes no difference who it is, but somebody. If one is killed his friends or family must kill in return.

You can trace it all down through the history of man. You can trace the burnings, the boilings, the drawings and quarterings, the hangings of people in England at the crossroads, carving them up and hanging them, as examples for all to see.

We can come down to the last century when nearly two hundred crimes were punishable by death, and by death in every form; not only hanging that was too humane, but burning, boiling, cutting into pieces, torturing in all conceivable forms.

I know that every step in the progress of humanity has been met and opposed by prosecutors, and many times by courts. I know that when poaching and petty larceny was punishable by death in England, juries refused to convict. They were too humane to obey the law; and judges refused to sentence. I know that when the delusion of witchcraft was spreading over Europe, claiming its victims by the millions, many a judge so shaped his cases that no crime of witchcraft could be punished in his court. I know that these trials were stopped in America because juries would no longer convict.

Gradually the laws have been changed and modified, and men look back with horror at the hangings and the killings of the past. What did they find in England? That as they got rid of these barbarous statutes, crimes decreased instead of increased; as the criminal law was modified and humanized, there was less crime instead of more. I will undertake to say, Your Honor, that you can scarcely find a single book written by a student, and I will include all the works on criminology of the past, that has not made the statement over and over again that as the penal code was made less terrible, crimes grew less frequent.

 Activity

❏ Describe the main linguistic register of this excerpt. Give examples of words, phrases and grammatical constructions to support your description. (You may find it useful to refer to concepts and terminology introduced in Thread 2, or to consult Halliday and Hasan (1976) or Biber and Conrad (2009).)

❏ Why does Darrow refer to the 'history of man', a very broad topic indeed given the circumstances? What overall point is he making by means of this reference?

❏ Darrow criticises capital punishment as a way of exacting retribution. What are the main features of the rhetorical strategies he uses in making this criticism?

C6

C6   DECIDING LEGAL MEANING

In this unit, we extend our exploration of similarities and differences between how meaning is understood in linguistic approaches to language and in statutory inter- pretation. We do this by examining the reasoning developed in one among a large number of cases worldwide that have looked at the meaning of the word *sculpture* for the purpose of copyright law. The main question in this case (on which a number of the legal issues turned) was: is a *Star Wars* Stormtrooper helmet a *sculpture*?

The task in this unit consists of two sections: first, a directed exploration of the meaning of the word *sculpture*; second, some questions that follow a description of essential points in the case. (Both accounts are quite long by comparison with material presented to introduce other activities in this book; but each is brief and selective in relation to the detail contained in the case in question.)

First, we approach the issues in the case by thinking about how the meaning of *sculpture* can be investigated outside the specialised sphere of legal interpretation.

1   Make a note of three or four objects or artefacts you consider to be obviously sculptures. They may have names or you may need to describe them.

2   Now make a second note of the same number of objects or artefacts, but ones you believe to be clearly not sculptures.

3   Now make a third note, of objects or artefacts you consider to be borderline cases: objects you think would divide people consulting their intuitions about whether the word *sculpture* fits.

4   Now, drawing on Unit A6, assess how the exemplars in your three lists might fit into a 'prototype' account of word meaning.

5   Your three lists begin to map your mental model of the **extension** of the word *sculpture*: the set of things in the world that the word can be used to refer to. How far do you detect historical and/or cultural variation in decisions whether objects will satisfy the concept 'sculpture'? How far is such variation also likely to exist within a single society?

6   Write a brief definition, looking at your three lists (but not at the paragraph that follows) that tries to capture what you think a *sculpture* is.

7   Now compare your definition with some definitions produced by scholars in relevant fields, including dictionary-writing:

7.1   In the *Concise Oxford Dictionary*, *sculpture* is 'the art of forming representa- tions of objects etc. or abstract designs in the round or in relief by chiselling stone, carving wood, modelling clay casting metal, or similar processes'.

7.2   Dictionaries arrive at their statements of meaning in different ways, however; so it is interesting to compare their entries for the same word. The *Collins COBUILD Dictionary*, for example, bases the order in which it presents different senses on their frequency of use in a corpus of several billion words;

and the full *Oxford English Dictionary (OED)* describes each word by showing the historical development and branching of interwoven senses. The *OED* entry for sculpture as a noun gives four main meanings, each divided into subsidiary senses, matched to periods of use and supported with illustrative quotations.

8 Develop your sense of *sculpture* further by considering the **sense relations** the word enters into with other words. For example, is *sculpture* a **hyponym** (type of) either *fine art* or *craft*? Of *hobby* or *pastime*? Of *furniture*? Beyond sense relations of this kind, you may also want to consult a **thesaurus**, which relates words to their neighbours and opposites by meaning in the same semantic field. *Roget's Thesaurus*, for example, locates *sculpture* next to 'carving, statuary, ceramics, plastic arts'. To develop a fuller understanding of sculpture as a concept, you might consult encyclopedias, either online or in print, and/or histories of relevant fields. Computer-generated **KWICs** ('key word in context' reports) can show a list of occasions of use of a given word in a given corpus, with a selected number of words on either side of the target word; these are also helpful in considering a word's behaviour in context. (It is possible to download a free **concordancer** software programme, such as Laurence Anthony's AntConc, to enable you to do this.)

9 Using these various methods and resources, try to build up a profile of possible and likely use of *sculpture*, including contexts in which the word occurs and the values and implications associated with it. Such a profile gives a picture of the word's ordinary use, subject to the proviso that such data will certainly show up variation on several dimensions rather than a single meaning.

10 Now we will go on to ask how, faced with such variation and complexity, a court can go about arriving at a singular, legally correct meaning for *sculpture* in a given legal context. To do this, first it is necessary to read a brief account of the case:

Lucasfilm v. Ainsworth

The case of *Lucasfilm v. Ainsworth* concerned the designs for Imperial Stormtrooper helmets and armour featured in the first *Star Wars* film (somewhat enigmatically called *Star Wars: Episode IV – A New Hope*, released in 1977). Ainsworth, the defendant, had created moulds and other materials to make the helmets and armour used during filming, based on initial storyboard sketches and a clay model prepared on behalf of Lucasfilm (the main claimant). The resulting white helmets and armour became known as the 'cheesegrater', 'jawbone', 'X-wing fighter pilot', 'rebel troop', 'chest box', and others. Roughly 30 years later, Ainsworth set up a website selling replicas of the helmets and armour online to *Star Wars* fans (who organise themselves as 'Garrisons' and enjoy costumes and other designs related to the continuing film series).

Lucasfilm alleged copyright infringement in California and obtained a default judgment against Ainsworth. They then sought to enforce that judgment against Ainsworth, or enforce their American copyright claim, in the UK (where Ainsworth was based). There were numerous claims, and issues both of fact and law, in the case. But the questions all buttressed a central claim and counterclaim, each of which depended on whether any of the helmets were either 'sculptures' or 'works of artistic craftsmanship' within the meaning of s. 4 ('Artistic works') of the Copyright, Designs and Patents Act 1988.

This central question occupied the English courts throughout three proceedings at successive levels: first instance court, Court of Appeal, and Supreme Court. At first instance, it was held that the Imperial Stormtrooper helmet was *not* a sculpture within the meaning of the Act. Rather, it was a mixture of costume and prop, whose function was utilitarian: it made a contribution to the film, which overall was the work of art. The same reasoning was applied to the armour, and analogous argument made on the different requirements for 'works of artistic craftsmanship'. Toy models marketed by Lucasfilm were also deemed not to be sculptures, because their primary purpose was to be used in play rather than 'exhibited, viewed or contemplated'. The Court of Appeal and Supreme Court concurred with that first instance judgment.

Because no copyright subsisted in the helmets or armour as sculptures under UK copyright law, and so were not protected as 'artistic works' by UK copyright law, only Lucasfilm's claim based on infringement under US law succeeded. The claimant's other claims (totalling USD 20 million) failed; and Ainsworth's counterclaim that he had produced artistic works (defending an income derived from sales of the helmets and armour of roughly USD 14,000) also failed.

Interpreting *sculpture*

The reasoning process through which the courts arrived at a correct, legal meaning for *sculpture* illustrates some key features of statutory interpretation outlined elsewhere in this thread.

At first instance, Mann, J (i.e. Mr Justice Mann, the judge) acknowledged difficulty with the concept that a sculpture is an artistic work under the 1988 Act (CDPA 1988). He noted that:

> There is no statutory definition of 'sculpture' for the purposes of this area of legislation. The only statutory assistance one has in relation to this question is a somewhat circular indication of what is included: '"sculpture" includes a cast or model made for purposes of sculpture' (s. 4(1)(2)(b)).

The judge looked to relevant authorities for guidance. He found that what such authorities provide is principally a series of examples, linked to factors taken into account by judges in deciding a particular case. Early authorities included an 1891 case applying an earlier Copyright Act in which artistic merit played a part that was no longer a feature of the 1988 legislation. In a 1995 case brought by the appliance manufacturer Breville, the claimants successfully claimed copyright in plaster shapes used as moulds for differently shaped sandwiches produced by their sandwich maker (though there was then found to have been no infringement). Another relevant case was a case in which it was claimed that a Frisbee (the plastic flying disc) was a sculpture, though the court found they were purely functional, indeed industrial objects.

In these and other cases, dictionary definitions, including one from the *Shorter Oxford English Dictionary* and one from *Webster's Third New International Dictionary*, were introduced. They were not used as authorities, but as aids to memory and more precise formulation. Judicial reference was also made to an article on 'Art of sculpture' in the *New Encyclopaedia Britannica*, which stated that:

> Sculpture is not a fixed term that applies to a permanently circumscribed category of objects or sets of activities. It is, rather, the name of an art that grows and changes and is continually extending the range of its activities and evolving new kinds of objects. The scope of the term is much wider in the second half of the 20th century than it was only two or three decades ago, and in the present fluid state of the visual arts, nobody can predict what its future extensions are likely to be.

Despite this description, the courts concluded that what was required was that a work in question should be a sculpture 'in the ordinary sense of that term' or 'as included in the extended definition of sculpture contained in the Act'. Interpretation could proceed, therefore, by reasoning from 'what is the normal understanding of the expression *sculpture*', despite the view of one judge suggesting that 'that is a pretty loose boundary'. In another case, the judge (Laddie, J) pointed to a sense of purpose inherent in whether the definition should be a broad or narrow one:

> The law has been bedevilled by attempts to widen out the field covered by the copyright Acts. It is not possible to say with precision what is and what is not sculpture, but [. . .] a sculpture is a three-dimensional work made by an artist's hand. It appears to me that there is no reason why the word 'sculpture' in the 1988 Act should be extended far beyond the meaning which that word has to ordinary members of the public.

Extending the process of analysis further in *Lucasfilm*, Mann, J proposed a 'multi-factorial' approach, formulating a list of eight 'points of guidance' to be taken into account in considering the meaning of the term *sculpture* for the purposes of the Copyright, Designs and Patents Act 1988.

The first three points of guidance appear merely to provide general orientation:

(i)   some regard had to be had to the normal use of the word;
(ii) nevertheless, the concept could be applicable to things going beyond what would normally be expected to be art in the sense of the sort of things expected to be found in art galleries; and
(iii) it was inappropriate to stray too far from what would normally be regarded as sculpture.

Mann, J's fourth point noted that, by statute, no judgment should be made as to artistic worth. His fifth point echoes Laddie, J's concern above, regarding possible overexpansion of the category of protectable sculptures:

(v)   not every three-dimensional representation of a concept could be regarded as a sculpture, otherwise every three-dimensional construction or fabrication would be a sculpture.

Points (vi) and (vii) highlight purpose and function:

(vi)   it was of the essence of a sculpture that it should have, as part of its purpose, a visual appeal in the sense that it might be enjoyed for that purpose alone, whether or not it might have another purpose as well [. . .]; and

(vii) the fact that the object had some other use did not necessarily disqualify it from being a sculpture, but it still had to have the intrinsic quality of being intended to be enjoyed as a visual thing.

The final point concerned materials or mode of production:

(viii) the process of fabrication was relevant but not determinative; there was no reason why a purely functional item, not intended to be at all decorative, should be treated as a sculpture 'simply because it had been (for example) carved out of wood or stone'.

Immediately following this list, the judge emphasised that the enumerated factors were guidelines, not rigid requirements. The question 'What is a sculpture?', he concluded, 'has some of the elements about it of the unanswerable question: "What is Art?"'. Analysed by multifactorial reasoning, nevertheless, the helmets were found to be intended to express something and to have interest as objects, but served the purpose principally of character portrayal within the film rather than being aesthetic in themselves. This did not give them the necessary quality of artistic creation required by the Act.

The Court of Appeal and Supreme Court commended multifactorial analysis for its adaptation of implicit understanding of normal usage in the direction of requirements specific to the protection afforded by copyright; and the first instance outcome was upheld. Reservation was nevertheless expressed about points (vi) and (vii), which draw a fine distinction between the purpose for which an object may actually be used and its purposive nature: what Mann, J had described as 'its intrinsic quality of being intended to be enjoyed as a visual thing'. The difficulty presented by that fine distinction was described by Jacob, LJ (i.e. Lord Justice Jacob) in the Court of Appeal as precisely the reason why the judge in the lower court had outlined 'a number of considerations which should act as signposts to the right answer'. Joining in commendation of the multifactorial approach, Jacob, LJ nevertheless appeared to undermine it with a comment pointing in a different direction (which was later queried in the Supreme Court):

The result of this analysis is that it is not possible or wise to attempt to devise a comprehensive or exclusive definition of 'sculpture' sufficient to determine the issue in any given case. Although this may be close to adopting the elephant test of knowing one when you see one, it is almost inevitable in this field.

Declaring, attributing and deciding meaning

Having read this condensed (but still quite long) account of the interpretation of *sculpture* in *Lucasfilm*, now address the following issues:

❏   How closely does the approach adopted by the judge at first instance (Mann, J) reflect your understanding of approaches to legal interpretation as outlined in Units A6 and B6?

❏   Is using 'ordinary' or 'normal' meaning helpful as a starting point in deciding what a word means, if whatever is decided as that meaning will then be modified to fit the requirements of a piece of legislation being applied?

❏   How successful do you consider the multifactorial test for *sculpture* approved by the Supreme Court? Is using some such test essential if problems of 'the elephant in the room test' or the 'What is Art?' question are to be avoided?

❏   Finally, one school of legal theory, known as **legal realism**, has seriously queried the sorts of reasoning judges engage in. It suggests that such approaches to interpretation serve merely as a vehicle for decisions that are ultimately made on other grounds. Do you consider this to be a risk with the kinds of semantic argument put forward by the courts in interpreting a statutory word such as *sculpture*?

SPOKEN AND WRITTEN PERFORMATIVES

In this unit, we look at how performative speech acts take place in three different mediums: in speech, in writing, and in electronic communication. We consider the history of performativity in changing linguistic and social relations brought about by the shift from orality to literacy, and speculate about challenges facing performatives that have accompanied the rise of electronic means of communication and increased frequency of legal transactions and interactions at a distance.

Identifying legal speech acts

Consider the following excerpt from the will made by the American actress Marilyn Monroe (1926–1962):

Last Will and Testament of Marilyn Monroe

I, MARILYN MONROE, do make, publish and declare this to be my Last Will and Testament.

FIRST: I hereby revoke all former Wills and Codicils by me made.

SECOND: I direct my Executor, hereinafter named, to pay all of my just debts, funeral expenses and testamentary charges as soon after my death as can conveniently be done.

THIRD: I direct that all succession, estate or inheritance taxes which may be levied against my estate and/or against any legacies and/or devises hereinafter set forth shall be paid out of my residuary estate.

FOURTH: (a) I give and bequeath to BERNICE MIRACLE, should she survive me, the sum of $10,000.00.

    (b) I give and bequeath to MAY REIS, should she survive me, the sum of $10,000.00.

    (c) I give and bequeath to NORMAN and HEDDA ROSTEN, or to the survivor of them, or if they should both predecease me, then to their daughter, PATRICIA ROSTEN, the sum of $5,000.00, it being my wish that such sum be used for the education of PATRICIA ROSTEN.

    (d) I give and bequeath all of my personal effects and clothing to LEE STRASBERG, or if he should predecease me, then to my Executor hereinafter named, it being my desire that he distribute these, in his sole discretion, among my friends, colleagues and those to whom I am devoted.

** Activity**

1 Identify the explicit performative acts in this excerpt, and list the performative verbs that realise them. You should end up with a (fairly elaborate) representation based on repeated application of Searle's formula **F(p)**.

2 What kinds of linguistic expression guide you in identifying phrases or sentences that constitute performative acts? You might, for example, consider **deictics** such as personal pronouns (e.g. *I*), use of simple present tense, use of modality, use of temporal adverbs such as *now*, etc.

3 Only performative verbs, Austin suggests, co-occur with the adverb *hereby* between first-person subject and verb. Inserting *hereby* at appropriate points in sentences throughout the document accordingly gives you one test of whether your list of performative verbs fits or conflicts with Austin's stipulation.

4 How much of the document is *not* performative in the sense you have followed in responding to the previous questions? This final question may expose difficulties in thinking about the scope of the content that falls within any given performative act.

Conditions on the effectiveness of legal enactments

Felicity conditions are requirements that need to be fulfilled for a speech act to achieve its conventional effect. With **institutional speech acts**, the kinds of condition in question may include whether procedural conventions are followed, whether the performative act is uttered by an appropriate person, in appropriate circumstances, and whether the act is completed without errors. Felicity conditions are usually understood implicitly. Searle's descriptions show how detailed an analysis must be if it is to specify the intuitive felicity conditions that satisfy the requirements of a particular speech act, such as *bequeath*.

In a chapter on what he calls 'reversible performatives', Kurzon examines *bequeath*, which he describes as a 'ceremonial performative' (Kurzon 1986: 41–2). For legal speech acts, Kurzon emphasises, felicity conditions are not intuitive, but are explicitly laid down in the applicable law or laws. We can explore this statement further by staying with wills but changing jurisdiction: here are some selected provisions in the Wills Act 1837 (UK, as amended). For some provisions, only a section heading is shown.

7. No will of a person under age valid.
9. Signing and attestation of wills
   No will shall be valid unless –

   (a) it is in writing, and signed by the testator, or by some other person in his presence and by his direction; and
   (b) it appears that the testator intended by his signature to give effect to the will; and
   (c) the signature is made or acknowledged by the testator in the presence of two or more witnesses present at the same time; and
   (d) each witness either –

       (i) attests and signs the will; or
       (ii) acknowledges his signature, in the presence of the testator (but not necessarily in the presence of any other witness)

   but no form of attestation shall be necessary.

13. Publication of will not be requisite.
14. Will not to be void on account of incompetency of attesting witness.
17. Executor shall be admitted a witness.
18. Wills to be revoked by marriage, except in certain cases.

Activity

❏ Following the exposition of Kurzon we give in Unit B7, describe how the sections above (none of which contains an explicit performative verb) function as performative acts. Remember to relate the provisions as a series to the effect of the **enacting formula**.

❏ If we apply Searle's (1969) model, some of the conditions that a speaker – in this case, a testator – has to fulfil are that he or she: (i) has authority (or power) to bequeath; (ii) has something to bequeath; and (iii) intends the act to be an act of bequeathing. How closely do these general felicity conditions on the speech act match the more detailed legal provisions presented here?

❏ Felicity conditions for conversational speech acts tell us what a particular act is. In law, such conditions work differently. They still define the constitutive issue (what is a will?); but they combine that function with specifying particular aims and protecting interests. What for example do you think s. 9(b) seeks to prevent? And what do you think the general presumption is behind s. 18?

Performativity, orality and literacy

Gibbons (2003) and other writers have pointed out that it is possible in some written legal documents to see traces of earlier, oral common-law traditions. One such trace is arguably use of clearly identifiable, first-person explicit performatives in documents such as wills. Such written performatives are fixed in permanent form but also convey the sense of a written 'record' of a situationally specific speech event (of a kind displaced by a shift of priority between the two mediums of speech and writing; Clanchy 1993).

In her paper 'Speech, writing and performativity: an evolutionary view of the history of constitutive ritual', Brenda Danet (1997) traces this development. She examines what she sees as 'one of the most prominent, universal features of language in all societies: providing recipes for the creation of new social relationships and social arrangements, and for transformations of the status of individuals or groups' (Danet 1997: 13). The performative dimension of language and society, she argues, has a complex history running from verbal formulas in preliterate social rituals, through their development and adaptation in customary law, into more recent practices based on production, adoption and retention of written documents.

Danet describes how constitutive ceremonies of this general kind, whether written or oral, are treated by members of society as legally binding, and how respect for obligations ratified by such means is typically embedded in a shifting combination of sacred and secular rituals. In illustrating such rituals, Danet also notes how linguistic stylisation is universally found in oral ritual genres of communication, and is sometimes carried over into the high, formal registers of more recent written legal styles (see unit B2).

In the course of her paper, Danet refers to earlier research she had undertaken with Bryna Bogoch on the history of wills during the crucial period of the early rise of literacy in medieval England. Danet and Bogoch (1992) assemble a corpus of the complete set of 62 wills in Old English that survive from the Anglo-Saxon period. Taking a combined linguistic and anthropological approach, the authors analyse the language of constitutive ritual in this corpus, describing different linguistic features in three main categories they identified as being of interest:

(i)   meta-comments about writing;
(ii)   linguistic realisation of the performative act of 'bequeathing'; and
(iii)   decontextualisation.

They then compare their historical data with modern wills. Here are some rows adapted from one of their tables (Danet and Bogoch 1992: 99).

Read the table and then consider the questions that follow.

Feature	Anglo-Saxon wills	Modern wills
1 Meta-comments about writing	Present	Absent
2 Realisation of the act of bequeathing	Linked to oral ceremony	Autonomous
3 Opening strategy	Non-standard	Standard
4 Witnesses	Reference only, or touching the document	Signature
5 Direct address	Present	Absent
6 Hedging	Present	Absent

Activity

1   What historical changes reported in the table suggest movement away from features of speech towards a written genre? Are there any changes that point in the opposite direction?

2   Row 1 of the table appears to suggest that while modern testators take the act of writing for granted, Anglo-Saxon wills show self-consciousness in using the new medium. Danet and Bogoch's examples from their corpus include:

(a) I, Ealdorman Alfred, command to be written and made known in this document to King Alfred and all his councillors . . .

(b) Then I wish it to be given out for my soul just as I now said to my friends with whom I spoke . . .

Explain in more detail how these two comments on writing and speaking might be thought to support an inference that wills underwent a transition during the period from earlier oral forms of social relationship into a recorded, literate legal culture.

3   In Danet and Bogoch's corpus, wills often refer explicitly to an oral ceremony that constituted the binding act of bequeathing, in advance of the written document. Performative significance was nevertheless marked in some ceremonies by witnesses touching a cross on the document with a sword or a hand (touching the cross was a medieval equivalent of a modern signature). How reasonable is it for Danet to see a link between verbal and physical aspects of this performative act?

4   Danet's inference is that the ritual reveals a transitional connection between physical manipulation of symbolic objects, common in oral ceremonies, and a new literacy, in that individuals are relating their movements to graphic marks on the parchment. How reasonable is this inference?

5   Finally, in their study Danet and Bogoch note the presence of an extra performative that has disappeared completely from modern wills. Over one-quarter of the wills in their corpus contain **curses** addressed to anyone who tampered with the will. Here is one example:

And he who shall detract from my will which I have now declared in the witness of God, may he be deprived of joy on this earth, and may [. . .] he be delivered into the abyss of hell to Satan the devil and all his accursed companions and there suffer with God's adversaries, without end, and never trouble my heirs.

In light of your thinking in response to the questions above, what would you consider an appropriate explanation of the historical disappearance of this performative?

Spoken and written contracts

Danet's arguments prompt fundamental questions about how legal performativity relates to linguistic medium. How effective, we might therefore ask, are explicit legal performatives in speech in the modern period of majority (though very uneven) literacy in most societies?

Contracts offer an interesting illustration. It is commonly assumed, but wrongly, that contracts are only enforceable if they are made in writing. Several shifts exist, historically. Before widespread literacy, in oral legal culture, spoken contracts and associated rituals were the norm (and remain so in many societies). With the rise of literacy, a gradual shift took place towards more frequent use of, and greater status accorded to, written documents, including contracts. Seventeenth-century English law required a large number of contracts to be made in writing (Baker 2002: 348–50). Today, the law generally only insists on writing where the subject matter or nature of a contract requires certain evidence, or where a cautionary element is introduced to impress on one of the parties the seriousness of the agreement being entered into (hence a requirement of writing consumer credit agreements, sales of an interest in land, and distance selling agreements).

There is still a tension in the mix of recorded written and unrecorded oral contracts, however. If a written contract was required every time someone bought a bottle of milk or loaf of bread, they would need to countersign an invoice; this would obstruct the multiplicity of transactions in modern everyday life. In most commercial dealings, written evidence is normally available in the form of electronically produced sales receipts, invoices and orders, but these are mostly not a legal requirement. In recent years, however, there has been a resurgence in what are called formality requirements (i.e. requirements of a particular form to make a contract enforceable; failure to comply can make a contract void, ineffective or without the consequences that should normally follow). This shift reflects a changing commercial environment and increased protection measures put in place for consumers.

C7

Performativity, now and in the future

Towards the end of the article discussed above, Danet turns from the advent of literacy to the recent rapid expansion of the online world, in order to address a further question: if a shift from orality to literacy prompted fundamental change in how performativity is achieved, is an equivalent transition now likely because of our current shift towards new kinds of **mediated orality**?

Two central insights organise Danet's discussion. One is her scepticism about the conventional wisdom that the prime incentive for the invention of writing was a need for record-keeping. She does not dispute the importance of record-keeping, but claims that her study with Bogoch shows how far preoccupation with the referential function of language can lead to overlooking the cultural importance of performativity. Her other main insight is that (as she highlights in claiming that the language of Anglo-Saxon wills was more context-dependent than modern wills) the historical development of written communication has been away from a presumption that other people will know who or what is meant on the basis of shared knowledge among members of a community.

In discussing the anthropological significance of decoupling the verbal content of documents from face-to-face ceremonies, Danet weighs up the possibility that, in future, video-recorded oral ceremonies and eventually fully virtual events may replace performative documents, in the way that documents took over from oral rituals. She draws attention to current developments, including legally binding electronic signatures and other technical and legal means to guarantee the authenticity and binding quality of **virtual ceremonies**. She even speculates about the form of video wills.

In our period of rapidly changing technological capabilities and international connectedness, a number of open-ended questions arise:

Activity

1   What factors (technological, economic, linguistic, legal) would you expect to be taken into account in developments in this area?
2   To what extent do new media of electronic transmission and dissemination of texts threaten our notion of the authoritative, binding document?
3   How far will mediated forms of orality encourage new techniques of impersonation and fraud, potentially undermining levels of trust in rapidly changing societies?
4   What will the effects of such new media be on the document-based legal culture mostly discussed in this book? Is it plausible, for example, to anticipate trials taking place completely in virtual courtrooms by means of synchronous electronic interaction? International treaties negotiated and signed without the signatories ever meeting, let alone signing?

C8 MISLEADING LANGUAGE IN ADVERTS

In this unit we look at a practical aspect of how advertising language is regulated: whether an advert that has been complained about is misleading. We provide a brief outline of advertising regulation, then work through three non-broadcast adverts about which complaints were made to the UK Advertising Standards Authority (the ASA; www.asa.org.uk). The disputed text of each advert is assessed in relation to the issue raised by complainants. Towards the end of the unit, the ASA judgments are summarised.

Introduction

In **free speech** theory, adverts fall within a category of **commercial speech**. Such speech is not prized as contributing as much to democratic society as political speech, but it is still protected to some degree (Barendt 2005: 392–416). Commercial speech is nevertheless regulated to some extent in all societies. Alongside consumer protection legislation, trading standards requirements and provisions related to health and safety and product liability, more general provisions regarding misrepresentation apply (Barendt *et al.* 2014: 229–73). There are also connections with other marketing communications, including use of online search keywords and the recently expanded 'advertising function' of trademarks (Waelde *et al.* 2014: 550–3, 702–6).

Front-line advertising regulation is dealt with in many countries by non-statutory bodies: a process often described as **soft law** because it involves codes administered by an extralegal body. But failure to comply with the relevant code can still result in litigation. The adverts we look at in this unit were displayed, and complained about, in the UK; the complaint details are adapted from reports published online on the ASA website. For reasons of space, we have removed irrelevant details and summarised where exact wording does not affect the issue in question. The gender of complainants is not indicated by the ASA; we have chosen to refer to all complainants as 'she' for the sake of consistency.

The CAP (non-broadcast) code and its implementation

The non-broadcast Code of Advertising Practice is drafted and periodically revised by the Committee of Advertising Practice (CAP), a body drawn from advertisers, agencies and trade organisations, and administered by the Advertising Standards Authority (ASA). The present 12th edition came into force in 2010, and contains 21 sections, including special provisions related to distance selling and shock tactics, slimming, gambling, motoring and tobacco (see the full code at www.cap.org.uk). We consider complaints dealt with under section 3, concerned with misleading advertising. Two preliminary points should be made:

❏ Advertising generally adopts a distinction between **product or service claims** (which are factual, and for which substantiation is required) and **trade puffs** (which are self-promoting, laudatory expressions not expected to be taken seriously and for which no evidence is needed).

❏ Implied meanings that give rise to claims are taken as part of the meaning of the advert. Implied meanings linked to trade puffs, or which merely evoke general positive feelings, may be complained about under other headings (e.g. that they are sexist or in some other way inappropriate).

In order to give a sense of the process through which UK advertising language is regulated, we now present the introductory subsections of section 3 of the Code, followed by three selected complaints. Each complaint concerned whether the advert was misleading. For each, we provide the company's response, then some questions. A summary of the complaint outcome is given at the end of the unit.

General provisions of section 3: misleading advertising

Section 3 of the Code consists of 57 subsections, dealing with matters including substantiation, exaggeration, prices, comparisons, denigration, endorsements and testimonials. The essential sections for analysing the complaints below are general sections 3.1–3.3. You may nevertheless find it interesting to consult the full code for fuller specification provided in other subsections.

3.1   Marketing communications must not materially mislead or be likely to do so.

3.2   Obvious exaggerations ('puffery') and claims that the average consumer who sees the marketing communication is unlikely to take literally are allowed provided they do not materially mislead.

3.3   Marketing communications must not mislead the consumer by omitting material information. They must not mislead by hiding material information or presenting it in an unclear, unintelligible, ambiguous or untimely manner.

Everything a pound

Text on a company's website stated 'Poundworld everything £1'.

A complainant had seen 'manager special' items in-store, costing £3 and £8.99. She challenged whether the claim 'everything £1' was misleading.

Response: Poundworld Retail Ltd saw the 'manager specials' as a service in addition to their £1 products. They said the manager specials were 'occasional' offers that usually ran during the Christmas selling period and at random and infrequent intervals for the remainder of the year. Following discussion with their home Trading Standards authority, they had identified strategies for marketing manager specials to ensure that the items were distinguishable in store from the £1 items and separate from them.

✪ Activity

- ❑ How is it possible to assess whether 'everything £1' is misleading in this context? Consider first the conventional meaning of 'everything'. Then consider inferences likely to be drawn from 'everything £1' in this sales context.
- ❑ Be as specific as you can about how much support for your assessment of inferences can be drawn from linguistic approaches you are familiar with (e.g. from work on speech acts, or work by Grice).
- ❑ Would a complainant have equivalent grounds for making a section 3 'misleading' complaint if she found products costing *less* than £1 in the shop? If not, why not?

Trading in

The website of a furniture and carpet company included a link to a leaflet headed 'We will pay you £500 for your old 3 piece suite'. Further text stated 'Trade your old furniture in for the furniture of your dreams, available on everything in store with absolutely no exceptions . . . we will pay you £100 per seat for your old sofa . . . on everything in store, nothing will be excluded, not even the famous brand names.

> *A complainant who asked to trade in her sofa against an item of bedroom furniture was told that this was not an option. She challenged whether the claim that the trade-in offer was 'available on everything in store with absolutely no exceptions' was misleading.*

Response: The company said a dictionary definition of a 'trade-in' was obtaining a fixed value for a like-for-like transaction. They believed customers would expect to need to trade in an item of the same kind as the one they wanted to obtain.

✪ Activity

- ❑ Do you agree with the company's meaning of *trade-in*? How useful is dictionary evidence in relation to such a claim?
- ❑ What features of the wording of their leaflet seem in tension with that claim? Consider in particular the use of the word *furniture*.
- ❑ Taking both the complaint and the response into account, should this claim be upheld? Briefly describe your reasoning.

Single travellers

A national press advert for a travel company stated 'The First Choice for Single Travellers'.

A competitor company challenged whether the claim 'The First Choice for Single Travellers' was misleading and whether it could be substantiated.

Response: The company said that 'Solitair – First choice for single travellers' had been a registered trademark since 2008. They provided evidence to demonstrate that, and said no issues had been raised when they registered the trademark and that they had not received any complaints about it since. The company argued that the claim did not relate to sales, but indicated that their services were the perfect fit for single travellers. They believed their company was the best choice for single travellers, and said repeat booking figures were approximately 60 per cent.

Activity

❑   Words and phrases such as *favourite* (famously used in adverts by British Airways), *foremost* and *first choice* are difficult. Does 'first choice' in this context convey a specific claim? Or could it be read as merely a trade puff, along the lines of 'best', 'outstanding', etc.?

❑   If the slogan 'First choice for single travellers' conveys a specific claim, how would you paraphrase that claim? Is such a claim necessarily a comparative claim in relation to other travel companies?

❑   The primary function of a registered trademark is as a badge of origin. It distinguishes goods or services originating from one commercial source from those that originate from another; in doing so, it prevents consumer confusion between products or services that may differ in quality. In your view, should the fact that 'First choice for single travellers' is used in this way as a trademark affect the outcome of the complaint?*

The complaint rulings

Everything a pound

The complaint was upheld. The ASA took the view that the advert suggested every item in the store would be priced at £1. It noted the precautions issued internally intended to ensure the price of items priced at more than £1 should be clear to consumers. Nevertheless, it considered that a significant draw of the claim would be that consumers would expect to pay no more than £1 for any item in the store.

Trading in

The complaint was upheld. The ASA considered there was likely to be a general expectation among consumers that a trade-in offer normally related to broadly similar products. However, it also took the view that the references to 'available on everything in store with absolutely no exceptions' and 'nothing will be excluded', in conjunction with photographs of other furniture in addition to sofas and armchairs and the logos of companies unlikely to be associated with sofas, suggested that the offer applied across the broad range of furniture, and that it would be possible to trade in one category of furniture against another category.

Single travellers

The complaint was upheld. Although the ASA acknowledged that 'Solitair – First choice for single travellers' was a registered trademark, it considered that consumers were nonetheless likely to interpret the claim as a comparative claim. Consumers would therefore expect Solitair to have a higher turnover or more unit sales from single travellers than their competitors within the travel market. Because no evidence had been produced to demonstrate that this was the case, the ASA concluded that the advert was misleading. In reaching this conclusion, the ASA instructed the advertisers to include a prominently displayed disclaimer to the registered trademark 'Solitair – First choice for single travellers', which made clear that they did not have a higher turnover or more unit sales than other single-traveller holiday companies.

Advertising standards and the average consumer

There is a considerable literature on advertising language in linguistics. Some of that work describes how language has been used in specific ways in advertising (e.g. Leech 1966); some celebrates, as well as analyses, the craft of copywriting (Myers 1994, 1998); some engages more directly with issues of regulation (Geis 1982; Preston 1994). The legal literature on advertising illustrates provisions with verbal examples from case law but mostly does not dwell on linguistic points related to promotional language.

Arguably, the main issue in understanding advertising language from a regulatory perspective is this: from what position is any interpretation of the meaning or effect of an advert to be judged? As we discuss in Unit B8, some such position is essential in assessing inferred meanings or other effects that reflect socially variable standards, including taste and decency. In this respect, problems in adjudicating advertising standards resemble issues that arise in defamation law; and an equivalent interpretive standard has evolved, in some respects similar to defamation's **ordinary reasonable reader**. In advertising (as well as in trademark law), the standard is that of the **average consumer**: a standard that emerged historically from problems of protecting credulous or gullible consumers while seeking not to limit opportunities for creative commercial communication styles. The resulting average consumer, as defined most precisely in trademark law, is held to be 'reasonably observant, reasonably well-informed and circumspect'; he or she behaves in ways that necessarily vary depending on what kind of product or service is being purchased, since the degree and kind of attention required in buying a new car, for example, are likely to differ from those used in buying a tube of toothpaste (Davis 2005). Applying the standard of an average consumer, however, is undertaken less explicitly in decisions arrived at by an extrajudicial body such as the ASA than in a court case, though in principle it could be problematic in either. It is interesting, therefore, finally to consider how far you feel the thinking you engaged in while working through the three adverts above matches your own notion of a general standard appropriate to the 'average consumer'.

The complaints (www.asa.org.uk):
Everything a pound: *Poundworld Retail Ltd*, 8 October 2014
Trading in: *Richard F. Mackay Ltd*, 15 October 2014
Single travellers: *Solitair Ltd*, 30 July 2014

LANGUAGE DATA AS EVIDENCE

To illustrate how linguistic evidence is analysed and presented in legal contexts, in this unit we explore some kinds of data that a forensic linguist may work with.

Who wrote this?

Consider a situation of a kind we discuss in Unit A9. Suppose, for example, that the police are trying to find out who issued a bomb threat, wrote a suicide note or impersonated someone in a faked letter. A forensic linguist might be able to help in the investigation by narrowing down the search for the writer by deploying linguistic methods of **authorship attribution** (Love 2002).

Despite people's often very careful efforts at linguistic disguise, habits of language use can still expose someone's individual and social identity. Specific features of a speaker's **idiolect**, or distinctive pattern of language use (the legal analysis of which is sometimes called **forensic stylistics**), can provide a lead.

Authorship attribution

The word *authorship* suggests written documents. But it is not essential that the texts to be examined are written. Spoken texts (e.g. a recording of a phone call) as well as written texts (SMS messages, Internet forum posts, ransom notes or wills) may become data for authorship analysis. Spoken texts call for phonetic/phonological analysis; written texts invite analysis of **handwriting** (if there are handwriting data). Either type of data, however, allows analysis of word choice, style and manner, as well as grammatical abnormalities. All of these are linguistic footprints left by the particular language user.

Authorship attribution addresses either of two issues:

❑ determining whether a specific Person P produced Text T (spoken/written); and
❑ what characteristics an unknown author of a text is likely to exhibit (this second question arises where the need is to narrow down the field of likely suspects).

If the question is whether a particular, known individual wrote a text, then a **negative identification** would be one that shows, on the basis of clear evidence, that P did not produce T. By contrast, a **positive identification** would show that P did, or probably did, produce T. A positive identification is far harder to achieve. It needs to demonstrate something to a high standard of proof that is nevertheless inevitably based on linguistic probabilities (with the result that all such authorship identification findings are presented as probability statements).

In circumstances where there is no suspect as regards the identity of the perpetrator of a crime, then instead of asking whether Person P produced Text T, investigators try to establish a general idea of who P might be by asking what sort of person might have produced Text T. This kind of analysis is called **speaker profiling** (and falls within the wider category of criminal profiling). A recording of a speech event might, for example, supply information about, or characterise, a suspect by suggesting his or her geographical origin or social characteristics. The oddly punctuated handwritten bomb threats left by the Mad Bomber (who planted homemade bombs in New York City during the 1940s and 1950s) are an instance of this: the threats offered clues that he might be an immigrant or first-generation American (Ewing and McCann 2006). This probability, along with additional psychological profiling data, helped locate the offender.

Methodologically, the basic principle for determining authorship is comparison. This can be done qualitatively or quantitatively, depending on the sample data set available. Here is an example of authorship detection of an unusual kind in an academic context. A professor of business information systems was puzzled by this line in an assignment written by one of his students (*Times Higher Education*, 7 August 2014):

> common mature musicians [and] recent liturgy providers are looking to satisfy . . . Herculean personalised liturgies.

After informal 'forensic' work, the professor discovered that the student had plagiarised from the following sentence in a source text:

> The current big players and new service providers are looking to supply more powerful personalised services.

Now ask yourself some analytical questions:

> ❑   In what ways do the two texts resemble each other, and how do they differ?
> ❑   What method do you think the student used in trying to cover up his or her plagiarism?
> ❑   How do you think the professor was able to find the source of the plagiarised text?

A complication with authorship attribution

Authorship analysis is complicated by the fact that authorship is not a clear-cut, single concept, even setting aside collaborative writing. Imagine a witness giving an account of events in a police station. The police officer summarises what she says, and requires her to sign the statement at the end of the document. In such circumstances, the witness is a **precursory author** (someone whose ideas inspire a text) and a **declarative author** (someone whose name is put down as the author); but the police officer is the **executive author** (the person who actually did the writing; for different types of authorship, see Love 2002: Chapter 3). These distinctions matter in cases where legal investigation is not primarily of the verbal behaviour of the defendant but whether, and if so how, police officers may have distorted words of an interviewee by fabricating a confession or altering a witness statement. As we discuss in Unit A9, Coulthard (2002) compared murder accomplice Derek Bentley's confession with a corpus of police language and submitted that some features of the confession resembled police sociolect far more than they resembled Bentley's.

Modern modes of communication can make analysis of some language crimes or disputes more challenging. There have been a number of libel lawsuits against search engine giant Google, for example, regarding its **autocomplete function**. An alleged defamatory imputation can be created when a person's name is entered into the search box and the search engine automatically suggests keywords that portray the person in a damaging light (such as 'rapist', 'bankrupt' or 'conman'). In defence, Google has argued that such suggestions are produced by computer algorithms based on searches by previous users, and are not actively published by Google itself. Similarly, smartphones speed up typing by providing predictive text based on complex algorithms; but authorship questions may arise in future in the event of claims as to liability for what is communicated as a result.

Activity

❏   Who do you think is the 'author' of potentially defamatory 'messages' communicated (in a hybrid, human–machine sense of communicated) by search engines and smartphones? Who, if anyone, should bear legal responsibility for such allegedly defamatory suggestions?

Did they commit a crime?

Perjury

Perjury is the crime of wilfully making a false statement on a material matter when testifying under oath in court. Consider one aspect of a widely discussed US perjury case, *Bronston v. United States*. At a bankruptcy examination, a lawyer representing the creditor engaged in the following exchange with the defendant, Bronston:

Q: Do you have any bank accounts in Swiss banks, Mr. Bronston?
A: No, sir.
Q: Have you ever?
A: The company had an account there for about six months, in Zurich.

It was later revealed that Bronston had had a large personal bank account in Switzerland for five years.

When Bronston was tried for perjury, a crucial question was whether a literally true but misleading answer falls within the scope of the offence. The trial court convicted Bronston and the Court of Appeals affirmed; but the Supreme Court reversed the decision, reasoning that perjury is about what the witness *states* rather than what he or she *implies*.

⊛ Activity

❏ Should the court have focused in this way on the literal meaning of a statement? Consider general arguments for and against.

❏ Now use Grice's account of implied meanings to develop your analysis. Did Bronston's answer fulfil the maxims of quality, quantity, relation and manner? What implicatures did his answer generate (construct a brief account of steps involved in how that implicature is produced)?

❏ Could a Gricean approach have been helpful to the court in this case, or are the underlying assumptions associated with such an approach in conflict with the adversarial nature of perjury proceedings?

Tiersma (1990) reviews this case extensively, drawing on a Gricean account of indirect communication.

A similar scenario can be found during the Clinton Grand Jury hearings. Consider this short extract from the transcript:

Q: Now, do you know a woman named Monica Lewinsky?
A: I do.
Q: How do you know her?
A: She worked in the White House for a while, first as an intern, and then in, as the, in the legislative affairs office. . . .
Q: . . . At any time were you and Monica Lewinsky together alone in the Oval Office?
A: I don't recall . . . She – it seems to me she brought things to me once or twice on the weekends. In that case, whatever time she would be in there, drop it off, exchange a few words and go, she was there. . . .

⊛ Activity

❏ President Clinton later admitted they had been alone on some 10–15 occasions. Had the president therefore made a false statement?

Throughout the hearing, President Clinton stuck to the literal meaning of words and to this extent appears to have misled his antagonists on numerous occasions. Read Tiersma's analysis at: www.languageandlaw.org/PERJURY.HTM.

Threat

Threats, as generally described, are a declaration of one's intention to do injury to a person or his or her property. Consider the following scenarios:

1 'Resign or you'll get your brains blown out' (in a young person's letter to a US president).
2 'Just a friendly little warning – if you date my girlfriend again, you're dead meat' (from a jealous boyfriend).
3 'I'm going to get you, bitch' (from a man to a woman he had assaulted earlier).
4 'I don't want to hurt you' (by a rapist to a victim).
5 'Are all the windows insured?' (from a litigant, who had just lost his case, to a judge).

Activity

❑ Discuss the difficulty of distinguishing threats such as these from predictions, warnings, and other questions and statements.

Now consider two more examples:

6 'We will kill Richard Nixon' (by an African American minister during a sermon).
7 'Let's hunt Sen. Tim Leslie for sport . . . I think it would be great if he were hunted down and skinned and mounted for our viewing pleasure' (posted online by a 19-year-old university student, in response to California state senator Tim Leslie's campaign to allow more hunting of mountain lions).

Activity

❑ These two examples concern the difference between making a political statement and a threat. What kind of contextual factors should be taken into account? (See also Unit A8 for discussion of the implications of speech act classification as regards free speech protection.)

The examples considered here are taken from Solan and Tiersma (2005); read Chapter 10 of their book to find out how judges decided these cases and to see in more detail how such decisions have been analysed from a variety of linguistic perspectives.

What is 'likelihood of confusion'?

In trademark cases, two verbal marks may be compared across different linguistic dimensions when there is a dispute concerning them (typically sound; form including morphology and grammatical behaviour; and meaning).

An Australian example is provided in Gibbons (2003). The issue arose whether two trade names for drugs, *Alkeran* and *Arclan*, were sufficiently similar to cause consumer confusion.

⭐ **Activity**

❑ How similar do these marks appear to you (assuming no additional features of design such as colour, font, etc.)? Describe similarities and differences.

Now consider the following additional information (adapted from Gibbons):

1 The most likely Australian pronunciation for these words is ælk əræn and ɑklæn.
2 The initial vowels in a phonemic transcription look distinct, but the æ-ɑ vowels (as in *had* versus *hard*) are relatively close in Australian English.
3 In English, the ə sound (the schwa) is often lost in consonant clusters (e.g. secretary is often pronounced sekrətri. This applies to the extra ə in *Alkeran*.
4 A significant proportion of the Australian population speak English as a second language.
5 'l' and 'r' sounds are often substituted one for the other in many languages of the world. This also occurred in the history of English, as with modern *turtle* being derived from Latin *turtur*.

⭐ **Activity**

❑ Now revisit the question above: do the two marks appear to you any more or less similar now?
❑ How clearly or effectively do you think the necessary distinctions regarding the sound of the two marks would emerge in court without assistance from a linguist?

What does this text say?

A US postal worker found guilty of destroying mail was sentenced to 60 months of probation and a fine, although the maximum sentence for the offence was six months of imprisonment. Some months later, he tested positive for cocaine. According to US law, the court should 'revoke the sentence of probation and sentence the defendant to not less than one-third of the original sentence' (18 U.S.C. § 3565(a)).

⭐ **Activity**

❑ Based on what the law says, calculate how long the new sentence should be.
❑ Is there ambiguity in the text – and if so, how would you explicate that ambiguity?

The ambiguity is whether 'original sentence' here refers to the actual probation sentence or the potential custodial range. The former interpretation leads to a sentence of 20 months of probation, resulting in a reduction of the penalty. The court decided instead that the former postal worker should serve 20 months in prison, a much longer term than the original maximum sentence. The court in fact sentenced the defendant to a term of *imprisonment* not less than one-third of the original term of *probation*.

> ☐ From the perspective of a linguist, construct an argument to explain to the judge why the court's decision is questionable.

Activity ✪

Three US linguists and a lawyer (Cunningham *et al.* 1994) wrote a journal article criticising the decision. They argued that an ambiguous term cannot simultaneously carry both of its possible meanings. The Court of Appeals cited their paper as a reference and released the accused (he had already served 11 months in prison by then, longer than one-third of the original maximum sentence).

Identifying problems of linguistic access to law

Child witnesses

Courtrooms, which are designed primarily for adults, may baffle a child participant. Brennan (1994) studied questions put to children in sexual abuse cases in an effort to understand children's comprehension of lawyers' questions. He asked children aged 6–15 to repeat questions from counsellors, teachers and lawyers. Counsellors' questions were almost always reproduced with their sense intact. Teachers' questions were reproduced with the sense intact about 80 per cent of the time. With lawyers, the main sense was missed 43 per cent of the time in random questions. When the questions were difficult, the main sense was reproduced only 15 per cent of the time. Problems lie in how questions are formulated as well as in what they ask.

Here are some cross-examination questions posed to children who were alleged victims of sexual abuse, as documented by Brennan (the first four examples are taken from Brennan 1995; the fifth example is taken from Brennan 1994).

EXAMPLE 1

Q: Were you the first to go into the shower that, after tea that night or not?
A: Yes.
Q: At any stage whilst you were in the bathroom did he ever enter the bathroom that previous week? (Transcript 11 years)

EXAMPLE 2

Q: December last year, and was that a weekend or week day?

A: I can't remember.

Q: Cannot remember. Were the circumstances much the same then as they were on the last occasion you can remember?

A: Yes, it was the same just about every time. (Transcript 8 years)

EXAMPLE 3

Q: How far was the trampoline from you when you were first helped on the bike by Mr Brown? (Transcript 7 years)

EXAMPLE 4

Q: Well you are not sure whether you said those things to the police which are wrong? (Transcript 11 years)

EXAMPLE 5

Q: You went to, went and got into the car outside your home, I withdraw that, whereabouts in relation to your home did you get into the car on this morning.

A: Well on the, when?

❏   Why do you think these questions appear difficult to understand, especially for children?

❏   How could the questions be rephrased so they would be understood by children more easily?

❏   In what ways do the questions exemplify unequal power relationships between the cross-examiner and the witness?

❏   Research (Brennan 1994; Brennan and Brown 1997) has shown that children can be reliable witnesses but that their reliability can be systematically destroyed by inappropriate interviewing techniques. One reason is that children are known to be 'suggestible' (i.e. children's beliefs and memories are susceptible to influence by suggestions made to them) and are generally eager to fit their behaviour to adult expectation, especially when under pressure. A second reason is that children are in a less powerful position than adults and do not have the language skills to negotiate power relations. Consider the implications and significance of these two reasons.

Second-language speakers

Below are some questions posed to second-language speakers, taken from Gibbons (2003). Consider why the second-language speakers answered the questions the way they did. What makes their response inappropriate? Read the examples and work through the questions that follow.

EXAMPLE 1 (POLICE INTERVIEW)

Q: But isn't it the case, that you decided prior to approaching those men, to steal from them?

A: I . . . say yes . . . or what? ['or what' not transcribed by police]

EXAMPLE 2 (POLICE INTERVIEW)

Q: Yes. Can you describe those two men?

A: Um – yeah. Yes.

EXAMPLE 3 (TRIAL)

A: When the child came, I initially examined the patient and I noted the moistness of the tongue, sunken eyes, the skin color, and everything was okay.

Q: Are you suggesting that there were no sunken eyes?

A: *No.*

Q: I think we better slow down a little bit more and make sure the record . . . did you observe sunken eyes?

A: No.

❑   In example 1, the interviewee shows clear signs of incomprehension and seeks help from the interviewer. Was the question posed to him difficult to understand? If so, why?

❑   Explain the witness's response in example 2 in terms of direct versus indirect speech acts and language proficiency.

❑   In example 3, language habits from the witness's first language may have affected how he responds to questions in English: in his first 'no' reply, is he answering the speech act or the propositional meaning of the question? What would have happened if the lawyer did not seek clarification?

❑   Is miscommunication avoidable in these circumstances?

Activity

SAME LAW, DIFFERENT TEXTS

C10

In this unit, we explore how courts resolve linguistic indeterminacy in bilingual and multilingual jurisdictions. Two legal cases are discussed.

Arriving at a legal meaning

Two major kinds of **linguistic indeterminacy** contribute to legal indeterminacy in statutory interpretation. **Intralingual indeterminacy** refers to uncertainties such as those created by ambiguity (semantic, syntactic, referential, pragmatic, etc.), vagueness and generality. **Interlingual indeterminacy** arises when two texts do not completely correspond (i.e. there are discrepancies between texts). In two examples below, we gain a glimpse of strategies adopted in bilingual and multilingual jurisdictions to resolve each type of indeterminacy.

Intralingual indeterminacy: is Perrier water a 'carbonated beverage'?

Having two or more legislative texts sometimes helps with interpretation, especially as regards intralingual indeterminacy. According to Beaupré (1986: 2–3), many cases would not have reached the courts 'had the parties compared the two versions of the law in the first place'.

Consider a Canadian case in which the main issue in dispute was whether Perrier, a carbonated mineral water sold in bottles or cans, should be taxed as a 'carbonated beverage' within the meaning of Schedule III of the Excise Tax Act. The following extract is taken from the judgment of *Perrier Group of Canada Inc. v. Canada*, delivered by Judge Linden.

In resolving the dispute, the court referred first to dictionary definitions of *beverage*, and found that some dictionaries define it as excluding water while others simply define it as 'a drink'. It also considered the relevant case law, which the court found inconclusive. The court then turned to the French version of the legislation:

24 An analysis of the French version of the legislation is most helpful. Subsection 18(1) of the *Constitution Act, 1982* states that the French and English versions of an Act are equally authoritative. This statement requires that, where the ordinary meanings of the French and English versions of a statute seem to point in different directions, the Court is obliged to choose an interpretation that best reconciles the wording used in both. MacGuigan J.A. commented on this obligation in *Nitrochem Inc. v. Deputy Minister of National Revenue for Customs and Excise*, [1984] C.T.C. 608, 53 N.R. 394 (F.C.A.), as follows:

> With respect to the reconciliation of English and French texts, a judge's responsibility is not to seek some primary instance of ordinary usage in one language to which the meaning in the other language must be made to conform, but rather to try to grasp the whole meaning in both languages.

25 The appellants have urged that we do what MacGuigan J.A. above suggests should not be done, that is, to accept "some primary instance of ordinary usage" in the English language version to which the French version would then be made to conform. The French version of section 1 uses "boisson" as the equivalent of three different English words used in the legislation, they being "drink", "water" and "beverage". Several observations may be made about this use of "boisson". First, it is a term of general meaning. It is not like the English word "beverage", which ordinarily connotes a more specialized sort of drink.

26 Rather, "boisson" ordinarily designates any kind of drink. Its primary definition given by *Le Petit Robert*[1] is "Tout liquide qui se boit". Translated, this definition means simply "a liquid suitable for drinking". Water is certainly such a liquid.

27 As a second observation, I note that the closest French equivalent to the English word "beverage" is not "boisson" but "breuvage". This latter term, as its spelling suggests, is the etymological equivalent to "beverage". One of the meanings of "boisson" set out in *Le Petit Robert* is "breuvage". Not surprisingly, the popular meanings of the two words are very similar. Again as given by *Le Petit Robert*, the primary definition of "breuvage" is:

1. Boisson d'une composition spécial ou ayant une vertu particulière.

28 Translated somewhat literally, this definition reads: "A drink having a special composition (mix) or particular property (characteristic)".

29 What is important about this definition is not its exactly translated meaning, but the simple fact that a "breuvage" is a specialized form of a "boisson". This much is plain from the definition and reinforces the first observation that the French version deliberately chose a term with a general rather than a specific meaning.

30 Counsel for the appellants referred the Court to a document published by l'Office de la langue française in the Province of Quebec, where it suggests that the words "boisson gazeuse" be used to denote soft drinks or soda pop, and that "eau gazeuse" be employed to describe "les eaux minérales gazeuses". This publication also stated "boisson englobe eau, eau n'englobe pas boisson," which contradicts the submissions counsel made earlier. As interesting as this document is, and though it may be influential in improving French usage in the future, its advice, like that of the dictionaries, cannot bind this Court. Thus, in my view, since both versions of the legislation are equally authentic, and since we must adopt the meaning that both versions share, "beverage" and "boisson", as used in the legislation, both mean any type of drink, including water.

31 If a server in a Canadian restaurant asked a customer which "beverage" to bring and the customer responded, "Perrier, please", would the server be surprised that the customer thought that Perrier was a beverage? I think not. Would the server respond to the customer saying, "Perrier is a water, and I shall bring it, but do you want a 'beverage' as well?" I think not. In our common speech, most Canadians, in my view, would include water, especially sparkling water, within the meaning of beverage, despite the many dictionary definitions excluding it. Similarly, if a server in French-speaking Canada asked what the customer wished as a "boisson", the response "Perrier" would not surprise the server. No one would think that Perrier is not a "boisson", despite the advice of the Office de la langue française. Though the word may not always be used to refer to water, therefore, I am of the opinion that it is more natural to interpret "beverage" as including water.

This case is one of many instances where a Canadian court has resolved ambiguity contained in a legislative text by referring to another language version of the same text. Consider the following questions:

> ❏ In para. 25, Judge Linden acknowledges that the English word *beverage* 'ordinarily connotes a more specialized sort of drink' (than water). Then in para. 31, he presents a hypothetical scenario in which treatment of Perrier as a beverage would not contradict ordinary usage, in order to justify that *beverage* should be interpreted as including water. Do you think the scenario is consistent with or contradicts the earlier point?
> ❏ In para. 29, Judge Linden argues that the French version 'deliberately chose' a general rather than specific term. Why do you think he did not consider the rendering of *beverage* as *boisson* to be possibly a translation error?
> ❏ Was the shared meaning rule applied in this case?

Interlingual indeterminacy: are boats vehicles?

Now consider the EU case *Fonden Marselisborg Lystbådehavn v. Skatteministeriet*. Fonden Marselisborg Lystbådehavn (the Marselisborg Pleasure Boat Port Trust) is an independent institution based at the pleasure boat port of Marselisborg in Denmark that lets out water-based mooring and dry berths and land sites for storing boats during winter. The Sixth Directive referred to below is EU legislation that specifies a common list of VAT exemptions, which include, in Article 13B(b) of Title X, 'the leasing or letting of immovable property' excluding 'the letting of premises and sites for parking vehicles'. The issue in dispute in this case was whether pleasure boats should be considered to be 'vehicles'.

41 The words used in the various language versions of Article 13B(b)(2) to designate 'vehicles' are not consistent. As the Commission rightly stated, a number of language versions, among which are the French, English, Italian, Spanish, Portuguese, German and Finnish versions, encompass means of transport in general in that definition, including aircraft and boats. On the other hand, other versions, such as the Danish, Swedish, Dutch and Greek versions, have selected a more precise term with a more limited meaning which serves to designate principally 'land-based means of transport'. More particularly, the Danish word 'kjøretøjer' refers to land-based transport on wheels.

42 In that connection it must be recalled that, according to settled case-law, where there is a difference between the language versions the provision in question must be interpreted by reference to the purpose and general scheme of the rules of which it forms a part (see, in particular, Case C-372/88 *Cricket St Thomas* [1990] ECR I-1345, paragraph 19, and Case C-384/98 D [2000] ECR I-6795, paragraph 16).

43 As regards the letting of premises and sites for parking vehicles, Article 13B(b)(2) of the Sixth Directive introduces an exception to the exemption laid down for the leasing and letting of immovable property. It thus makes the transactions to which it refers subject to the general rule laid down in that directive, namely that VAT is to be charged on all taxable transactions, except in the case of derogations expressly provided for. That

provision cannot therefore be interpreted strictly (see Case C-346/95 *Blasi* [1998] ECR I-481, paragraph 19).

44 Therefore, the term 'vehicles' used in that provision must be interpreted as covering all means of transport, including boats.

45 Letting mooring berths for boats is not limited solely to the right to privately occupy the surface of the water, but also involves making available various port equipment for mooring the boat, landing-stages for the crew and the use of various sanitary or other facilities. As the Advocate General points out in paragraph 51 of her Opinion, none of the reasons, including the social ones, that originally justified allowing the exemption from VAT for immovable property may be applied to the letting of mooring berths for pleasure boats in the circumstances in the main proceedings.

46 In those circumstances, having regard to the objectives of Article 13B(b) of the Sixth Directive, point 2 of that provision, which excludes the letting of premises and sites for parking vehicles from the exemption from VAT, must be interpreted as meaning that it is generally applicable to the letting of premises and sites for parking all means of transport, including boats.

47 In the light of the foregoing, the answer to the second question must be that Article 13B(b)(2) of the Sixth Directive is to be interpreted as meaning that the definition of 'vehicles' includes boats.

 Activity

❏ On what basis did the court decide that 'vehicles' must include boats?
❏ Do you think neither, either, or both of the following considerations should be relevant to a decision in this case?

(a) What the 'majority' of the language versions say.
(b) The fact that the case concerns a Danish company and that the Danish version of the Directive referred only to land-based transport on wheels.

❏ Based on this case, what advantages and disadvantages do you see in purposive (rather than narrower text-based) interpretation in a multilingual jurisdiction?

Notes:

* The combined name and slogan, in a distinctive font with graphic embellishment, were registered as a trademark in the UK in 2008 (UK00002484595), for three classes of goods/services: printed matter and publications; television advertising; and travel agency services (case details can be searched at www.ipo.gov.uk).

1 *Le Petit Robert* is a popular and widely used French dictionary.

Section D

EXTENSION

ENGAGING WITH PUBLISHED SCHOLARSHIP

The readings that make up Section D provide you with relevant background and will familiarise you with important research directions. The readings are excerpts from books and articles written by leading scholars, and have been brought together here to give you an overview of key issues.

Editorial note

We have omitted bibliographic references where it seemed reasonable to do so in order to keep the text relatively uncluttered. References that have been kept in can be followed up in the bibliography at the end of the book.

Where words or sentences have been omitted from the original text, this is indicated by [...].

The typeface of the original works, and other features of presentation including italics and boldface, have been modified where necessary to achieve consistency when presented together in a single volume.

How to use the extracts

As you engage with the readings in this section, consider these aspects of 'reading' published academic work:

1   Comprehension: grasping both stated, and what is implied. You may need to read each passage more than once – possibly several times, looking up words or references and taking notes as necessary.
2   Summary or paraphrase: taking 'ownership' of the text, by recreating parts of it in your own words and so becoming able to use its ideas (e.g. working its ideas into an argument of your own).
3   Establishing significance: identifying the main claims being made, as well as their implications.
4   Evaluating evidence: seeing how the argument is put together, singling out examples or illustrations and looking for counter-examples or exceptions that may go against what the passage is saying.
5   Comparison: putting what is said in a larger context to see how it compares with other viewpoints you may be familiar with.

These are not separate approaches. When you set out to 'read' an extract, keep in mind that what will be needed is some combination of all these processes. This is especially the case because you should try to link the extracts to material presented in other sections of the book.

LAW AS A PROFESSION OF WORDS

In this unit we read two short extracts that examine common presumptions held about legal language.

Extract 1: the precision of legal language

Our first extract, not inappropriately in view of the author's status as virtually founder of the modern study of legal language, comes from David Mellinkoff's *The Language of Law* (1963). Mellinkoff's book consists of two main strands: a detailed historical description of legal English; and a critique of excesses associated with that variety and the need for reform. This extract is Mellinkoff's comment on the claim that, for all its oddities, legal English allows greater precision than alternative forms of expression.

Reproduced from Mellinkoff, D. (1963) *The Language of the Law*, Eugene, OR: Resource Publications, pp. 393–5.

Section 129: The limits of precision: The impossible and the undesirable

Along with his continued striving for precision in the small area where law language can be more precise than the ordinary speech, the lawyer can take a surer hold on the instruments of his [*sic*] craft, can flog himself less with vague and debilitating misgivings, if he recognizes once and for all that it is impossible that the language of the law become completely precise. Not that this should signal an end of the striving, nor license sloppy pleading and general literary mush. Only that the striving must not be confused with arriving, and the attainability of near goals not discouraged by the unattainability of absolutes.

It would be a most strange and wonderful thing if lawyers had indeed been able to succeed where the rest of talking and writing humanity had failed. The quest for a precise language is as ancient as the search for the fountain of youth, and less capable of fulfilment than the alchemist's dream of turning lead into gold. Marvellous it would be if lawyers had fashioned an exact instrument out of language – a substance that Plato found "more pliable than wax."

But they have not done so.

Maitland spoke of his prize specimen of law French precision in glowing, prideful words:

Precise ideas are here expressed in precise terms, every one of which is French: the geometer or the chemist could hardly wish for terms that are more exact or less liable to have their edges worn away by the vulgar.

These words, applied to the merest speck of the language of the law, suggest a comparison between the languages of law, mathematics, and the natural sciences, a comparison that can only be embarrassing to the lawyer and disappointing to his clients.

The geometer may speak with assurance of a line, for it lives only in a succession of moving dots. The law's most bloodless abstractions – a corporation, property, justice – concern living people, their hopes, their whims, their aching backs. Tomorrow the back no longer aches, and the concept of justice and property has changed a little with the relief.

Nor does the lawyer – unlike his fellow professional, the chemist– deal with universal phenomena, with fixed points of boiling and freezing. The common law speaks of "Willy the milman; Robin the pannierman, etc.", each with his own unpredictable thoughts and acts. If the law is a science, it is not an exact science, and its language must share some of the ambiguity of life.

[. . .] Made for people, the common law has long suffered a further tribulation largely unknown to the exact sciences. The law must not only speak about people but to them. Not that the law has always done this. Quite the contrary. But when the law speaks in a "hidden tongue," it is occasionally berated – if not reformed. The scientist has been able to talk to himself unmolested. The day may now be here, but it is still not officially recognized of science, as it long has been of law, that ignorance is no excuse.

As a corollary to that maxim, there is an underlying feeling in the nations of the common law that law must in some degree be comprehensible not merely to those who work at it but to those who are expected to be governed by it. Accordingly, the law must communicate within professional ranks and beyond – into an ever-widening area of literacy. And the wider that area of communication becomes the more impossible the attainment of precision. The finest minds may sharpen the finest tools – e.g., symbolic logic – and use them to analyse the problems of the law, but ultimately the law must talk with people – many people – about their problems. And in that communication it is impossible to speak in the precise measures of the mathematician. The law ministers to living needs, and in speaking to the living its language shares some of the imperfections of the common tongue.

Notes

Frederic William Maitland: late nineteenth-century professor of law who specialised in the history of English law.

Geometer: a mathematician whose field of study is geometry.

Questions/discussion

1   What attitudes towards legal language does Mellinkoff attribute to lawyers? And what connection is he making between such professional attitudes and perceptions of authority associated with legal language?

2   Mellinkoff quotes Maitland's implication that there is an almost unique suitability of 'Law French' – now for many centuries merely an etymological substratum of legal English (see Unit A2) – for achieving precision. What point do you think he is making by means of this reference?

3   The passage makes a contrast between precision of scientific language and precision in legal language. What difference is Mellinkoff suggesting there is between the two?

4   A further contrast is drawn in the passage: between (a) legal language expressing an abstract formal system of rules; and (b) legal language as a medium of communication between lawmakers and people governed by the law. Do you agree

with the balance Mellinkoff suggests is desirable between these different functions of legal language?

Extract 2: the different senses of 'law as a profession of words'

This extract comes near the end of an influential article by Marianne Constable, Professor of Rhetoric at Berkeley, USA; the author reflects on a widely quoted expression with which Mellinkoff opened his book: that law is 'a profession of words'. Constable dissects this phrase. In discussing different ways that scholarship concerned with law and society understands the power wielded by legal language, she points out that almost all such studies engage in one way or another with law 'as a profession of words'. But the phrase, she shows, conceals different presumptions about what a 'profession of words' might actually be.

Reproduced from Constable, M. (1998) 'Reflections on law as a profession of words', in B. Garth and A. Sarat (eds), *Justice and Power in Sociolegal Research*, Evanston, IL: Northwestern University Press, pp. 19–35, at pp. 28–9, available at: www.mcgill.ca/files/crclaw-discourse/Constable.pdf (accessed 20 November 2015).

"Profession" here has three relevant meanings: an open declaration or public avowal; an avowal in appearance only or a pretence; and an occupation, vocation, calling, or business in which proficiency or expertise is claimed. While studies of the legal profession, a significant subfield in law and society studies, draw the third definition into play most clearly, other studies engage – contest and affirm – other senses of the phrase.

That phrase, "profession of words," is complicated not only because of the multiple senses of "profession" but also because "of" has two grammatical senses. "Knowledge of God," for instance, may mean (roughly) either "knowledge belonging to God [that God possesses]" or "knowledge [one possesses that is] about God." "Profession of words" thus has six – or more, depending on the constancy of "words" – different senses.

Most studies of law engage continually with one or more of these aspects of the profession of words that is law. In doing so, they do not simply accept a particular meaning of the phrase as definitive of law; instead they explore relations between law and language that they may express in terms of power but that also have implications – which may or may not be verbalized as such – for justice. [. . .]

Law in the first sense of a profession of words, as an open declaration or public avowal of words, may be taken to affirm words, principles, rules as proper ways of dealing with disputes and controversies. Although one usually thinks of a declaration or avowal as taking place through words, it need not.

Public declarations of law may occur through statements and enactments, but they may also occur through the actions of legal actors or institutions who display rather than verbally articulate a commitment to speech. Hence historical studies, pursuing this first sense of law as a profession of words, may consider the extent to which public declarations of law-statements or actions affirm the value of speech, or of particular rules of law, or of a rule of law. [. . .]

In the second sense of law as a profession of words, the avowal made by law occurs through words or consists of words. In constitutional theory as well as in anthropology of law, scholars turn to particular language as evidence of what is called law (even when such language paradoxically serves to recall the listener to a silent or exemplary rather than propositional law). Social psychologists and other researchers use judges' instructions as standards by which to measure jury performance and accept such statements as law. Some scholars point explicitly to the use of claims and counterclaims to express legal differences (Perelman and Tyreca 1969); many others take for granted that argument and interpretation characterize law, filling law journals with the fruit of their participation in such activity. The stature of written vs. spoken texts, the authoritativeness of the U.S. Constitution as a founding document, controversies over so-called activist judges' deviations from established legal doctrine, and discussions of judicial decision-making all concern the words through which law makes public declarations.

While some theorists, such as Ronald Dworkin and Jürgen Habermas, seek the conditions of law as conditions under which a sincere exchange of words may occur, other scholars suggest that viewing law as all exchange of words (as in the second sense of a profession of words) or as a commitment to speech (as in the first) is naive, disingenuous, or worse. Invoking a third and a fourth sense of law as a profession of words, such scholars see law as a pretence of words – as involving a falseness that belongs either to words themselves or to law insofar as it claims to be about words rather than something else.

Claims as to the obfuscation produced by legal language or of the inability of language of any sort to map reality involve this third sense; claims as to the falseness of legal assertions of neutrality or law's commitment to speech over violence involve the fourth sense of a profession of words, in which law's avowal of words is contrasted to its less neutral, or even violently oppressive or irrational, conduct.

In a fifth sense, law as a profession of words is the subject matter of studies of the legal profession which "draw attention to how the occupation, vocation, calling, or business of law claims proficiency or expertise about words." Even studies that do not focus on legal training acknowledge that learning law is like learning a language (or unlearning one) and that practicing law involves communication, if not traditional skills of oratory and argument (Plato; White 1985, 1990; Wydick 1994).

Finally, if the fifth sense of law as a profession of words refers to a vocation or calling that specializes in or is about words, a sixth sense takes the "profession of words" to refer to a calling belonging to words. That is, while the expertise of the legal profession is linguistic, the occupation or business of words concerns law; their vocation or calling lies in or consists of law. But while the first five senses of law as a profession of words may or may not involve justice, this sixth sense is different. For the concern of speech with law, its calling to law, is a call for justice, never a call for mere power.

Questions/discussion

1   Constable suggests that the various meanings of 'profession of words' depend on two linguistic features: (a) alternative meanings of 'profession'; and (b) different relationships between entities connected by 'of'. Referring to points Constable makes in the passage, explain and illustrate these two kinds of potential for multiple meaning.

2   This is a challenging passage. It condenses a complex view of legal scholarship into a brief argument about the meaning of just one phrase. However, the argument

depends less on familiarity with law or legal theory than may first appear. Perhaps the best way into grasping what Constable is arguing is to express each of her six possible meanings in your own words. Then, as a separate stage, consider the implications of each as regards the role of language in ensuring that law delivers something more: justice.

3   Constable's argument is, in microcosm, an example of legal reasoning: she dissects an expression in order to show different meanings it may contain and ultimately to argue for one emphasis over others. What does the form of her argument suggest about a theme she shares with, but interprets differently from, Mellinkoff: the accessibility and potential for precision of legal language?

MAKING LEGAL LANGUAGE COMPREHENSIBLE

In this unit we present two extracts that tackle arguments for and against reform of legal language from a practical, campaigning perspective.

Extract 1: are arguments against plain English drafting valid?

In the UK, an organisation called the Plain English Campaign describes itself as 'fighting for crystal-clear communication since 1979', a fight that consists of 'attacking the use of jargon in various industries'. Legal language has been a major focus of their campaign. The following extract is the Campaign's online reply to a series of common criticisms:

1. *'Plain English is simple, restrictive language, and takes away the skills of the drafter.'*
Drafting a document in plain English takes a lot of skill. Communicating your points clearly so that the reader can accurately interpret your meaning is the most important task in writing. The draftsman's job is to communicate precise ideas, not produce a work of literature.

2. *'There is no need to make legislation easy to read. It's not meant to be the same as a newspaper. People who want to read laws should educate themselves.'*
Using plain English does not mean writing everything in the style of a tabloid newspaper. It means writing documents in a way that is appropriate for the audience. If a law affects people (for example, an employment law affecting small business), those people should have a fighting chance of understanding it. The language used in a law should depend on who the law affects, taking account of how familiar they are with the subject. Saying it is impossible to produce laws that everybody understands is no reason not to make it understandable to as many people as possible. Plain English is not dumbing down.

3. *'Plain English is not legally accurate or precise.'*
This myth has been steadily and repeatedly shattered. In the United States, 44 of the 50 states have some form of requirement for insurance contracts to be written in plain

English. Contrary to lawyers' expectations, there has never been a case where a contract has been declared less legally valid though being written in plain English.

Attempts to make text legally accurate through excessive (and impenetrable) detail are often flawed. For example, trying to define an organisation's powers through a comprehensive list will inevitably lead to problems. Eventually a situation that the drafter had not foreseen will arise. A perfect example is when new technology arises, such as when courts have to decide if a law applying to a posted letter also applies to an e-mail. Courts can use their discretion to settle such disputes, taking account of the law's intended purpose as well as its exact content.

In any case, this argument is based on the idea that existing legalese is perfectly accurate. If this were true, there would be far less need for lawyers to debate conflicting interpretations of a law or document. Drafters should aim for clarity and precision rather than choosing between the two.

4. 'Plain-English drafting is too expensive and time-consuming.'
Our experience shows that rewriting legalese into plain English can take time, but this can be avoided by using clearer drafting in the first place. Even if the drafting takes longer, the new law or document will take less time to understand, and there will be less need for its meaning to be debated and explained. Studies in the Australian state of Victoria, which uses plain-English drafting, show that lawyers can understand and use a plain-English version of an act in between a half and a third of the time it takes with the traditional version.

5. What use would a purpose clause serve?
Given that English courts take into account the intention behind an Act, the purpose clause would be an extremely useful way for the drafter to give guidance for future disputes. The purpose clause would give a clear explanation of what a law should achieve, overriding any interpretation of its contents that appeared to contradict this aim. The purpose clause would also help the drafter, as a writer who starts with a clear outline of his message is far more likely to write that message clearly.

6. Is plain-English drafting really possible?
Realistically, the idea of producing legal documents that everyone can understand on a single reading is unlikely, but not impossible. The law is the most important example of how words affect people's lives. If we cannot understand our rights, we have no rights.

Notes
Adapted from: www.plainenglish.co.uk

Since 1990, the Plain English Campaign has awarded a 'Crystal Mark' to over 21,000 documents worldwide, distributed by over 1,600 organisations. A broadly similar international organisation, PLAIN (the Plain Language Association InterNational) is an analogous, non-profit, international organisation of advocates, professionals, and organisations (www.plainlanguagenetwork.org/).

Questions/discussion
1   Do you think the grounds for opposition to reforming legal language being rebutted here are (a) sensible; (b) unduly defensive? Give reasons.

2   Other than the criticisms listed here, do you think there are further arguments against plain English reforms that may be stronger and should have been included in the Campaign's online list?

3   The second criticism in the list in the extract makes an assumption about the audience for legislation. (The same assumption is addressed in extract 2, below, but in a different context.) What complications do you see with this assumption, if any? How are anticipated complications addressed in the response?

4   The reply to the third criticism tackles the issue of long lists contained in legal documents (in this case, lists of an organisation's powers). What alternative approach is implied for expressing such provisions, and how effective do you think that alternative approach would be?

5   Most of us see some, but not a huge number of, legal documents during our lives. In your experience, do the documents you have encountered (e.g. phone, tenancy or utilities contracts) resemble the style of legal language that, it is claimed, needs fundamental reform? Or are such documents already in a simpler style, particularly where companies are trying to attract and retain younger, possibly sceptical, customers?

Extract 2: the legitimacy conferred by ordinary language

Our second extract is also concerned with whether people, as plain English campaigners put it, need to understand their rights in order to *have* rights. It comes from an extended critique of legal language and interpretation in Peter Goodrich's 1986 book *Reading the Law*. In the passage reproduced below, Goodrich focuses on the claim often made that common-law systems work largely through 'ordinary language' that is accessible to those governed by the law, and that this adds significantly to the legitimacy of the legal system. The selected passage states Goodrich's disagreement with this claim.

Reproduced from Goodrich, P. (1986) *Reading the Law: A Critical Introduction to Legal Method and Techniques*, Oxford: Blackwell, pp. 119–20.

The command to know the law or the maxim that ignorance of the law is no defence to civil or criminal liability has a linguistic correlate in the construction of statutory provisions. Where general words are used in a statute or, more importantly, where a statute is intended to be of general effect and is designed to regulate everyday activities, then the language of the Act will be interpreted as common or ordinary language.

The logic behind this interpretative rule is simply that if 'ordinary' people are affected by the Act then the language of the Act itself should, where possible, be given its ordinary meaning. In linguistic terms, however, this assumption is a debatable one: it is neither an accurate description of the practice of modern legislation and codes, nor is it a linguistically justifiable approach to statutory provisions; it is rather a common-sense justificatory argument which lacks any very clear linguistic substance or support.

The argument concerning ordinary meaning is descriptively inaccurate. The point is one of simple observation; the practice of contemporary legislative drafting is immensely complicated and it is simply untrue that generally effective provisions are comprehensible to the major portion of the population. The reasons underlying such a statement are numerous.

The vast majority of the population do not know where to find the law, neither is it likely that if they did have access to the statutory instruments they would be able accurately to assess the legal meaning of a contemporary statute, irrespective of its intended audience. At the end of the day, statutes are addressed to lawyers or on occasion to other professional bodies but hardly ever to the general populace. To understand even such generally applicable legislation as that concerning theft or taxation is a notoriously complex professional task and is not always even particularly easy for lawyers or the judiciary themselves. These statutes are drafted in a professional register, they are frequently litigated and amended, and even in the case of seemingly simple provisions their proper interpretation requires a knowledge of prior law, principles of interpretation and legal procedure generally. Such knowledge is by definition professional knowledge; it is not generally available and the task of the professional bodies is precisely that of translating legal language into ordinary language, for which task they are richly rewarded.

Questions/discussion

1   Goodrich argues against the combined claim that statutes: (a) are expressed in ordinary language; and (b) should be interpreted accordingly. He suggests that, linguistically, the proposition in (a) is inaccurate. What reasons does he give for this view?

2   When you have identified Goodrich's reasons, consider each one individually. Are the reasons given equally compelling, and do they all relate to the same claim about language and language use?

3   It might be suggested that this passage is not really concerned with public comprehension of the law, but with something else: the principle according to which a court should interpret statutory language. Members of the public being deemed to understand laws could be merely a presumption needed to guide what a court should do (and may be saying nothing about what real people do or can do). If so, the claim about public understanding may have little to do with empirical evidence. How would such a 'systemic' or procedural viewpoint affect your assessment of Goodrich's criticism?

THE LANGUAGE OF JURY TRIAL

The two extracts below both come from Chris Heffer's *The Language of Jury Trial* (2005), an extended empirical investigation of a legal genre.

Using collected Crown Court data, Heffer examines the discourse that results when legal professionals interact with laypeople during court proceedings involving a jury. His overall argument is that such discourse shows a tension between two different ways of talking about, and in fact conceptualising, what is going on in a trial. One uses genre features associated with crime narrative; the other uses resources associated with legal exposition and analysis. Articulated together, the two views produce a hybrid, 'complex genre'. The potentially contrasting dimensions of this genre are addressed, so Heffer argues, to two different audiences. He suggests that an 'ongoing dialectic' between the two modes of thought brings two conceptual schemas together in pursuing a goal shared by the different legal participants: identifying and weighing up issues in the case.

The first excerpt comes from Heffer's Introduction, and sets up the study in outline. The second comes from his Conclusion, where Heffer reviews his findings.

Reproduced from Heffer, C. (2005) *The Language of Jury Trial: A Corpus-Aided Analysis of Legal-Lay Discourse*, Basingstoke: Palgrave (page numbers below).

Extract 1: legal professionals' dual modes of thought during jury trial

In the context of jury trial, legal professionals have been taught to follow paradigmatic legal principles and procedures, and are well aware of the contribution an evidential point might make to their logic-based legal case. At the same time, they are equally well aware of the need to communicate with and persuade a group of lay people (the jurors) who are unlikely to reason in a paradigmatic fashion with respect to evidence detailing the crime narrative at the heart of the case. Both paradigmatic and narrative modes of thought are indispensable, then, to the criminal trial process, but they are also incommensurable: neither can be fully stated in the vocabulary of the other and so they are incapable of being measured against a common standard.

(p. xv)

Extract 2: the nature of legal-lay discourse

Review of the evidence: legal-lay discourse in jury trial

From our explorations of both the communicational context and microlinguistic detail of the language of legal professionals in jury trial, we are now able to draw a number of general conclusions about the nature of legal-lay discourse.

In the first place, legal-lay discourse is essentially a hybrid form of discourse arising from the encounter between legal professionals, who are trained to think about legal cases in a paradigmatic fashion, and lay participants, who are used to reasoning about crime stories in a narrative fashion. Both the law and courtroom procedure are highly paradigmatic, while lawyers are trained to conceptualize the contextual vicissitudes of life in abstract paradigmatic terms. Yet the fundamental function of legal-lay discourse in jury trial is to persuade the jury, and it is the narrative mode that is our primary means of sense-making, particularly in the sphere of personal experience of life on which so many crucial jury decisions are made. In attempting to accommodate both the lay jury and their professional discourse community, legal professionals draw on both narrative and paradigmatic discoursal strategies.

The textual product that results in most cases bears little relation to written legal register but is still quite distinct from everyday lay genres. At the level of the trial as a whole, we saw that counsel attempt to construct both a legal argument and a crime story from within a structure which combines procedural, adversarial and adjudicatory features. The distinct nature of the legal-lay discourse that is produced in this way can be seen in the form of evidential narrative in witness examination, in which counsel might follow the general structure of oral narrative discourse but with a much greater emphasis on the specification of orientational features and the construction of primary evaluation through legal evidential points. And at the level of individual expressions, we see counsel preferring to use the apparently everyday *I suggest* to put their case rather than the more legal and 'pompous' *I put it to you* but with an assertive sense which is virtually unknown outside the trial context. And we see the judge doing a very similar thing with their distinctive summing-up expression *you may think.*

Secondly, although the majority of time in a trial is spent on counsel's interaction with witnesses, when seen in relation to the ultimate goal of jury trial, legal-lay discourse is primarily unidirectional: counsel and judges are communicating with the jury, who essentially do not answer back until they give their verdicts. This can explain some apparent discoursal oddities: that witnesses are asked to look at the jury rather than their addressee when they reply; that counsel's turns, even in examination-in-chief, are longer than those of witnesses; that most 'questions' in cross-examination are effectively declarations rather than requests for information; that cross-examiners can virtually narrate to the jury ignoring the witness altogether and can focus on creating solidarity with the jury rather than eliciting information from the witness.

Thirdly, although it is essentially unidirectional, it involves multiple reception roles. Counsel are speaking minimally to the lay witness, the jury and the judge, all of whom are likely to interpret their words in slightly different ways. Similarly, in summing-up, the judge is not only directing the jury, but also informing the higher tribunals that might subsequently take up the case. This, in particular, explains why most judges will not go too far down the line of accommodating only the jury and why the legal directions in particular remain so problematic for jury comprehension.

Fourthly, legal-lay discourse is essentially persuasive. Plentiful evidence has been adduced here which tends to show that the primary function of legal-lay discourse is to persuade rather than inform the jury. This is hardly new with respect to counsel: it is common knowledge that their primary aim is to win their case. I have attempted to show, though, through an analysis of narrative construction and subjectivity, how these persuasive devices and strategies depend on the narrative mode. Analysis of some of the more subtle subjectivity-based evaluative devices (namely, projection and evaluative pointing) shows just how richly and persuasively cross-examiners manage to exploit the narrative mode despite the paradigmatic constraints.

While persuasion can be taken for granted with respect to the barrister, I claim more controversially that the summing-up is essentially also a persuasive genre. Since the jury are under no obligation to provide reasons for their decision, the judge needs to persuade them to take up and act on his legal directions. The evidence (presented in the book in Chapter 6) suggests that there are some signs that judges in English courts will narrativize to some extent highly paradigmatic legal directions in order to converge with lay juror discourse expectations. In the review of evidence, on the other hand, the problem seems to be quite the opposite since it is not clear how a judge can effectively summarize the evidence without constructing crime and trial stories, which are necessarily partial, subjective and therefore persuasive.

Fifthly, and vitally, legal-lay discourse is the product of a strategic tension between the legal professional's conflicting paradigmatic and narrative needs. But this tension between the need to conform to the paradigmatic linguistic conventions of the legal setting and the desire to get across to the jury through the narrative mode is one which is dynamic and ongoing rather than simply being enshrined in conventional institutional practice. Consequently, it results in considerable variation between individual speakers. This tension comes to the fore particularly in the judge's summing-up to the jury. The study of judicial variation in delivery of the proof directions showed that there was a very considerable difference between judges with a narrativizing tendency and those with a preference for categorizing. This might well reflect a tension between making an attempt to engage with the juror and remaining legally safe. The tension is also reflected well in judges' modifications of their comments in the summary of evidence where, in attempting to balance strategies of influence and impartiality, they can end up sounding quite contused.

Finally, although legal-lay discourse, wherever it is found in jury trial, will tend to show the above features, it is also genre dependent: it varies very significantly according to the specific trial genre in which it is found. We have seen that examination-in-chief and cross-examination are highly distinctive in form despite involving the same participants in the same setting with apparently the same 'interview' structure. It is purely the communicative goal of counsel which thoroughly alters the linguistic nature of the two types of examination. Similarly, the judge's legal directions and review of evidence are very different in nature despite being produced in the same monologue. So while I have attempted to identify some features which are probably shared by most forms of legal-lay discourse, it would be very misleading to talk about 'trial language' as a category of discourse.

(pp. 208–10)

Notes

Paradigmatic: Heffer explains this relatively uncommon term (pp. 20–1). 'Paradigmatic' mode is a form of logical/scientific reasoning thought to have emerged more recently than storytelling in evolutionary terms and which appears later in child development. It is typically writing-based, analytic, and abstract (standing apart from the messy facts of life). Narrative reasoning, by contrast, is common in oratory and advocacy, and is considered closer to lived experience and everyday detail.

Questions/discussion

(As with all Section D passages, you will need to read these extracts more than once and to refer back to them in answering the questions.)

1   In extract 1, Heffer suggests that the two modes of reasoning involved in the complex genre of jury trial are 'incommensurable'. Consider in what ways the two discourses might be 'incommensurable'.

2   What features of discourse does Heffer point to as evidence for each component genre? (He gives examples.)

3   How conclusive can Heffer's linguistic corpus evidence be, given his emphasis on genre as also a matter of intentions and interpretations, and of people pursuing an activity with a recognised goal – not only a matter of discourse form?

4   Are hybrid genres of the kind Heffer claims unusual in modern communication? (Think of political media interviews, etc.) In fact, Heffer suggests that more than two audiences are involved: who are the other audiences, besides the judge and jury?

5   How do you feel each of the audiences identified would respond, if made aware that there may be different channels of communication working simultaneously in a process as important as a trial, emphasising different points or at least presenting the same points in different ways?

D4   COURTROOM LANGUAGE

Theory and Practice

In the other three units of Thread 4, we look at courtroom discourse from a descriptive, third-person perspective ('objective' in the sense of being looked at as an object, from outside). The extract presented in this unit allows us to switch perspective, and to view the communicative functions of each stage of a trial from a lawyer's point of view.

Below, we reproduce an excerpt from a book chapter entitled 'Rhetoric in the law', by Robert P. Burns (2004), professor of law at Northwestern University, USA. Burns argues that law in action is different from law 'on the books'; it is a simplification, he argues, to view law wholly as a system of rules. Here is his compressed account of linguistic practices involved in a trial.

Reproduced from Burns, R. P. (2004) 'Rhetoric in the law', In W. Jost and W. Olmsted (eds), *A Companion to Rhetoric and Rhetorical Criticism*, Malden, MA: Blackwell Publishing, pp. 442–56, at pp. 445–9.

> The opening statements present God's-eye narratives of what the evidence will show. Done artfully, this will be more than a recitation of expected evidence. It will rather be a "continuous dream" (Gardner 1983: 31) that weaves all of the evidence into a coherent narrative that illustrates, *shows*, the meaning of the events that have brought the case to trial. The opening statement answers in narrative fashion the rhetorical question that lawyers often put to themselves in opening statement, "What is this case about?" or, in the language of hermeneutics, "What should this case be seen *as*?" The opening is woven around what trial lawyers call a "theme," an implicit moral argument much like the plot of a novel, based on the values implicit in the life-world of the jury, the rhetorical resources implicit in "the tacit practices, habits, cultural values, personal and social commitments, and so on that comprise our hermeneutical and rhetorical horizon of understanding: what Ludwig Wittgenstein calls *Lebensformen*, and Cavell our 'mutual attunements'" (Jost 2000: 103).
>
> The story told in opening statement is itself the result of earlier conversations, those between lawyer and client, conversations that have their own rhetoric. Here the desires and perceived needs of the client are mediated by the lawyer's projection of how they may be

presented in narrative form in the trial, to the extent to which "I want" can become "I am entitled to" (Pitkin 1994: 282), and the extent to which desires have to take account of – and must change in the light of – all the norms that make for a persuasive opening statement.

These opening statements are not simply comprehensive statements of past fact. Since the lawyer is ethically obliged to defer to his client's "objectives" and different factual theories of the case may have different consequences, the lawyer will be obliged, within ethical restrictions, to present that version of events that will support his client's objectives. The opening statements are, from this perspective, narrativized statements of client objectives. Facts, as presented by both lawyers, are purposes, their client's purposes. Thus the court will decide between competing purposes insofar as they can be narrativized and so presented through the lens of the community's *sensus communis*. Of course, that common sense is interested in understanding the situation in which it operates, and so "the facts" of the case and their accuracy have important moral significance; the trial is practical all the way down.

Story structure is almost always built around the sequence of legitimate social equilibrium, a disruption of that equilibrium, and its restoration. This is precisely the structure of Aristotle's commutative justice (Aristotle 1926a: 1129a–1138b, 253–323). But notice how the plaintiff's story told in opening statement must be intrinsically incomplete. When the opening statement is given, when its story is told, there has not yet been restoration, the world remains broken. Only the practical intervention of the jury can recreate a just world. The rhetoric of opening statement reminds the jury that it is not a simple "finder of fact" that has only historical or theoretical interest. Quietly and with assurance, they enact the jury's moral responsibility for the problematic situation that brings the case to court and places the jury within the unfolding drama.

But the opening statement has a competing performative function. It is a promise, a promise that the highly characterized story told in the opening will be supported by admissible evidence. However compelling the *meaning* of the events urged in the opening statement, however attractive the implicit pragmatic argument about what ought to be done or the mode of social ordering the case calls for, the opening will ultimately fail if its story turns out not to be *true*, turns out to be *only* a pretty story. The opening begins the tension between (1) the meaning of the events and so the relative importance of the norms embedded in the opening's theme and (2) the truth of the story, the extent to which it corresponds to what occurred (Bruner 1990: 44). And the mere fact that there are two opening statements dramatizes the inevitable gap between a story and the telling of it.

The trial's central tension begins when the plaintiff calls his first witness. The tension on the level of language is no longer between two opposed narratives but between radically different forms of narrative. On direct examination witnesses must tell their stories in their own words (in response to non-leading questions) and in the language of perception (with a minimum of opinion and interpretation). Simple, clear language. But witnesses remember an event as a meaningful gestalt, so that even this form of testimony comes with the imprint of the witness's understanding. This creates a tension between the relatively public norms that shape the opening and the quite personal, apolitical perspectives of most witnesses: "They do not speak diplomatically and the full significance of their accounts often cannot be subsumed by the more public norms around which theories of the case are spun. By giving particularity and empirical truth their due, the trial *disciplines and clarifies* the norms and purposes embedded in the openings" (Burns 2001: 205). The combination of the relatively "political" narratives of opening and the detailed and particular narratives of direct provide the ideal medium for forging public identity. We define and clarify who we are less by providing a general definition of what injustice is for us than by saying *this*, this densely complex human situation, is what *we* call injustice. And so the form of direct testimony drives the mind downward toward concrete events and away from the easy generalizations and clichés of mass culture. And so witnesses are permitted only to recount facts, and are forbidden the full range of speech acts. They may not make promises about future behavior or make recommendations to the tribunal as to how it should rule. These chaste narratives preserve the "forensic" character of trial rhetoric, for, to paraphrase Aristotle, narrative is the natural home of language about individual justice (Aristotle 1926b: 1414b, 424–5).

Much is revealed in the tension between opening's attempts to assimilate the case to the most important of the values of the life-world, on the one hand, and the often resistant particularities of direct examination on the other. This tension is illuminating because both narratives are so tightly constrained. They are constrained principally by the anticipation of the devices of the adversary trial that can be deployed against them, but they are also constrained by the rules of ethics and of evidence – Plato's revenge on the Sophists. The rules of ethics place the lawyer in a tension between duties of zealous representation to the client and of candor to the tribunal, a tension between energy and constraint. The lawyers may not allude to any matter in opening of which there will not be admissible evidence. It is the law of evidence that determines what is admissible. One generative principle of evidence law requires that the evidence be relevant, that is, that it can be linked through a plausible argument with one of the norms embedded in the jury instructions, in the technical language, that it have some tendency to make the existence of any fact that is of consequence to the determination of the action more probable or less probable than it would be without the evidence. Thus the trial's rhetoric presses these very different kinds of narratives toward each other, toward the law, and toward the evidence, while each struggles within these constraints to appeal to the jury's entire sensibility.

The trial's forward momentum is achieved by the construction and deconstruction of narrative. The pretenses of direct examination – its implicit and often quite convincing claim to be "the whole truth and nothing but the truth" of a past event – can be shattered by cross-examination. The heart of cross-examination is a series of short, clear, undeniable statements that suggest a perspective hidden by the smooth and apparently sincere surface of direct. After a convincing direct examination, the deconstructive blow of a short and effective cross-examination can be stunning. It can shock a jury into understanding that they are "on their own" in understanding the case, that they can rely only on their own insight and reflective judgment.

The cross-examiner deploys a number of rhetorical tools. He can retell the same story told on direct while showing the jury that a different selection of details, a different ordering of those details, and fair, indeed undeniable characterization of those details, yield a wholly different interpretation of the events at issue. (Crossexaminers are quite aware of the "artifice" that goes into even the most chaste narrative.) The cross-examiner can explore all those things of which the witness is ignorant, where the unknown could, once again, change the meaning of events. He can point out the ways in which the witness's "sense-data" could have been synthesized in a different way, and the way the witness saw that it was the result of some undisclosed interest or passion. He can more directly challenge the witness's credibility, showing how the witness's version of events is inconsistent, given the commonsense web of belief shared by witness, lawyer, and jury, with other undeniable facts. The witness can be challenged in a way that requires him to show relevant moral dispositions, most importantly willfulness in face of unpleasant truths, in ways that radiate out throughout the case. For our often-tacit understanding of the human psyche in action and conversation is subtle and profound (see chapter 17, this volume), occurring "before predication" (Fergusson 1949: 239). Where the witness is also a party, performance under cross-examination shows the jury what kind of person played a role in the real-world drama that led to the trial.

Cross-examination rarely tells; it shows. What is manifest is seldom said. Cross is one of the devices that allows the jury to work through *all* of the implications of its prejudgments under the discipline of the evidence. This is true whether it reveals the most willful aspects of the witness's story or his moral dispositions. Cross is an important element in the emergence at trial of a truth beyond mere storytelling, for it deconstructs narrative, and narrative is the only means we have to understand human action. It continues the process of looking *through* narrative toward a practical truth that cannot be represented like the dramatization of a story can be. And this will be, as we will observe, what the jury needs.

The case proceeds in spirals of construction, deconstruction, and partial reconstruction from witness to witness and on to closing argument. In closing argument, the lawyer will move back and forth between meaning and truth, between the importance of the values and policies implicit in the continuous dreams of opening statements, on the one hand, and the deep values implicit in the respect for the persons "on trial" that are embedded in respect for simple factual truth. By the time of closing, the simple stories of opening statement have almost always run aground on the jagged particularities of persons and memories of events that resist being "subsumed" even under the most carefully wrought theory of the case. All that the lawyer who "argues the evidence" can do in closing argument is to try to coax the jury back to imagining the entire case through his theory and theme. For judgment cannot be compelled, it can only be wooed. The closing shows the jury that the advocate's position can be maintained within the best interpretation of the norms that inhabit the jury's lifeworld. The result is not logically compelled, but it can be responsibly embraced in that space of freedom between fact and norm, between respect for individual persons and politically mediated purposes.

The rhetorical methods of closing feature examples from and analogies to familiar experiences, for "the greatest weapon in the arsenal of persuasion is the analogy, the story, the simple comparison with a familiar object," since "nothing can move the jurors more convincingly than an apt comparison to something they know from their own experience is true" (Spangenberg 1977: 16). That means, in arguing the importance of circumstantial evidence, "If you go into the woods and find a turtle on a tree stump, you know he didn't get there by himself." As for the witness caught in a single, perhaps relatively unimportant lie, "If you order beef stew and the first bit of meat is rancid, you are not expected to carefully remove that bit and accept the rest" (Burns 1999: 69).

Notes

The phrase 'direct examination' is often contracted by Burns in this extract as simply 'direct' (in lawyerly jargon which contrasts with the assumed formality of 'legal language'; Tiersma 1999). In some other common-law jurisdictions, including the UK, 'direct' examination is referred to as 'examination-in-chief'.

Questions/discussion

1   (a) What significance does the author attribute to the 'fact that there are *two* opening statements'?

    (b) What contrast is created by the author's use of italics in the phrase 'what *we* call injustice'?

    (c) What do the examples of 'turtle on a tree stump' and 'rancid meat' represent, and what does such imagery add to Burns's description?

2   Does the passage as a whole give a coherent impression of the author's view of the perceived role of the jury in a trial?

3   What, according to Burns, is the contribution made by language to a trial? Piece together his statements and other sources of evidence presented in the passage to support your view.

D5   TALKING THE LANGUAGE OF LAWYERS

Below we present two extracts, each of which explores what it means to describe the language of lawyers as a specialised, acquired 'rhetoric'. Our first extract examines the training in language that law students receive before they qualify. Rather than focusing, as in advocacy manuals, on particular techniques, the extract explores a deeper, ideological process that brings about a change in how students believe language works. Our second passage also looks beyond 'rhetoric' in law as being only concerned with specific verbal techniques. It develops a social view of a kind of 'constitutive rhetoric': an ordered but evolving system of communicative rules and values that reproduce and develop legal culture.

Extract 1: learning to think like a lawyer

Reproduced from: Mertz, E. (2007) *The Language of Law School: Learning to 'Think Like a Lawyer'*, New York: Oxford University Press, pp. 215–16.

In this influential book, the legal anthropologist Elizabeth Mertz presents observation data collected from various American law schools. She analyses how becoming a lawyer involves learning to shift one's 'attention away from accustomed social contextual anchors and toward new legal-contextual frameworks' (Mertz 2007: 211). The author suggests in particular that morality and social context are marginalised in legal discourse through a linguistic transformation: 'the inculcation of approaches to text, reading, and language' (Mertz 2007: 207).

As we have seen, there is an unusually central role for linguistic ideology (note 1) in law school socialization, because it is in and through manipulations of language that nascent attorneys learn to wield the special power of their profession. Proper application of the legal tests and categories, gleaned from a proper legal reading of written legal texts, is the foundation on which legally trained professionals draw in claiming authority. Thus, the linguistic ideology that undergirds legal training orients students' attention to layers of legal-textual authority. There is no need to claim that we will generate factual accuracy (in the usual sense) from such a reading, for the core compass orienting the reader remains "what the court, or legislature, said" – and then, in turn, what the position of that court or legislature was in the hierarchy of legal text generators. What we accept as true for the purposes of making a legal decision may not conform accurately to what happened, but that is rarely a matter of concern; once a court has met certain threshold requirements (it has jurisdiction to decide the matter, its decision was not clearly erroneous, etc.), it has the performative power to *find* facts. Thus, the legal reader's task is not to uncover what actually happened (more usually the mandate of the social scientist), but to correctly discern the facts as found by the authoritative court. These facts, read through a filter of doctrinal language also extracted from written legal texts, must then be sorted out in a way that permits the building of analogies.

To accomplish this requires a reading focused on layers of authoritative language and oriented by linguistic ideology. This linguistic ideology equates the proper alignment of language with authoritative legal knowledge, and thus also with proper application of the law. Legal epistemology rests on linguistic processes: expert deciphering of written legal texts, appropriate use of analogies and concomitant legal-linguistic frames, making arguments within these frames, ability to speak in the various voices and from the various stances required to argue effectively (sometimes to anticipate your opponent's argument, sometimes to make an argument for your client, or, if you are a judge, to weave between alternative positions in coming to a decision, which may in turn instantiate yet another point of view). In other words, in legal language, we know this fact because it was found and written down (entextualized; note 2) by an authoritative court, operating under correct metalinguistic rules and with the proper authority. One of the miracles of this system is its ability to combine certainty with such a flexible – indeed, at times deliberately agnostic – approach to social reality. The legal epistemology taught in the prototypical first-year U.S. law classroom, embodied in the practice of learning to read cases, employs a set of linguistic procedures to generate knowledge that is at once flexible enough to encompass almost any conceivable content, while still generating certainty (defined within linguistic parameters) and rules with knowable parameters (again linguistic), that nevertheless change as they are applied.

From a world in which normative judgment is circumscribed by a rich sense of social context – who someone was, the full depth of feelings and motives that inspired certain actions, the circumstances that conspired to push events in one way or another, personal histories, social inequalities, and more – law students are moved into a new world, in which legal judgment is circumscribed by linguistic norms, texts and the arguments they permit, and layers of authoritative language. The orienting compass that guides them is metalinguistic in the strongest sense: an ideology of language that circumscribes social reality completely. Justice is done if the proper linguistic protocols are observed, if the opposition of voices is literally represented in apparently dialogic form in court and in written opinions – as it is also in law school classrooms. Gal and Irvine would call this "iconicity" (note 3): linguistic ideology reading language form as a mirror of social phenomena (it is also an example of "erasure" (note 4), because a focus on procedure renders invisible the ways some oppositional voices and viewpoints are not making it into the discussion at all). As Morris explains, a core aim of legal reasoning is "to rupture linguistic forms, polite forms, non-lawyerly forms, and to introduce a necessary pugilism" (note 5) as it imposes "a limiting order, an institutionalized order, a boundarying of rationality." As I've demonstrated, this reorientation in epistemology is accomplished in large part through a shift in linguistic practices, effectuated in and through a shift in linguistic ideologies.

Notes

1   *Linguistic ideology* involves ideas, assumptions and beliefs that people have about the nature, structure and use of language. Efforts to understand linguistic ideology are interesting because they help to trace the social origins, development and cultural variation of thought (for discussion, see Woolard and Schieffelin 1994).
2   *Entextualized* refers to taking some piece of language (e.g. a word or longer stretch of text) out of context (decontextualised) and reusing it in a new discourse (recontextualised). The process requires the power to do so of an **extextualising** agent, who creates a relationship between the original and new discourses. The process is considered a way of borrowing institutional power in order to serve new political goals, if the extextualising agent interprets the original discourse in a new light.
3   Gal and Irvine (1995) use the term **iconicity** to refer to social images conjured up by linguistic practices (e.g. a Southern US accent is taken by some to signify laziness). Speech characteristics of an individual speaker are sometimes mistakenly thought to be 'naturally' linked with certain social groups. Iconisation is one of three main processes at work in constructing linguistic ideologies.
4   Erasure, in this context, is a process in which ideology renders some people or activities virtually invisible (e.g. the belief that a language community is homo-geneous may make someone unable to see internal variation by sociolect, since such variants are not compatible with that person's more general vision).
5   *Pugilism*: the profession or hobby of boxing.

Questions/discussion

The questions below require you to pay close attention to individual points that cumulatively build up a difficult argument about how lawyers' world view is shaped by a process of being made to think in a new way about the relation between language and reality. The questions below may appear to be closed comprehension questions, but the subject matter invites very open-ended discussion.

1   According to the argument being developed, what is unusual about how legal texts are read?
2   Explain the 'miracle' discussed by the author.

3   According to Mertz, what shift in linguistic ideology do law students undergo during their studies? For example, what do you think is meant by the statement that 'linguistic ideology equates the proper alignment of language with authoritative legal knowledge'?

4   *Epistemology* is the science or investigation of how we know things. But the word is not usually modified by a preceding adjective, as it is here: 'legal epistemology'. How would you explain to someone what 'legal epistemology' might be?

5   *Metalinguistic* means 'concerned with or about language, examining or talking about language as an object'. What contribution is the author suggesting 'metalinguistic rules' make to how law works?

Extract 2: law as a 'constitutive rhetoric'

Reproduced from: White, J. (1985) 'Law as rhetoric, rhetoric as law: the arts of cultural and communal life', *University of Chicago Law Review*, 52(3): 684–792, at pp. 688–90.

I want to direct attention to three related aspects of lawyer's work. The first is the fact that the lawyer, like any rhetorician, must always start by speaking the language of his or her audience, whatever it may be. This is just a version of the general truth that to persuade anybody you must in the first instance speak a language that he or she regards as valid and intelligible. If you are a lawyer, this means that you must speak either the technical language of the law – the rules, cases, statutes, maxims, and so forth, that constitute the domain of your professional talk – or, if you are speaking to jurors or clients or the public at large, some version of the ordinary English of your time and place. Law is in this sense always culture-specific. It always starts with an external, empirically discoverable set of cultural resources into which it is an intervention.

[. . .] These means of persuasion can be described with some degree of accuracy and completeness, so that most lawyers would agree that such-and-such a case or statute or principle is relevant, and another is not. But the agreement is always imperfect: one lawyer will see an analogy that another will deny, for example. And when attention shifts to the value or weight that different parts of the material should have, disagreement becomes widespread and deep. Ultimately, then, the identity, the meaning, and the authority of the materials are always arguable, always uncertain. There is a sense in which the materials can be regarded in the first instance as objective, external to the self; but they are always remade in argument. Their discovery is, in a sense, an empirical process, their reformulation and use an inventive or creative one.

This suggests that the lawyer's work has a second essential element, the creative process to which I have just alluded. For in speaking the language of the law, the lawyer must always be ready to try to change it: to add or to drop a distinction, to admit a new voice, to claim a new source of authority, and so on. One's performance is in this sense always argumentative, not only about the result one seeks to obtain but also about the version of the legal discourse that one uses – that one creates – in one's speech and writing. That is, the lawyer is always saying not only, "Here is how this case should be decided," but also, "Here – in this language – is the way this case and similar cases should be talked about. The language I am speaking is the proper language of justice in our culture." The legal speaker always acts upon the language that he or she uses, to modify or rearrange it; in this sense legal rhetoric is always argumentatively constitutive of the language it employs.

The third aspect of legal rhetoric is that what might be called its ethical or communal character, or its socially constitutive nature. Every time one speaks as a lawyer, one establishes for the moment a character – an ethical identity, or what the Greeks called an ethos – for oneself, for one's audience, and for those one talks about, and in addition one proposes a relation among the characters one defines. One creates, or proposes to create, a community of people, talking to and about each other. The lawyer's speech is thus always implicitly argumentative not only about the result – how should the case be decided? – and about the language – in what terms should it be defined and talked about? – but also about the rhetorical community of which one is at that moment a part. The lawyer is always establishing in performance a response to the questions, "What kind of community should we, who are talking about the language of the law, establish with each other, with our clients, and with the rest of the world? What kind of conversation should the law constitute, should constitute the law?"

Each of the three aspects of the lawyer's rhetorical life can be analyzed and criticized: the discourse one is given by one's culture to speak; the argumentative reconstitution of it; and the argumentative constitution of a rhetorical community in one's speech or writing. The study of this process – of constitutive rhetoric – is the study of the ways we constitute ourselves as individuals, as communities, and as cultures, whenever we speak. [. . .] Both the lawyer and the lawyer's audience live in a world in which their language and community are not fixed and certain but fluid, constantly remade, as their possibilities and limits are tested. The law is an art of persuasion that creates the objects of its persuasion, for it constitutes both the community and the culture it commends.

Questions/discussion

1   In what respects does White suggest that legal use of language is not fixed or static?
2   What evidence does he present for that view?
3   Why does the author call this kind of rhetoric 'constitutive'? How does 'constitutive rhetoric' differ from other kinds (e.g. what does it constitute)?
4   How well does this view of legal communication fit with other views of lawyers and their use of language you have encountered in other units in this book?

D6   PERSPECTIVES ON LEGAL INTERPRETATION

This unit brings together two extracts that each look, in different ways, at aspects of judicial interpretation from the perspective of linguistics and cognitive science/psychology.

Extract 1: two approaches to meaning and legal construction

In the first of two brief extracts from Solan's *The Language of Statutes*, the author discusses the two kinds of approach to meaning we outline in Unit A6: an approach involving rules (including definitions) and an approach involving prototypes. Solan suggests that the two coexist in everyday interpretive behaviour. Building on his discussion of these alternative approaches, Solan assesses the interaction between these different ways of understanding meaning in US statutory interpretation.

Reproduced from Solan, L. (2010) *The Language of Statutes: Laws and their Interpretation*, Chicago, IL: University of Chicago Press, pp. 64–6.

Most psychologists now believe that we think both ways. We think in terms of prototypes in some circumstances and in terms of rules in others. Medin, Wattenmaker, and Hampson found that people prefer to rely on defining features when they do not have much information about the surrounding circumstances. They also found, however, that when people have greater information about context, they use family resemblance models based on prototypes. Psychologist Steven Sloman suggests that people employ both rule-based and associative systems in reasoning and that conflicts between the two occur frequently in everyday life. As an example, he suggests the dilemma of deciding whether to wear a seat belt for a car ride of a very short distance, say moving one's car from one parking space to an adjacent one. An individual can rely upon experience-based intuitions about danger and not don the seat belt or can apply a rule: always wear a seat belt. Many other psychologists have reached similar conclusions [. . .].

What all this means for legal interpretation is that the choice between definitional and ordinary meaning is only natural. It appears that people reason about concepts from both the top down, consistent with the classical model, and from the bottom up, consistent with prototype analysis. [. . .] The two approaches to legal construction – definitional meaning and ordinary meaning – capture both the fact that people reach different conclusions and the ambivalence within each individual. Judges routinely use both methods, although the definitional-meaning approach is the more common.

This is not a surprising observation given that the definitional approach appears, at least superficially, to be the more "law-like" of the two. As we saw in the previous chapter, laws are themselves structured as definitions. If, to win a conviction, the state must prove that a defendant has violated all elements of a crime, then it is natural to analyze similarly the words that make up the elements. In this way, the state must prove all the elements of all the elements. Prototype, or ordinary-meaning analysis, is to some extent methodologically inconsistent with this standard approach to applying laws in that it reduces the uniformity with which the law applies.

Although the ordinary-meaning approach reduces the likelihood of judicial decisions at odds with what the legislature would have wanted, problems remain. First, it is not always as easy as it may seem to abandon the definitional approach, and it is not always clearly legitimate to do so if the goal is to establish a reliable proxy for actual legislative intent. Second, once one chooses the ordinary-meaning approach, it is not always clear what the ordinary meaning is. [. . .] Given the way our minds work, we should not expect it to be a simple matter to eschew the definitional-meaning approach to word meaning in favour of the ordinary-meaning approach as a matter of doctrinal imperative. They are both firmly embedded in the way we think, and a definitional approach to meaning feels consistent with our basic notions of how laws work.

Questions/discussion

1   Solan suggests that an ordinary-meaning approach, based on prototypical categories rather than definition, may fit better with legislative purpose but at the cost of less precision and greater risk of inconsistency in application. How fair do you find that assessment?

2   How much interaction between the two approaches to meaning can be found in judicial efforts to settle the legal meaning of *sculpture* in *Lucasfilm v. Ainsworth*, as outlined in Unit C6?

In the second short extract from Solan, the author identifies challenges in the availability of two different approaches to meaning to judges as they interpret statutory language. In particular, he draws attention to increased reliance on dictionaries in establishing 'ordinary meaning'.

Without question, though, the biggest change in the search for word meaning is the almost obsessive attention courts now pay to dictionaries, using them as authority for ordinary meaning. Until the late twentieth century, Supreme Court justices only infrequently used the dictionary as a source of ordinary meaning. For example, in the almost two hundred years prior to Scalia's appointment to the Supreme Court in 1986, the Court referred to "ordinary meaning" in close proximity to "dictionary" only six times. From the time of his appointment through 2008, the Court did so an additional twenty-one times. [...]

The problem with using dictionaries to determine the ordinary meaning of a word is that the principal purpose of a dictionary is to determine the outer boundaries of appropriate usage for each sense of a word. But most of the time, the issue before a court is not whether the legislature intended one distinct sense of a word as opposed to another (e.g., "riverbank" vs. "savings bank"). Rather, the question is whether the facts of the case are sufficiently close to the circumstances in which it feels comfortable to use the statutory word that it is fair to conclude that the legislature most likely would have expected the statute to apply. Other than providing an articulate expression of the general meaning to assist in that inquiry, dictionary definitions most often do little to aid in that inquiry. Once judges begin to fight over which dictionary to consult, the use of dictionaries to determine ordinary meaning is virtually futile.

(Solan 2010: 76)

Questions/discussion

3   Solan suggests that the definitions of words offered by a general dictionary provide useful information that is nevertheless not well-suited to solving the interpretive problems that courts face. Why is this?

4   If judges refer to dictionaries, how serious is the risk of 'fights over which dictionary to consult'?

5   Solan's overall view is that US statutory interpretation generally succeeds in arriving at sensible and fair interpretations that are less disrupted by semantic and pragmatic side issues than might be imagined. He concludes that 'law works . . . most of the time' (Solan 2010: 5). How do you respond to that conclusion, in the light of the material and issues introduced in this unit?

Extract 2: relevance theory and legal interpretation

Our second extract comes from a paper by Robyn Carston, 'Legal texts and canons of construction: a view from current pragmatic theory'. Carston examines a highly topical issue in philosophy of law: how far legal use of language shares pragmatic characteristics with colloquial or conversational uses. In an influential paper, Andrei Marmor (2008) suggested that, in crucial respects, the pragmatics of legal language is unique in foregrounding strategic considerations absent from ordinary conversational contexts. The Gricean framework of implicature is based on an underlying principle of cooperation; but Marmor argues that the idea that rational communicators orient themselves towards successful communication is suspended both in legal 'enactments' (legislation) and in the adversarial practice of litigation. In contrast with that view, Carston identifies convergence between interpretive heuristics as expressed in modern pragmatics and in long-established legal maxims. Partly through dialogue with Marmor, she goes on to consider how far relevance theory in particular might shed light on legal interpretation.

Reproduced from Carston, R. (2011) 'Legal texts and canons of construction: a view from current pragmatic theory', in M. Freeman and F. Smith (eds), *Law and Language: Current Legal Issues*, Vol. 15, Oxford: Oxford University Press, pp. 8–33, at pp. 31–3.

A similar sort of case, discussed by Marmor (and many others), concerns a (fictional, but highly plausible) enactment which stipulates that 'It shall be a misdemeanour . . . to sleep in any railway station.' The word whose interpretation is at issue is 'sleep,' a word which is surely among the least ambiguous or vague words in the language. Consider now the case of a passenger who, while sitting waiting for a delayed train at 3 a.m., falls asleep for a few minutes; does he, thereby, commit a misdemeanour? Marmor considers the possibility that while what the law literally *says* is that it is an offence to sleep in the railway station, the prescriptive *content* of the law is, roughly, to prohibit attempts to *use the railway station as a place to sleep in*. However, he dismisses this interpretation as not having sufficient foundation, as being too much of 'a stretch.' This suggested content, or something very similar to it, seems to me to be the right interpretation. No (rational) policeman who noticed the briefly dozing passenger would feel impelled to bring the force of the law down on him. On the other hand, the policeman might well take the law to apply to a man who throws a blanket onto the station platform, lies down on it, and stares up at the ceiling, showing no signs of intending to move on, but who does not in fact sleep. Again, my interpretation of 'sleep' here, as being both narrower in denotation than its literal encoded meaning (it excludes the briefly dozing passenger) and also broader (it includes the awake man on the blanket), can be explained in RT terms: the relevance (or purpose) of the law lies with obvious contextual implications concerning preventing people from treating a railway station as a place to spend the night or set up home in, and this, in turn, by mutual parallel adjustment, leads to an adjustment of the meaning of the word 'sleep'.

As already noted, Sperber and Wilson's claim that utterances (and other communicative acts) come with a presumption of their own *optimal relevance* unpacks as an implied guarantee that the speaker/author has been as relevant as possible (to the addressee) within the parameters of her *abilities and preferences*. This proviso is interesting as it seems to mesh with interpretive practices sometimes made explicit in legal interpretation. [. . .]

Not all speaker/author preferences are transparent to the interpreter, or intended to be. When there is a sufficiently relevant interpretation derivable without seeking them out, that is the warranted interpretation. Without doubt, the question of whether the RT account of ordinary everyday utterance interpretation can, perhaps with certain provisos and/or modifications, be carried over to the case of legal interpretation needs much more consideration than I've given it here. It should be that the first-pass reading of any legal document does fall quite straightforwardly within the general pragmatic story. However, one of the ways in which legal interpretation is special is in the kind of conscious effortful scrutiny a legal text may be subjected to in a bid to find an interpretation which may benefit a particular individual's case in a situation where the stakes are very high for that individual. To extrapolate validly from the one kind of interpretive process to the other and to provide cognitively grounded reasons for favouring a particular interpretation in the case of an explicit interpretive dispute is an important challenge for relevance theory. [. . .]

It remains something of an article of faith on my part that this effort would be enhanced by paying close attention to an account of the cognitive processes of and the constraints on ordinary utterance comprehension, such as those offered by relevance theory. Ultimately, though, even if the situation can be improved and judges come to interpret from a position of deeper understanding of language and communication, genuine disagreements about the correct interpretation of a legal text are inevitable, given the nature of language, that is, its under-determinacy of the propositions it is used to express, and the defeasibility of the pragmatic inferences employed to fill the interpretive gaps.

Questions/discussion

1   Is it possible that a definition of the word *sleep* might be devised that could cope with Carston's problem cases?

2   In their approach to the meaning of *sculpture* in *Lucasfilm v. Ainsworth*, English judges espoused a multifactorial approach. Based on the likely purposes of a 'no sleeping in the station' rule, formulate an equivalent list of points that might link the ordinary meaning of *sleep* to the purpose of the regulation.

3   Carston concludes her article with the observation that the major challenge thrown up in examining legal interpretation from the perspective of pragmatics is the scope of 'relevant context' within which any legal utterance should be interpreted. Importantly, she notes, 'relevant context' in pragmatics is not a constant: the purpose of the concept is precisely to point to *varying* assumptions mobilised in interpretation. How damaging is this observation as regards convergence or collaboration between pragmatic and legal approaches to explicating meaning in legal contexts?

UNDERSTANDING LEGAL SPEECH ACTS AND RULES

D7

The two extracts in this unit relate to our discussion throughout Thread 7 of the contribution made by particular uses of language (especially speech acts) to the exercise of legal power. Our first extract works through Searle's speech act categories, pointing out legal connections and implications. Our second extract focuses on the linguistic properties of generality and 'displacement' (the second of these being the property of human language, in contrast with other sign systems, by means of which language can refer to contexts removed from the speaker's immediate situation). The extract relates these fundamental capabilities of language to the difference between commands and legal rules.

Extract 1: law as speech acts

Reproduced from Danet, B. (1980) 'Language in the legal process', *Law and Society Review*, 14(3): 445–564, at pp. 458–60.

Searle (1976) and Hancher (1979), among others, have attempted to develop typologies of speech acts, drawing on Austin's earlier efforts (1970b). It is useful to cross-classify Searle's categories with our two sets of functions of law.

1. Representatives

These are utterances that commit the speaker to something being the case or assert the truth of a proposition; they match words to the world. Searle distinguishes between speech acts whose illocutionary force or point (to use his preferred term) is strong, such as testifying or swearing, and those whose illocutionary point is weak, such as asserting, claiming, and stating.

2. Directives

These are future-oriented speech acts that seek not to match words to some current state of things but to change the world, to get someone to do something. Within the facilitative-regulative functions of law, they are most prominent in legislation that imposes obligations. The notion of directives clearly lies behind the Austinian view (1873) of the law as a set of commands. Strong directives are also prominent in dispute processing. Questions should be seen as a special form of request – to *tell* something rather than to do something. When a witness is under oath and on the witness stand, a question is not just a request but an *order* to tell something. Subpoenas, jury instructions, and appeals are all directives. Lawyers believe that the inclusion of an "enacting clause," as in "Be it enacted by the Parliament that all citizens aged 18 shall be eligible for army duty," is what provides the authority of such utterances. However, it is the matching of the form and content of the utterance with the context of its use – in a set of mainly nonlinguistic, i.e., legal, conditions – that invests it with authority (cf. Hancher, 1979). Criminal law relies heavily on this use of language.

3. Commissives

These utterances commit the speaker to do something in the future. The major category in legal settings is, of course, contracts. Promises between friends are weaker commissives than contracts. Both the parties to a contract and the guarantors engage in commissive acts. Marriage ceremonies and wills are other examples. Societies and languages differ in the conventions, linguistic and nonlinguistic, that define these speech acts. They must be performed "just right" in order to count. These conventions, with all their ambiguities, often become explicit only when a dispute arises about what the parties understood by a commissive. Drawing on Grice's (1975) notion of the cooperative principle, Hancher (1979) proposes that contracts should be recognized as *cooperative commissives*, speech acts that cannot be said to have taken place unless the other party also commits himself or herself. In modern legal parlance, this is a *bilateral contract*.

4. Expressives

These express the speaker's psychological state about a proposition and include such speech acts as apologizing, excusing, condemning, deploring, forgiving, and blaming – what Goffman (1971) would call ritual demonstrations of one's position in relation to societal rules. In modern trials, the tradition of asking convicted persons just before sentencing whether they have anything to say is an opportunity for them to display publicly whether their relation to the rules has changed.

5. Declarations

These are utterances whose successful performance brings about a correspondence between their propositional content and reality. The change in reality occurs solely because of the utterance of the speaker, provided he or she has the authority to engage in such acts and regardless of any subsequent acts on the part of the hearers. To say "You're fired" is not merely to depict reality, as in a representative, but to change it. [. . .]

Within the facilitative-regulative functions of law, regular declarations include marriage ceremonies (the speech act of the person conducting the ceremony, not that of those getting married), bills of sale or receipts, appointments and nominations, and the legislative stipulation of rights and of definitions of concepts. In dispute processing, regular declarations include lawyers' objections, sentences, and appellate opinions, all of which "count' because of the institutionalized authority of speakers to engage in these acts; examples of representative declarations are indictments, confessions, pleas of guilty/not guilty, and verdicts.

Notes

1   *Facilitative-regulative function of law*: Towards the end of Unit B7, we draw attention to criticisms (associated with the work of Hart) levelled against a view of law as a regulative system of commands. Such criticisms emphasise that law also performs enabling (facilitative) functions: establishing companies, creating married couples from individual persons, making possible transfers of property, etc.

2   *Subpoena*: A written order compelling an individual to appear before a court and provide a testimony.

Questions/discussion

1   After reading through the extract, consider which of the categories described best fits the following actions:

(a) A tenant signing a contract to lease an apartment.
(b) A judge settling a rowdy audience down in the courtroom with the word: 'Order!'
(c) An expert witness explaining skid marks created by a car accident.
(d) A computer user checking the box 'I agree' to terms and conditions when installing a piece of software.
(e) A lawyer cross-examining a witness.
(f) Plea-bargaining between a prosecutor and a defendant.

2   What kinds of difficulties arise in mapping legal functions onto speech acts in this way? What implications if any follow from those difficulties?

3   Having noted that the class of 'declarations' overlaps with that of 'representatives' (in other descriptions, 'assertives'), Searle proposed creating a new subcategory: 'representative declarations': a category he suggests would be especially relevant to law. Searle argues that judgments pronounced by judges (e.g. 'Guilty') involve both a factual claim and a declaration imposing institutionalised authority on the outcome. Do you see any tension between these two aspects of the function of judgments, as both representatives and declarations?

4   At least two alternative approaches might be followed in dealing with legal utterances that seem to fit two categories: one would consider utterances to be capable of performing more than one speech act at a time. Another (seemingly preferred by Sperber and Wilson 1995) would view speech act classification as usefully descriptive but theoretically inadequate. Instead, some more general framework of utterance interpretation might be thought to be needed, in which contextual inference would play a far larger role. Discuss the merits of these alternative approaches as regards the interpretation of performative legal pronouncements and documents.

Extract 2: language capabilities and general rules

Our second extract comes from Frederick Schauer's editorial introduction to a collection of republished articles on language and law that had become difficult to get hold of. (Schauer takes up themes he touches on in this Introduction in his own chapter in the volume, 'Rules and the rule-following argument'; Schauer 1993: 313–18).

Reprinted from Schauer, F. (ed.) (1993a) *Law and Language*, Aldershot: Dartmouth Press, pp. xi–xii.

Language is many things, but one of them is that it is general, having rules (or, some would say, practices or, others would say, conventions) that are neither speaker- nor situation-specific. Indeed, that is just what makes for rules (or practices or conventions). Thus, nouns other than proper names do or at least can refer to many things or events, and the compositional nature of language, pursuant to which a speaker of a language can understand a sentence he or she has never heard before, is facilitated (or defined) by the way in which rules of grammar and structure are similarly applicable wholesale rather than being made up anew instance-by-instance.

In much the same way, law as an institution differs from other forms of social interaction largely because of its generality. When John Austin in *The Province of Jurisprudence Determined* distinguished laws from commands according to the generality of the former and the particularity of the latter, he identified something widely held to be at the heart of understanding the operation of law and legal systems. Although special legislation is not unknown to the law, and although numerous jurisdictional rules often empower judges and other decision-makers to make largely particularistic determinations, law in one way or another commonly extends over time, over persons and over events.

Numerous devices of the law reflect this generality. More often and more strongly than other forms of decision-making, law commonly takes the constraints of precedent seriously, requiring that prior decisions be followed just because they are prior. More frequently than most other decision-making institutions, the decision-making institutions of the law ordinarily provide written reasons for their decisions, preserving those reasons in elaborately indexed series of books so that they will be available (by way of guidance or constraint) to future decision-makers. And with especial frequency law employs statutes, regulations, codes and other instruments by which those in power attempt to order or control large numbers of future actions and events.

Were law not so much about obeisance to the past and control of the future, were it focused more on now, and were it not so commonly spatially-general rather than situation-specific, the relationship between law and language would be important, but less specially so. But because law so often is the instrument of temporal and spatial generality, it has a special use for language shorn of many of the normal conversational and contextual embellishments ordinarily discussed under the heading of pragmatics. Language is part and parcel of most interpersonal transactions, but removing language from an interpersonal context puts particular weight on language in its own right, on what is called in the speech-act tradition 'utterance meaning' rather than speaker's meaning. In all of the variations just mentioned, decision-makers attempt to project decisions made here and now into a larger and less-known future; they do this by relying on the generality of language – on the ability of what they say now to be understood by unknown others in the future, and on the ability to say things now that will apply to a large and open-ended number of situations. Because legal decision-makers can do this only insofar as language allows them to do, language plays a central role in the operation of law that is different from, even if not necessarily greater than, the role it plays in facilitating many other forms of human interaction.

Notes

Rules, practices, conventions: Schauer is alluding here to theoretical debates in linguistics and philosophy: is language a matter of rules (e.g. grammatical rules as formulated by, for instance, Noam Chomsky)? Or a matter of conventions or discourse practices (i.e. looser, socially constituted regularities or, for instance, Wittgenstein's still more varied 'language games')?

Compositional nature of language: The hierarchical organisation of language structure, in which larger units (e.g. grammatical units) are seen as being 'composed' of smaller units; as regards meaning, the notion that the meaning of a whole utterance can be predicted from the meaning of its parts.

John Austin: As noted in Unit B7, John Austin (1790–1859), the jurist author of *The Province of Jurisprudence Determined* (1832), is a different John Austin from the Oxford 'ordinary language philosopher' J. L. Austin (1911–1960), also John, who wrote *How to Do Things with Words* (1962).

Questions/discussion

Schauer distinguishes 'utterance meaning' and 'speaker-meaning', and suggests that statements of law depend largely on their meaning as utterances written or said in a particular context (e.g. published as a statute; posted on a notice or sign); nevertheless, those utterances are intended, he suggests, to be interpreted in many different situations, including unknown future situations.

1   (a) List as many features of language use as you can that have the effect of embedding an utterance in a particular situation (these are Schauer's 'normal conversational and contextual embellishments ordinarily discussed under the heading of pragmatics').

   (b) Schauer suggests that if law were more concerned with current situations and less with being applicable at different times and in different places, the relationship between law and language would be less important than it is. Explain why that might be the case. How far do you agree with this claim?

2   Schauer implies a close relationship between the capability of language to refer beyond an immediate speech-situation (into the past, to other places, into the future, and to hypothetical circumstances) and the development in law of the language-based machinery we have looked at throughout this book (archives of law reports, reasoned judicial decisions, rules formulated in general terms, etc.). How far are these two aspects of language use – ability to operate across time and space, and complex, interlocking documentary procedures – complementary with one another?

LANGUAGE STRUGGLES ONLINE

D8

Our extract in this unit is followed by more open-ended questions than in most other units. It comes from an article by Lyrissa Barnett Lidsky: 'Silencing John Doe: defamation and discourse in cyberspace'. The article brings together two topics we juxtapose in Unit B8:

❏   the challenge of defining the meaning conveyed by allegedly defamatory statements, so that one specified meaning can be used as a basis for assessing the damage to reputation it could inflict; and

❏   legal challenges facing the regulation of new styles of public discourse in cyberspace.

Lidsky's article focuses on a category of US libel suits that grew rapidly with the rise of the Internet: actions brought by large companies against unnamed (anonymous) Internet-user defendants. Unusually for lawsuits, even if the claimants in such actions are successful they are unlikely to recover damages, because the defendants in question would not be able to pay. In the questions below, however, we focus on a more serious challenge presented by Internet language: how we should think in future about language regulation online. Most current regulatory frameworks were introduced to respond to print discourse or developed in response to twentieth-century broadcast mass media; but they are now also applied to online language use.

Republished from Lidsky, L. B. (2000) 'Silencing John Doe: defamation and discourse in cyberspace', *Duke Law Journal*, 49(4): 855–945, at pp. 861–5.

What is unique about these new Internet suits is the threat they pose to the new realm of discourse that has sprung up on the Internet. The promise of the Internet is empowerment: it empowers ordinary individuals with limited financial resources to "publish" their views on matters of public concern. The Internet is therefore a powerful tool for equalizing imbalances of power by giving voice to the disenfranchised and by allowing more democratic participation in public discourse. In other words, the Internet allows ordinary John Does to participate as never before in public discourse, and hence, to shape public policy. Yet, suits [*like the hypothetical suit discussed at the beginning of the article*] threaten to re-establish existing hierarchies of power, as powerful corporate Goliaths sue their critics for speaking their minds. Defendants like John Doe typically lack the resources necessary to defend against a defamation action, much less the resources to satisfy a judgment. Thus, these Internet defamation actions threaten not only to deter the individual who is sued from speaking out, but also to encourage undue self-censorship among the other John Does who frequent Internet discussion fora.

Although one might intuitively expect the First Amendment to prevent powerful plaintiffs from silencing their critics, the First Amendment extends only limited protections in such circumstances. Beginning with the landmark decision of *New York Times Co. v. Sullivan*, the Supreme Court grafted numerous constitutional limitations onto the structure of the defamation tort. But Sullivan and much of its progeny involved an individual plaintiff (often a public official or public figure) challenging statements made by a relatively powerful media defendant. The First Amendment jurisprudence that developed was therefore responsive to the culture of the institutional press and its need to deliver information quickly without risking crippling liability for minor mistakes of fact. It is little wonder that this same jurisprudence may not be responsive to the emerging institutional culture – or, more appropriately, cultures – of the Internet.

Although Internet communications are almost invariably "written" communications, they lack the formal characteristics of written communications in the "real world." In the real world, the author is separated from her audience by both space and time, and this separation interposes a formal distance between author and audience, a distance reinforced by the conventions of written communication. Internet communications lack this formal distance. Because communication can occur almost instantaneously, participants in online discussions place a premium on speed. Indeed, in many fora, speed takes precedence over all other values, including not just accuracy but even grammar, spelling, and punctuation. Hyperbole and exaggeration are common, and "venting" is at least as common as careful and considered argumentation. The fact that many Internet speakers employ online pseudonyms tends to heighten this sense that "anything goes," and some commentators have likened cyberspace to a frontier society free from the conventions and constraints that limit discourse in the real world. While this view is undoubtedly overstated, certainly the immediacy and informality of Internet communications may be central to its widespread appeal.

Although Internet communications may have the ephemeral qualities of gossip with regard to accuracy, they are communicated through a medium more pervasive than print, and for this reason they have tremendous power to harm reputation. Once a message enters cyberspace, millions of people worldwide can gain access to it. Even if the message is posted in a discussion forum frequented by only a handful of people, any one of them can republish the message by printing it or, as is more likely, by forwarding it instantly to a different discussion forum. And if the message is sufficiently provocative, it may be republished again and again. The extraordinary capacity of the Internet to replicate almost endlessly any defamatory message lends credence to the notion that "the truth rarely catches up with a lie." The problem for libel law, then, is how to protect reputation without squelching the potential of the Internet as a medium of public discourse.

Notes

John Doe: Not a real name, but a generic name (Joe Bloggs in the UK), with Jane Doe used for females: a placeholder name for a party whose true identity is unknown or must be withheld in a legal action. Lidksy says John Doe is named as defendant in such cases until disclosure of the user's actual identity by an ISP is authorised.

Goliath: See the Biblical story of David and Goliath. Figuratively, a large and powerful opponent pitted against a heroic but conventionally disadvantaged protagonist (David's slingshot aimed into the eye of the giant).

First Amendment: To the US Constitution, adopted 1791: 'Congress shall make no law . . . abridging the freedom of speech, or of the press . . .'

New York Times Co. v. Sullivan: A landmark case in US defamation law; defamatory speech had traditionally been dismissed as beyond First Amendment protection (a kind of 'fighting words'; see Unit A8). *Sullivan* was an action brought by an Alabama police commissioner complaining of derogatory treatment in an advertisement sponsored by civil liberties campaigners in the *New York Times*. In the Supreme Court, the constitutional position of defamation of public figures was clarified; the case also restricted the circumstances in which public figure claimants can sue.

Tort: Field of civil law concerned with breaches of duty imposed by law, including topics such as negligence, employers' liability, trespass and defamation.

Jurisprudence: Philosophical or theoretical analysis of law.

Republish: In libel, republishing a defamatory statement amounts to a new instance of defamatory publication.

'The truth rarely catches up with a lie': Popular folk-wisdom, that falsehoods tend to be disseminated faster than truths.

Questions/discussion

1   What are the key features of Internet interaction that Lidsky suggests distinguish it from conventions associated with written communication?

2   How far do you think such features are technological characteristics of the Internet, and how far are they interactional styles that may continue to evolve for non-technological reasons? (For instance, compare the role books played in social relationships of the late fifteenth century, on the invention of printing, with the role they played by the late sixteenth century, after the Reformation; or that audiovisual media played in cinemas during the 1930s with the functioning of clips on YouTube now.)

3   Lidsky draws attention to how Internet activists initially likened cyberspace to a frontier society, free from conventions and constraints that limit discourse in the real world – including, it was sometimes wrongly supposed, legal liability. What view do you take of unrestricted and unregulated communication online?

4   Into this imagined communication paradise, Lidsky introduces the idea of power. She describes how the Internet appeared to promise empowerment of ordinary individuals by allowing them greater democratic participation in public discourse. But the libel actions she describes appear to do the opposite. What wider – rather than specific, technical – issues are raised by such struggles over online discourse?

5   Opponents of the kinds of lawsuit Lidsky outlines view them as David and Goliath struggles: the powerful use defamation to chill free speech by terrorising the powerless into silence. Others have viewed such actions as legitimate vindication of personal and corporate reputation in the face of what amounts to industrial espionage. To highlight the financial aspect of tensions in the 'marketplace of ideas', Lidsky focuses in her article on cases in which the defamatory statements were published on share-trading bulletin boards. Such statements could, if believed, have an effect on day-to-day share values. On the basis of what you have read, which is the fairer assessment: chilling free speech or vindicating personal and corporate reputation?

6   To make your discussion of Q5 more concrete, consider two (simplified) potentially defamatory statements adapted from Lidsky's article: (i) an online statement, which turned out to be false, identifying failings in a company's investment strategy; and (ii) a claim that the message writer, calling himself Dirk Diggler (the protagonist in a film about the porn industry, *Boogie Nights*) is regularly having sex with the CEO's wife.

7   Lidsky's overall concern in the article is to explore how defamation law's approach to new styles of communication can avoid suppressing ('squelching') legitimate social criticism along with the many reckless and damaging falsehoods published online. In general, she is in favour of defamation law being applied online as it is in relation to other forms of discourse. How far do you agree?

RESOLVING DISPUTED MEANING IN COURT

The following extracts are taken from a series of US cases that dealt with the meaning of 'carrying' or 'using' a firearm: an offence contained in the firearms chapter of the Federal Criminal Code (18 U. S. C. § 924(c)(1)), a provision that carries a five-year mandatory prison term. We consider how the courts resolved the disputed meaning of the terms in question.

Extract 1: 'using' a firearm

In *Bailey v. United States*, the police stopped and searched Bailey's car. They found cocaine in the passenger compartment and a loaded 9 mm pistol in the trunk (in UK English, the 'boot'). The defendant was charged on several counts, but one disputed charge was whether he should be convicted of 'using' a firearm during and in relation to a drug trafficking crime. A prosecution expert testified that it is common for drug dealers to carry a firearm to protect themselves in transactions. The following extract is taken from Justice O'Connor's opinion:

> We agree with petitioners, and hold that § 924(c)(1) requires evidence sufficient to show an *active employment* of the firearm by the defendant, a use that makes the firearm an operative factor in relation to the predicate offense.
>
> This action is not the first one in which the Court has grappled with the proper understanding of "use" in § 924(c)(1). In *Smith*, we faced the question whether the barter of a gun for drugs was a "use," and concluded that it was. *Smith v. United States*, 508 U. S. 223 (1993). As the debate in Smith illustrated, the word "use" poses some interpretational difficulties because of the different meanings attributable to it. Consider the paradoxical statement: "I *use* a gun to protect my house, but I've never had to *use* it." "Use" draws meaning from its context, and we will look not only to the word itself, but also to the statute and the sentencing scheme, to determine the meaning Congress intended.
>
> We agree with the majority below that "use" must connote more than mere possession of a firearm by a person who commits a drug offense [. . .]. Had Congress intended possession alone to trigger liability under § 924(c)(1), it easily could have so provided. This obvious conclusion is supported by the frequent use of the term "possess" in the gun-crime statutes to describe prohibited gun-related conduct.

Questions/discussion

1   Describe the possible meanings of *use* that the court had to decide between.
2   Although the court did not cite the source, the 'paradoxical statement' it took into account involving two different uses of *use* was taken from a journal article co-written by a lawyer and a linguist, published while the court was deciding the case (Solan 2010). What did this illustration contribute to the court's reasoning?

3   Do you agree with the court's judgment that *use* must mean more than mere possession in this context? Why – or why not?

Extract 2: 'carrying' a firearm

The facts in *Muscarello v. United States* are strikingly similar. Both marijuana and a handgun were found in the trunk/boot of the defendant's vehicle. Perhaps due to the reasoning in *Bailey*, this time the government charged the defendant with 'carrying a firearm'. What stands out in the judgment is the judges' eagerness to use informal corpora to establish the meaning they should ascribe to the word *carry*. The following extract is part of the majority opinion delivered by Justice Breyer.

We begin with the statute's language. The parties vigorously contest the ordinary English meaning of the phrase "carries a firearm." Because they essentially agree that Congress intended the phrase to convey its ordinary, and not some special legal, meaning, and because they argue the linguistic point at length, we too have looked into the matter in more than usual depth. Although the word "carry" has many different meanings, only two are relevant here. When one uses the word in the first, or primary, meaning, one can, as a matter of ordinary English, "carry firearms" in a wagon, car, truck, or other vehicle that one accompanies. When one uses the word in a different, rather special, way, to mean, for example, "bearing" or (in slang) "packing" (as in "packing a gun"), the matter is less clear. But, for reasons we shall set out below, we believe Congress intended to use the word in its primary sense and not in this latter, special way.

Consider first the word's primary meaning. The *Oxford English Dictionary* gives as its first definition "convey, originally by cart or wagon, hence in any vehicle, by ship, on horseback, etc." 2 *Oxford English Dictionary* 919 (2d ed. 1989); see also Webster's *Third New International Dictionary* 343 (1986) (first definition: "move while supporting (*as in a vehicle* or in one's hands or arms)"); *Random House Dictionary of the English Language Unabridged* 319 (2d ed. 1987) (first definition: "to take or support from one place to another; convey; transport").

The origin of the word "carries" explains why the first, or basic, meaning of the word "carry" includes conveyance in a vehicle. See *Barnhart Dictionary of Etymology* 146 (1988) (tracing the word from Latin "carum," which means "car" or "cart"); 2 *Oxford English Dictionary*, supra, at 919 (tracing the word from Old French "carier" and the late Latin "carricare," which meant to "convey in a car"); *Oxford Dictionary of English Etymology* 148 (C. Onions ed. 1966) (same); *Barnhart Dictionary of Etymology*, supra, at 143 (explaining that the term "car" has been used to refer to the automobile since 1896).

The greatest of writers have used the word with this meaning. See, *e.g., The King James Bible*, 2 Kings 9:28 ("[H]is servants carried him in a chariot to Jerusalem"); *id.,* Isaiah 30:6 ("[T]hey will carry their riches upon the shoulders of young asses"). Robinson Crusoe says, "[w]ith my boat, I carry'd away every Thing." D. Defoe, *Robinson Crusoe* 174 (J. Crowley ed. 1972). And the owners of Queequeg's ship, Melville writes, "had lent him a [wheelbarrow], in which to carry his heavy chest to his boarding-house." H. Melville, *Moby Dick* 43 (U. Chicago 1952). This Court, too, has spoken of the "carrying" of drugs in a car or in its "trunk." *California v. Acevedo*, 500 U. S. 565, 572–573 (1991); *Florida v. Jimeno*, 500 U. S. 248, 249 (1991).

These examples do not speak directly about carrying guns. But there is nothing linguistically special about the fact that weapons, rather than drugs, are being carried. Robinson Crusoe might have carried a gun in his boat; Queequeg might have borrowed a wheelbarrow in which to carry not a chest but a harpoon. And, to make certain that there is no special ordinary English restriction (unmentioned in dictionaries) upon the use of "carry" in respect to guns, we have surveyed modern press usage, albeit crudely, by searching computerized newspaper data bases—both the New York Times data base in Lexis/Nexis, and the "US News" data base in Westlaw. We looked for sentences in which the words "carry," "vehicle," and "weapon" (or variations thereof) all appear. We found thousands of such sentences, and random sampling suggests that many, perhaps more than one-third, are sentences used to convey the meaning at issue here, *i.e.*, the carrying of guns in a car.

The *New York Times*, for example, writes about "an ex-con" who "arrives home driving a stolen car and carrying a load of handguns," Mar. 21, 1992, section 1, p. 18, col. 1, and an "official peace officer who carries a shotgun in his boat," June 19, 1988, section 12WC, p. 2, col. 1; cf. *The New York Times Manual of Style and Usage, a Desk Book of Guidelines for Writers and Editors*, foreword (L. Jordan rev. ed. 1976) (restricting *Times* journalists and editors to the use of proper English). The *Boston Globe* refers to the arrest of a professional baseball player "for carrying a semi-loaded automatic weapon in his car." Dec. 10, 1994, p. 75, col. 5. The *Colorado Springs Gazette Telegraph* speaks of one "Russell" who "carries a gun hidden in his car." May 2, 1993, p. B1, col. 2. The *Arkansas Gazette* refers to a "house" that was "searched" in an effort to find "items that could be carried in a car, such as . . . guns." Mar. 10, 1991, p. A1, col. 2. The *San Diego Union-Tribune* asks, "What, do they carry guns aboard these boats now?" Feb. 18, 1992, p.D2, col. 5.

Now consider a different, somewhat special meaning of the word "carry"—a meaning upon which the linguistic arguments of petitioners and the dissent must rest. The *Oxford English Dictionary*'s twenty-sixth definition of "carry" is "bear, wear, hold up, or sustain, as one moves about; habitually to bear about with one." 2 *Oxford English Dictionary*, at 921. Webster's defines "carry" as "to move while supporting," not just in a vehicle, but also "in one's hands or arms." *Webster's Third New International Dictionary*, supra, at 343. And *Black's Law Dictionary* defines the entire phrase "carry arms or weapons" as

> "To wear, bear or carry them upon the person or in the clothing or in a pocket, for the purpose of use, or for the purpose of being armed and ready for offensive or defensive action in case of a conflict with another person." *Black's Law Dictionary* 214 (6th ed. 1990).

These special definitions, however, do not purport to *limit* the "carrying of arms" to the circumstances they describe. No one doubts that one who bears arms on his person "carries a weapon." But to say that is not to deny that one may also "carry a weapon" tied to the saddle of a horse or placed in a bag in a car.

Nor is there any linguistic reason to think that Congress intended to limit the word "carries" in the statute to any of these special definitions. To the contrary, all these special definitions embody a form of an important, but secondary, meaning of "carry," a meaning that suggests support rather than movement or transportation, as when, for example, a column "carries" the weight of an arch. 2 *Oxford English Dictionary*, at 919, 921. In this sense a gangster might "carry" a gun (in colloquial language, he might "pack a gun") even though he does not move from his chair. It is difficult to believe, however, that Congress intended to limit the statutory word to this definition—imposing special punishment upon the comatose gangster while ignoring drug lords who drive to a sale carrying an arsenal of weapons in their van.

We recognize, as the dissent emphasizes, that the word "carry" has other meanings as well. But those other meanings (*e. g.*, "carry all he knew," "carries no colours"), see *post*, at 143–144, are not relevant here. And the fact that speakers often do *not* add to the phrase "carry a gun" the words "in a car" is of no greater relevance here than the fact that millions of Americans did *not* see Muscarello carry a gun in his truck. The relevant linguistic facts are that the word "carry" in its ordinary sense includes carrying in a car and that the word, used in its ordinary sense, keeps the same meaning whether one carries a gun, a suitcase, or a banana.

Given the ordinary meaning of the word "carry," it is not surprising to find that the Federal Courts of Appeals have unanimously concluded that "carry" is not limited to the carrying of weapons directly on the person but can include their carriage in a car.

Questions/discussion

1   (a) Which (and what type of) sources did the court consult in establishing the meaning of *carry*?

     (b) What would the advantages and disadvantages have been of relying on dictionary meaning alone in considering a case such as this?

     (c) The court found that the word *carry* shares its etymology with the word *car*. From a linguistic perspective, should any significance be attributed to this finding in relation to the case?

     (d) Does it matter, for the purpose of the court's argument, that the Bible was not originally written in English?

2   The dissenting judges in the case cited other dictionaries, other Bible passages and other literature to support the defendant's position. Justice Ginsburg also pointed out that many English translations of the Bible do not use the word *carry* in the passages cited in the majority opinion.

     (a) Overall, do you think the sources and method adopted were appropriate and sufficient for the court's purpose? Do you see any danger in the adoption of such approaches by the court – by both the majority and dissenting judges?

     (b) Linguists interested in contributing to law are often warned off playing at being lawyers. Are there risks of the reverse happening: judges setting themselves up as if they were linguists?

     (c) How might a corpus linguist have tackled the task of establishing the relevant meaning of *carry* in this context?

BILINGUALISM AND JURY SERVICE

Units A10 and B10 are concerned with how law responds to linguistic diversity in society, at different levels and in different ways. Many of the issues that arise are contentious. In this final unit of the book, we broaden our discussion to consider a situation in which law faces a dilemma in adjusting its established practice to a language policy that applies not only to the legal system, but to all public services, reflecting a country's overall political orientation. Designating a language as an official language creates the expectation of a right. But does a defendant who enjoys that right have a related right to be tried before jurors who can understand just one, or more than one, official language?

Wales provides our case study. As preparation, consider the linguistic demographics of the country. In Wales, everyone speaks English; but in addition, 23 per cent of the Welsh population self-report that they speak Welsh, and among that section of the population 11 per cent say they speak it fluently (source: *The Welsh Language Use Survey 2013/14*). Welsh and English are both official languages of the country: the Welsh Language Act 1993 places Welsh on equal footing with English in Wales. As a result of this legislation, defendants enjoy a right to have their case heard in Welsh before a Welsh-speaking judge, if they request this. A more difficult question, however, is whether competence in Welsh should also be made a criterion of jury selection in trials where Welsh may be used. Public consultation on this issue took place in 2005. Our first extract, from a public consultation document, outlines some of the background to existing practice governing use of Welsh in criminal proceedings.

Republished from Office for Criminal Justice Reform (2005) 'The use of bilingual (English and Welsh-speaking) juries in certain criminal trials in Wales: a consultation paper', pp. 10–11.

> Following the 1993 Act, Welsh Language Schemes have been adopted by all the major players in the criminal justice system – the police, the Crown Prosecution Service, the Probation Service, the Home Office and Her Majesty's Courts Service. Arrangements made under these Schemes have facilitated the use of Welsh in all aspects of the criminal justice system and at all levels.
>
> However, the Juries Act 1974, which applies to both England and Wales, takes a different approach. It is a statutory requirement under this Act that jurors have sufficient understanding of English to act as a juror, whether in England or in Wales. In practice, potential jurors are released from their service if they indicate, or it becomes apparent that they do not have sufficient understanding of English to follow the case. There is no comparable requirement for jurors in trials in Wales to understand Welsh, even if a significant amount, or indeed most of the trial is conducted in Welsh. The relevant provision, in section 10 of the Juries Act, reads as follows:
>
> > (4) Where it appears to the appropriate officer, in the case of a person attending in pursuance of a summons under this Act, that on account of . . . insufficient

understanding of English there is doubt as to his capacity to act effectively as a juror, the person may be brought before the judge, who shall determine whether or not he should act as a juror and, if not, shall discharge the summons.

In cases where a substantial amount of Welsh is used in a trial in Wales, it is currently the practice to provide simultaneous professional interpretation for everyone in the courtroom. Thus if, for example, the defendant is giving evidence in Welsh and ten of the twelve jurors are only able to understand English, these jurors will wear headphones in the courtroom and will hear a simultaneous translation into English of the defendant's evidence. If witnesses are giving evidence in Welsh and the defendant is only able to understand English, the defendant and such of the jurors as are unable to understand Welsh will hear the evidence interpreted into English via headphones.

With this background to the debate in place, consider some of the arguments for bilingual juries listed slightly later in the same document (pp. 11–12):

It has been suggested that bilingual juries might represent a threat to individuals' rights in areas of Wales where English is the main or only language. For example, the question has been posed whether a monoglot English speaking victim would feel comfortable with the idea of a Welsh-speaking defendant making an application for the case to be heard before a bilingual jury made up entirely of Welsh speakers. However, a Welsh-speaking victim may be equally insecure when faced with the prospect of a monoglot English speaking defendant presenting the case before a jury composed entirely of English speakers.
    Furthermore, without bilingual juries, Welsh speakers who give evidence in Welsh courts in their own language, a language which has equal legal status with English, will continue to be denied the knowledge that it has been understood at first hand by the jury. Bilingual juries would allow victims, witnesses and defendants to give evidence in English or Welsh and know that it was being understood at first hand. It would avoid the oddity that at present, different members of the jury may hear different versions of the same evidence, one the original Welsh and another the translated English version (or vice versa). It could be argued that allowing Welsh-speaking jurors to hear evidence given in Welsh would advance the rights of Welsh speakers whilst not affecting the rights of monoglot English speakers whose evidence, given in English, would also be understood by the jury.

A proposal to adopt bilingual juries in Wales was tabled in 2006 but rejected by the UK government in 2010. Our third extract is taken from a response by the Ministry of Justice to the proposal.
    Republished from Office for Criminal Justice Reform (2010) 'The use of bilingual (English and Welsh-speaking) juries in certain criminal trials in Wales: response to consultation', pp. 17–19.

Juries are selected at random from the whole community. Much of the authority of, and widespread public confidence in, the jury system derives from its socially inclusive nature. Members of the public are not excluded from jury service by their sex, wealth, class, education or any other irrelevant factor. Juries are made up of ordinary people. Random selection makes the jury a representative of society as a whole. It helps to give the jury its independence and impartiality, which are vital components of a fair trial and hence of justice itself.

There is a linkage between the ever greater element of randomness in the selection of juries and increasing democracy. Over the centuries, the historical direction has been towards greater social inclusiveness in jury selection. For example, the property qualification for jury service was abolished a long time ago and women are no longer excluded from jury service as they once were. These developments have run hand in hand with the increasing long-term democratisation of society.

The long term trend towards greater random selection of juries has been strengthened still further in recent years. The Criminal Justice Act 2003, brought forward by this Government, removed virtually all of the then remaining grounds for exclusion from jury service (the small number of exceptions being, for example, people with certain criminal records).

The main objection to bilingual juries has always been their interference with this key principle of random selection. If bilingual juries were proceeded with in Wales, they would probably only be used in a small minority of trials. Where they were used, however, they would be limited to the minority of people who can speak Welsh as well as English. On the face of it, bilingual juries would run directly counter not only to the long term historical development in favour of greater social inclusiveness in jury selection, but also to recent developments championed by the present Government.

Bilingual juries in Wales would involve a significant interference with the random selection principle. According to 2001 census results, 21% of people in Wales said they could speak Welsh (of whatever level or usage). This would amount to the exclusion from the jury, in every case involving a bilingual jury, of about four fifths of the population of Wales.

Furthermore, research conducted as part of the Ministry of Justice's 2007 report into "Diversity and Fairness in the Jury System" found that a far larger percentage of the Welsh population declared they were fluent in Welsh in the 2001 census than in a summoning survey conducted as part of the research. The census shows that 16.5% of the population in Wales speaks, reads and writes Welsh. This was not reflected in the proportion of those summoned for jury service for Welsh courts who declared that they were fluent in Welsh (a much lower figure of 6.4%). On the basis of this research, where bilingual juries were used, they would exclude well over nine tenths of the population of Wales. [. . .]

Two main arguments were provided as to why the principle of random selection should be overridden in the case of bilingual juries. The first was that the present legal prohibition on selecting a bilingual jury in Wales was inconsistent with legislation which gives participants in trials in Wales the right to use Welsh in court. The second was that bilingual juries would enable best evidence to be given, in that a witness or other speaker using Welsh or English would always be understood directly by the jury, rather than through an interpreter.

With regard to the first argument, reference to the current legal status of the Welsh language is not persuasive. There is also legislation on jury selection which makes it clear that jury selection procedures cannot be manipulated to generate a jury composed of members of any particular social group, including Welsh speakers. Indeed, it is noticeable that the juries legislation, the Juries Act 1974, was not amended in consequence of the enactment of the Welsh Language Act 1993.

Turning to the question of best evidence, it is a moot point whether evidence is best understood directly, rather than through a professional simultaneous interpreter, where two languages are in use during a trial. Certainly, one would have to have a very high level of understanding of both languages – in effect, perfect bilingualism – to be able to understand evidence given in both languages better than one would be able to understand one's weaker language through a professional interpreter.

It is questionable how many Welsh and English speakers would have this high degree of bilingualism (having regard to the statistical information mentioned above). Indeed, a bilingual juror could feel obliged to listen without using the interpreter and consequently may understand less well than through an interpreter, increasing the risk of miscarriages of justice. The evidential argument has not been made out.

Notes

'*Over the centuries, the historical direction has been towards greater social inclusiveness in jury selection*': In medieval England, jurors were drawn from privileged classes (people of rank, landowners, etc.) and were exclusively male. It was only in the twentieth century that trial by superiors gradually became trial by peers, as eligibility for jury service was extended to all adults aged 18–70. Today, eligibility for jury service is often seen as a marker of citizenship, although exclusion or disqualification criteria apply, varying between jurisdictions.

Questions/discussion

1   Summarise the major arguments presented in the extracts for and against the bilingual jury proposal.

2   One of the issues debated was whether it is desirable for jurors to hear evidence directly.

    (a) Do you consider not being able to be understood directly by the jury, but instead via simultaneous interpretation through headphones, to be no disadvantage? A minor disadvantage? A significant disadvantage?

    (b) On what basis does the 2010 report argue that a Welsh defendant may not be disadvantaged but better off having an interpreter than being heard directly?

3   Random selection is widely considered a means for ensuring representativeness. Although this method of selection is objective, and so may be viewed as fair, it can mean that minority groups in a community are tried by dominant linguistic groups. In the case of Wales, this means that minority Welsh speakers are often tried before English-speaking monolingual jurors.

    (a) Do you think of such a situation as 'fair'?

    (b) Would exclusion of non-Welsh speakers in trials where Welsh may be used compromise the independence and impartiality of the jury?

4   There is divergence in how jurisdictions handle this issue. Analogously with the decision on Welsh, the Irish Supreme Court declined a request for Irish-speaking or bilingual juries. By contrast, in Canada there is a right to be tried by a judge or

judge and jury who all speak the official language of the accused (i.e. English or French). Do decisions on the language requirement for jurors significantly affect the meaning of *peers* in the concept of trial by peers? Discuss the meaning of *peers* in this context.

FURTHER READING AND RESOURCES

The suggestions that follow for further reading should be read along with references in individual units and the consolidated References list. It would be impossible to include all important works here; instead, our aim is simply to launch further reading in relation to each thread by drawing attention to works that are likely to be easily accessible (mostly books) and which are in many cases introductory (but also have useful bibliographies to stimulate further possibilities). Since reading about language and law presents extra challenges associated with interdisciplinary enquiry, we also offer suggestions below for general resources.

Thread 1: legal language

Most writers about language and law agree that Mellinkoff (1963) put issues about what legal language is and whether it requires reform on the academic agenda. A more recent and accessible (but less detailed) account is Tiersma (1999), which can be read in summary versions both in print and online, including Tiersma (2000, 2008). The most widely cited stylistic study of legal documents remains Crystal and Davy (1969), though Crystal also touches on legal language interestingly in other works, including edited reference works such as Crystal (2010). General accounts of legal language need to be read with some degree of familiarity with descriptive linguistic work on grammatical structure and language varieties; many suitable introductions are available and are not listed here. If you are a non-native speaker of English, you may also benefit from the combined introduction to English proficiency and legal institutions in Riley and Sours (2014). Academic treatments of legal language in ESP (English for specific purposes) are analysed in Northcott (2013). Debates and proposals about reform of legal language are best followed online, starting with publications by international associations concerned with reform of legal language, including the Plain English Campaign and Clarity (the latter has an online archive of issues of *The Clarity Journal*), and reading publicly available documents about relevant areas of legal policy (e.g. by the UK Law Commission or similar bodies in other jurisdictions). A less direct but also interesting follow-up suggestion for this thread is to research language use and variation in fictional and film representations of law.

Thread 2: history and functions

General histories of English, especially ones that relate changes in the language to social institutions, provide essential background. A history of English law is also likely to be useful; selective reading of Baker (2002) is an obvious choice. Mellinkoff (1963) is essential for the specific history of legal language, with particular emphasis on the development of vocabulary. More specialised studies include Danet's (1980) review of scholarship on how language contributes to legal processes, and Danet and Bogoch (1992) on the transition from orality to literacy in law (a topic recently examined in detail from the perspective of legal publishing in Harvey 2015).

Thread 3: discourse types

Two contrasting routes present themselves into further reading on this topic. One is to read legal exposition on specific legal genres (e.g. in Butt 2013) or practical guidance on how language should be used in such genres (e.g. in Haigh 2015), then explore wider linguistic issues related to discourse types in non-legal fields, in works such as Swales (1990) or Biber and Conrad (2009). The other is to start with general works on genre, a topic investigated across many areas of discourse, then read into legal works in particular for exemplification and specific problems and issues. Intersection between the two approaches is glimpsed in Bhatia (1993).

Thread 4: courtroom discourse

Two starting points for this topic, historically, are Danet and Kermish (1978) and Atkinson and Drew (1979); the latter can be followed up in more recent studies using conversation analysis as a method. Matoesian (1993) provides detailed analysis in relation to rape trials; and O'Barr and Conley (1990) report findings linking features of courtroom discourse to wider social patterns and inequality. An ambitious and thought-provoking study of the complexity of courtroom speech events is Heffer (2005), which contains a useful list of further reading.

Thread 5: advocacy

Many works on legal advocacy are either anthologies of extracts from great legal speeches or how-to guides by lawyers or law teachers (e.g. Stone 2009; McPeake 2014). Du Cann (1993) and Morley (2009) provide the most successful combinations of the two approaches. More scholarly studies of trial techniques include Brennan (1994, 1995), Evans (1998), Mauet (2002), Burns (2004) and Bradshaw (2011). Specialised reading needs to be combined, however, with wider context: in this case, primary readings in rhetoric (e.g. Aristotle's *The Art of Rhetoric*) or on the history of and techniques involved in rhetoric (Vickers 2002). A landmark study bringing together law, rhetoric and hermeneutics is Goodrich (1986). Transcripts of entire legal cases, and a far larger number of selected speeches, can be readily found online (e.g. the closing argument we discuss that was delivered by defence counsel Clarence Darrow in the 1924 US case of *State of Illinois v. Nathan Leopold & Richard Loeb* can be read online at: http://law2.umkc.edu/faculty/projects/ftrials/leoploeb/darrowclosing.html).

Thread 6: legal meaning

There is a huge literature on legal interpretation, which combines essential learning for law students (e.g. Manchester and Salter 2011) with theoretical analysis (Hart 1994 [1961]; Scalia 1997; Barak 2005; Greenawalt 2012; Scalia and Garner 2012). Approaches vary between legal systems, and should be read with that in mind. The two most useful starting points in relation to this thread are Solan (2010) and Hutton (2014); advanced linguistic arguments can be found in Carston (2011), and philosophical analysis in the contributions to Marmor and Soames (2011).

Thread 7: speech acts

Reading into the literature on speech acts used in legal settings requires basic familiarity with speech acts gained from introductory guides to pragmatics. The two essential primary references here are Austin (1962) and Searle (1969). For related topics, familiarity with concepts in Gricean approaches to indirect meaning (Grice 1989) is recommended; see Durant and Leung (2016) for a summary in relation to law. The most referred to study of legal speech acts is Kurzon (1986), though this work now seems dated. An introduction to how speech act analysis relates to freedom of expression (and to US First Amendment jurisprudence) is Greenawalt (1989). Greenawalt's more recent publications also examine pragmatic issues in legal contexts: offensiveness (Greenawalt 1995) and legal interpretation (Greenawalt 2010, 2012). On the wider topic of performatives, see MacKinnon (1993) and Butler (1997) for arguments regarding pornography. Danet (1997) opened up lines of simultaneously historical and predictive research into legal performatives that have yet to be improved on. Wider discussion of the relation between performative utterances and legal rules can be found in Twining and Miers (2010).

Thread 8: language as regulated content

Some topics in this area can be approached by highlighting social (especially regulatory) issues implied in stylistic work on adverts (e.g. Geis 1982; Myers 1994, 1998; Preston 1994). Advertising should, however, be seen as one topic among others, including defamation and offensive language, that are analysed in media law (for a legal overview, see Barendt *et al.* 2014). A work that brings together linguistic and legal approaches is Durant (2010a). In order to locate questions in this area in their social contexts, it can also be helpful to read into the wider topic of freedom of expression. Warburton (2009) is a very short introduction; Kalven (1988) traces legal deliberations over problems of language interpretation in US First Amendment law; and Barendt (2005) provides a comprehensive analysis of free speech from a political and philosophical, as well as legal, perspective.

Thread 9: forensic evidence

The best way to stay abreast of current work in the specialised field of forensic linguistics is to consult the *International Journal of Speech, Language and the Law* (the official publication of IAFL, the International Association of Forensic Linguists). Further material can be found on the Association's website. Authoritative overviews include Coulthard and Johnson (2007) and Gibbons and Turrell (2008); collections of essays on particular topics and cases include Gibbons (2003) and Cotterill (2004). Exposition of expert evidence given in cases by a pioneer in the field can be found in Shuy (1993, 2003, 2010, 2012). However, 'language and law', as we explore it in this book, is a wider field than giving expert evidence in legal cases. Useful readings on the larger perspective include the analyses presented in Schane (2006), the critical account developed in Conley and O'Barr (2005) and a contrasting celebration in Berman (2013). A number of substantial edited collections giving a sense of the scope and directions of this rapidly expanding field are also notable: Schauer (1993), Freeman and Smith (2011), Solan and Tiersma (2012) and Visconti (forthcoming).

Thread 10: multilingual law

Most works on this topic are concerned with specific aspects of bilingual or multilingual practice. However, legal interpretation in bilingual and multilingual jurisdictions has received book-length scholarly treatment in Tabory (1980), Beaupré (1986) and Bastarache *et al.* (2008), with Tabory focusing on the international law context and the other works on the Canadian bijural and bilingual legal system. Šarčević (1997, 2012) discusses multilingual legal translation in the EU; see also discussion of institutional practices in the EU language regime in McAuliffe (2012). Issues arising in the bilingual courtroom are explored in Berk-Seligson (2002 [1990]), Powell (2008) and Ng (2009). Philosophical and political analyses of minority language rights are offered in Kymlicka and Patten (2003) and Pupavac (2012). A combined analysis of theoretical and practical issues in legal multilingualism, including a global review of current practice, is presented in Leung (2016).

Additional resources

Alongside further reading, what will make studying in this area satisfying is if you also access extra data to investigate, including examples of sources of law, law reports, legal blogs and other material. A massive amount of such material is freely available online; the following suggestions are merely places to start:

1   Constitutions of the legal systems of different countries (e.g. the US Constitution, about which there is a great deal of historical, textual and interpretive material available; or the constitutions of other countries, such as India). Search for the database 'Oxford Constitutions of the World'; then type in a jurisdiction/country.
2   International treaties and conventions (ITCs), including: European Union treaties such as TEU, TFEU (http://eur-lex.europa.eu/; this site also contains European legislation and case law); the United Nations treaty collection (https://treaties.un.org/); the European Convention on Human Rights; the Berne Convention, Paris Convention, and many others that will be relevant to topics discussed in the book.
3   National legislation, preferably in more than one jurisdiction (e.g. UK law, Australian law, Hong Kong basic law, legislation in your own country). As an example, UK databases that will help you do this include: www.legislation.gov.uk; Westlaw (legislation, case law and journal article database – but a subscription is required); Lexis Library (the same range, plus official forms such as Land Registry forms – subscription also required); British and Irish Legal Information Institute: www.bailii.org/ (legislation and cases, plus links to similar sites in many other jurisdictions).
4   Law reports (from different courts in national and international court hierarchies, presented in different degrees of detail and ranging from official transcripts to

newspaper digests). Search via: Westlaw, LexisNexis, Bailli, Lex-Europa, HK Legal Information Institute, etc. See also cases of the International Criminal Court (www.icc-cpi.int/en_menus/icc/Pages/default.aspx); judgments of the European Court of Human Rights (www.echr.coe.int/Pages/home.aspx?p=home). Don't only look for major, international cases; also look for local, apparently minor actions where these are reported (and compare official law reports with styles of journal and newspaper reporting of the same case).

5 Complaint adjudications by extrajudicial regulatory bodies (e.g. bodies governing advertising or press standards, trade competition and monopolies). A good UK example is the bulletin of weekly adjudications issued by the Advertising Standards Authority (www.asa.org.uk), but there are many others.

6 Legal blogs and news feeds, which exist in many fields. Two good UK/European examples are the Inforrm's Blog (the International Forum for Responsible Media) and, related to content introduced in Thread 8, the IPKAT: an entertaining but massively informative digest of IP law cases and issues (http://ipkitten.blogspot.co.uk/).

7 You can also enrich your reading of this book by visiting courts to listen. Arrangements for attending short periods of a court case vary, but it is usually possible to enter and leave without difficulty. If you are able to attend two different courts, pick courts that occupy different places in the legal hierarchy. In general, the higher up in a court hierarchy, the more 'legal discussion' you will hear; lower down in the court hierarchy, you will hear more procedural discourse used in processing people and cases. Remember to observe court rules where stated.

REFERENCES

Adler, J. (2007) *Constitutional and Administrative Law*, 6th edn, Basingstoke: Palgrave.

Atkinson, J. and Drew, P. (1979) *Order in Court: The Organisation of Verbal Interaction in Judicial Settings*, London/Basingstoke: Macmillan.

Austin, J. (1962) *How to Do Things with Words*, Oxford: Clarendon Press.

Baaij, C. (2012) 'Fifty years of multilingual interpretation in the European Union', in P. Tiersma and L. Solan (eds), *The Oxford Handbook of Language and Law*, Oxford: Oxford University Press, pp. 217–31.

Baker, J. (2002) *An Introduction to English Legal History*, Oxford: Oxford University Press.

Barak, A. (2005) *Purposive Interpretation in Law*, Princeton, NJ: Princeton University Press.

Barendt, E. (2005) *Freedom of Speech*, 2nd edn, Oxford: Oxford University Press.

Barendt, E., Hitchens, L., Crauford-Smith, R. and Bosland, J. (2014) *Media Law: Text, Cases and Materials*, 2nd edn, Harlow: Pearson.

Bastarache, M., Metallic, N., Morris, R. and Essert, C. (2008) *The Law of Bilingual Interpretation*, LexisNexis.

Beaupré, M. (1986) *Interpreting Bilingual Legislation*, 2nd edn, Toronto: Carswell.

Bennion, F. (2001) *Understanding Common Law Legislation: Drafting and Interpretation*, Oxford: Oxford University Press.

Bentham, J. (1838–1843) *The Works of Jeremy Bentham*, 11 vols, edited by J. Bowring, Edinburgh: William Tait.

Berg, D. (2005) 'The trial lawyer', *Litigation*, 31(4): 8–15.

Berk-Seligson, S. (2002) *The Bilingual Courtroom: Court Interpreters in the Judicial Process*, 2nd edn, Chicago, IL/London: University of Chicago Press.

Berman, H. (2013) *Law and Language: Effective Symbols of Community*, Cambridge: Cambridge University Press.

Beyerstein, B. and Beyerstein, D. (1992) *The Write Stuff: Evaluations of Graphology – The Study of Handwriting Analysis*, Buffalo, NY: Prometheus Books.

Bhatia, V. (1993) *Analysing Genre: Language Use in Professional Settings*, London: Longman.

Biber, D. and Conrad, S. (2009) *Register, Genre, and Style*, Cambridge: Cambridge University Press.

Bourdieu, P. (1992) *Language and Symbolic Power*, Oxford: Polity.

Bradshaw, B. (2011) *The Science of Persuasion: A Litigator's Guide to Juror Decision-Making*, Chicago, IL: American Bar Association.

Brennan, M. (1994) 'The battle for credibility: themes in the cross examination of child victim witnesses', *International Journal for the Semiotics of Law*, 7(1): 51–73.

Brennan, M. (1995) 'The discourse of denial: cross-examining child victim witnesses', *Journal of Pragmatics*, 23: 71–91.

Brennan, M. and Brown, R. (1997) *Equality before the Law: Deaf People's Access to Justice*, Durham: Deaf Studies Research Unit, University of Durham.

Burgoon, J. K. and Bacue, A. (2003) 'Nonverbal communication skills', in B. R. Burleson and J. O. Greene (eds), *Handbook of Communication and Social Interaction Skills*, Mahwah, NJ: Erlbaum, pp. 179–219.

Burke, E. (1975 [1788]) 'Speech in Opening the Impeachment of Warren Hastings'. In B. Harris (ed.) *Edmund Burke on Government, Politics and Society*, Brighton: Harvester Press, pp. 263–76.

Burns, R. P. (2004) 'Rhetoric in the law', in W. Jost and W. Olmsted (eds), *A Companion to Rhetoric and Rhetorical Criticism*, Malden, MA: Blackwell, pp. 442–56.

Butler, J. (1997) *Excitable Speech: The Politics of the Performative*, London: Routledge.

Butt, P. (2013) *Modern Legal Drafting: A Guide to Using Clearer Language*, 3rd edn, Cambridge: Cambridge University Press.

Butters, R. R. (2008) 'Trademarks and other proprietary terms', in J. Gibbons and M. Turell (eds), *Dimensions of Forensic Linguistics*, Amsterdam: John Benjamins, pp. 231–48.

Carston, R. (2011) 'Legal texts and canons of construction: a view from current pragmatic theory', in M. Freeman and F. Smith (eds), *Law and Language: Current Legal Issues 2011*, Vol. 15, Oxford: Oxford University Press, pp. 8–33.

Charrow, R. P. and Charrow, V. R. (1979) 'Making legal language understandable: a psycholinguistic study of jury instructions', *Columbia Law Review*, 79(7): 1306–74.

Cialdini, R. B. (2008) *Influence: Science and Practice*, 5th edn, Boston, MA: Allyn & Bacon.

Clanchy, M. (1993) *From Memory to Written Record*, Oxford: Blackwell.

Conley, J. M. and O'Barr, W. M. (2005) *Just Words: Law, Language and Power*, 2nd edn, Chicago, IL: University of Chicago Press.

Constable, M. (1998) 'Reflections on law as a profession of words', in B. Garth and A. Sarat (eds), *Justice and Power in Sociolegal Research*, Evanston, IL: Northwestern University Press, pp. 19–35, available at: www.mcgill.ca/files/crclaw-discourse/Constable.pdf (accessed 20 November 2015).

Cooke, M. (1995) 'Aboriginal evidence in the cross-cultural courtroom', in D. Eades (ed.), *Language in Evidence: Issues Confronting Aboriginal and Multicultural Australia*, Sydney, NSW: University of New South Wales Press, pp. 55–96.

Cotterill, J. (ed.) (2004) *Language in the Legal Process*, Basingstoke: Palgrave.

Coulthard, M. (2002) 'Whose voice is it? Invented and concealed dialogue in written records of verbal evidence produced by the police', in J. Cotterill (ed.), *Language in the Legal Process*, London: Palgrave Macmillan, pp. 19–34.

Coulthard, M. and Johnson, A. (2007) *An Introduction to Forensic Linguistics: Language in Evidence*, London: Routledge.

Croft, W. and Cruse, D. (2004) *Cognitive Linguistics*, Cambridge: Cambridge University Press.

Crystal, D. (2008) *A Concise Dictionary of Linguistics and Phonetics*, 6th edn, London: Longman.

Crystal, D. (2010) *The Cambridge Encyclopedia of the English Language*, 2nd edn, Cambridge: Cambridge University Press.

Crystal, D. and Davy, D. (1969) *Investigating English Style*, London: Longman.

Cunningham, C. D., Levi, J. N., Green, G. M. and Kaplan, J. P. (1994) 'Plain meaning and hard cases (review of Solan, 1993)', *Yale Law Journal*, 103: 1561–625.

Danet, B. (1980) 'Language in the legal process', *Law & Society Review*, 14: 445–564.

Danet, B. (1997) 'Speech, writing and performativity: an evolutionary view of the history of constitutive ritual', in B.-L. Gunnarsson, P. Linell and B. Nordberg (eds), *The Construction of Professional Discourse*, London: Longman, pp. 13–41.

Danet, B. and Bogoch, B. (1992) 'From oral ceremony to written document: the transitional language of Anglo-Saxon wills', *Language and Communication*, 12(2): 95–122.

Danet, B. and Kermish, N. (1978) 'Courtroom questioning: a sociolinguistic perspective', in L. Massery II (ed.), *Psychology and Persuasion in Advocacy*, Association of Trial Lawyers of America, pp. 413–41.

Davis, J. (2005) 'Locating the average consumer: his judicial origins, intellectual influences and current role in European trade mark law', *Intellectual Property Quarterly*, 2: 183–203.

Du Cann, R. (1993) *The Art of the Advocate*, revised edn, Harmondsworth: Penguin.

Dumas, B. K. (2002) 'Reasonable doubt about reasonable doubt: assessing jury instruction adequacy in a capital case', in J. Cotterill (ed.), *Language in the Legal Process*, London: Palgrave Macmillan, pp. 246–59.

Dunstan, R. (1980) 'Contexts for coercion: analysing properties of courtroom "questions"', *British Journal of Law and Society*, 7: 61–77.

Durant, A. (2010a) *Meaning in the Media: Discourse, Controversy and Debate*, Cambridge: Cambridge University Press.

Durant, A. (2010b) 'How does "substantial similarity of expression" in infringement actions look from a linguistic point of view?', in L. Bently, J. Davis and J. Ginsburg (eds), *Copyright and Piracy: An Interdisciplinary Critique*, Cambridge: Cambridge University Press, pp. 147–93.

Durant, A. (2012) 'Reading cases in interdisciplinary studies of law and literature', in M. Wan (ed.), *The Legal Case: Crosscurrents between Law and the Humanities*, London: Routledge, pp. 11–28.

Durant, A. and Leung, H. C. (in press) 'Pragmatics in legal interpretation', in A. Barron, P. Grundy and Y. Gu (eds), *The Routledge Handbook of Pragmatics*, London: Routledge.

Eades, D. (2002) '"Evidence given in unequivocal terms": gaining consent of Aboriginal young people in court', in J. Cotterill (ed.), *Language in the Legal Process*, London: Palgrave Macmillan, pp. 162–79.

Eades, D. (2003) 'Participation of second language and second dialect speakers in the legal system', *Annual Review of Applied Linguistics*, 23: 113–33.

Eades, D. (2005) 'Applied linguistics and language analysis in asylum seeker cases', *Applied Linguistics*, 26(4): 503–26.

Eades, D. (2010) *Sociolinguistics and the Legal Process*, London: Multilingual Matters.

Erickson, B., Lind, E. A., Johnson, B. C. and O'Barr, W. M. (1978) 'Speech style and impression formation in a court setting: the effects of "powerful" and "powerless" speech', *Journal of Experimental Social Psychology*, 14(3): 266–79.

Evans, K. (1998) *The Language of Advocacy*, London: Blackstone Press.

Ewing, C. P. and McCann, J. T. (2006) *Minds on Trial: Great Cases in Law and Psychology*, New York: Oxford University Press.

Ferguson, R. A. (1990) 'The rhetorics of the judicial opinion: the judicial opinion as literary genre', *Yale Journal of Law and the Humanities*, 2(1): 201–19.

Finch, E. and Fafinski, S. (2011) *Legal Skills*, 3rd edn, Oxford: Oxford University Press.

Findley, J. D. and Sales, B. D. (2012) *The Science of Attorney Advocacy: How Courtroom Behaviour Affects Jury Decision Making*, Washington, DC: American Psychological Association.

Foulkes, P. and French, P. (2012) 'Forensic speaker comparison: a linguistic-acoustic perspective', in L. M. Solan and P. M. Tiersma (eds), *The Oxford Handbook of Language and Law*, Oxford: Oxford University Press, pp. 557–72.

Freeman, M. and Smith, F. (eds) (2011) *Law and Language: Current Legal Issues 2011*, Oxford: Oxford University Press.

Frumkin, L. (2007) 'Influences of accent and ethnic background on perceptions of eyewitness testimony', *Psychology, Crime & Law*, 13(3): 317–31.

Fuller, J. (2009) 'Hearing between the lines: style switching in a courtroom setting', *Pragmatics*, 3(1): 29–43.

Gal, S. and Irvine, J. (1995) 'The boundaries of languages and disciplines: how ideologies construct difference', *Social Research*, 62(4): 967–1001.

Geis, M. (1982) *The Language of Television Advertising*, New York: Academic Press.

Gibbons, J. (2003) *Forensic Linguistics: An Introduction to Language in the Justice System*, Oxford/Malden, MA: Blackwell.

Gibbons, J. and Turrell, M. (2008) *Dimensions of Forensic Linguistics*, Amsterdam: John Benjamins.

Giles, H. (1970) 'Evaluative reactions to accents', *Educational Review*, 22(3): 211–27.

Giles, H. and Coupland, N. (1991) *Language, Contexts and Consequences*, Milton Keynes: Open University Press.

Goffman, E. (1981) *Forms of Talk*, Oxford: Oxford University Press.

Goodrich, P. (1986) *Reading the Law: A Critical Introduction to Legal Method and Techniques*, Oxford: Blackwell.

Greenawalt, K. (1989) *Speech, Crime and the Uses of Language*, Oxford: Oxford University Press.

Greenawalt, K. (1995) *Fighting Words: Individuals, Communities, and Liberties of Speech*, Princeton, NJ: Princeton University Press.

Greenawalt, K. (2010) *Legal Interpretation: Perspectives from Other Disciplines and Private Texts*, New York: Oxford University Press.

Greenawalt, K. (2012) *Statutory and Common Law Interpretation*, New York: Oxford University Press.

Greenberg, M. (2011) 'Legislation is communication? Legal interpretation and the study of linguistic communication', in A. Marmor and S. Soames (eds), *Philosophical Foundations of Language in the Law*, Oxford: Oxford University Press, pp. 217–57.

Grice, H. P. (1989) *Studies in the Way of Words*, Cambridge, MA: Harvard University Press.

Haigh, R. (2015) *Legal English*, 3rd edn, London: Routledge.

Halliday, M. (2004) *An Introduction to Functional Grammar*, London: Hodder Arnold.

Halliday, M. and Hasan, R. (1976) *Cohesion in English*, London: Longman.

Harris, B. (1998) *The Literature of the Law: A Thoughtful Entertainment for Lawyers and Others*, London: Blackstone Press.

Hart, H. L. A. (1994 [1961]) *The Concept of Law*, 2nd edn, Oxford: Clarendon.

Harvey, D. (2015) *The Law Emprynted and Englysshed: The Printing Press as an Agent of Change in Law and Legal Culture 1475–1642*, London: Hart.

Hayek, F. (1978) *Law, Legislation and Liberty, Volume 1: Rules and Order*, Chicago, IL: University of Chicago Press.

Heffer, C. (2005) *The Language of Jury Trial: A Corpus-Aided Analysis of Legal-Lay Discourse*, Basingstoke: Palgrave.

Heffer, C. (2008) 'The language and communication of jury instruction', in J. Gibbons and M. T. Turell (eds), *Dimensions of Forensic Linguistics*, Amsterdam: John Benjamins, pp. 47–66.

Heller, K. J. (2006) 'The cognitive psychology of circumstantial evidence', *Michigan Law Review*, 105: 241–306.

Hirst, P. (1979) *On Law and Ideology*, Basingstoke: Macmillan.

Hobbes, T. (2008 [1651]) *Leviathan*, edited by J. C. A. Gaskin, Oxford: Oxford University Press.

Hutchby, I. and Wooffitt, R. (2008) *Conversation Analysis*, Cambridge: Polity.

Hutton, C. (2014) *Word Meaning and Legal Interpretation: An Introductory Guide*, Basingstoke: Palgrave.

Jakobson, R. (1960) 'Closing statement: linguistics and poetics', in T. Sebeok (ed.), *Style in Language*, Cambridge, MA: MIT Press, pp. 350–77.

Kalven, H., Jr (1988) *A Worthy Tradition: Freedom of Speech in America*, New York: Harper & Row.

Katz, J. and Fodor, J. (1963) 'The structure of a semantic theory', *Language*, 39: 170–210.

Kurzon, D. (1986) *It is Hereby Performed: Explorations in Legal Speech Acts*, Amsterdam/Philadelphia, PA: John Benjamins.

Kymlicka, W. and Patten, A. (2003) *Language Rights and Political Theory*, Oxford: Oxford University Press.

Leech, G. (1966) *English in Advertising: A Linguistic Study of Advertising in Great Britain*, London: Longman.

Lerm, H. (1997) 'Language manipulation in court cross-examination: "how powerful is thy sword"', in K. Müller and S. Newman (eds), *Language in Court*, Port Elizabeth, South Africa: Vista University, pp. 167–81.

Leung, E. (2008) 'Interpreting for the minority, interpreting for the power', in J. Gibbons and M. T. Turell (eds), *Dimensions of Forensic Linguistics*, Amsterdam: John Benjamins, pp. 197–211.

Leung, H. C. (2012) 'Statutory interpretation in multilingual jurisdictions: typology and trends', *Journal of Multilingual and Multicultural Development*, 33(5): 481–95.

Leung, H. C. (2015) 'Lay litigation behaviour in postcolonial Hong Kong courtrooms', *Language and Law/Linguagem e Direito*, 2(1): 32–52.

Leung, H. C. (2016) *Multilingual Legal Order*, New York: Oxford University Press.

Levi, J. (1994) 'Language as evidence: the linguist as expert in North American courts', *Forensic Linguistics*, 1: 1–26.

Levinson, S. (1983) *Pragmatics*, Cambridge: Cambridge University Press.

Levinson, S. (1988) 'Putting linguistics on a proper footing: explorations in Goffman's participation framework', in P. Drew and A. Wootton (eds), *Goffman: Exploring the Interaction Order*, Oxford: Polity Press, pp. 161–227.

Liang, Z. (1989) 'Explicating "law": a comparative perspective of Chinese and Western legal culture', *Journal of Chinese Law*, 3: 55–91.

Lidsky, L. B. (2000) 'Silencing John Doe: defamation and discourse in cyberspace', *Duke Law Journal*, 49(4): 855–945.

Love, H. (2002) *Attributing Authorship: An Introduction*, Cambridge: Cambridge University Press.

MacKinnon, C. (1993) *Only Words*, Cambridge, MA: Harvard University Press.

Maley, Y. and Fahey, R. (1991) 'Presenting the evidence: constructions of reality in court', *International Journal for the Semiotics of Law*, 4(10): 3–17.

Manchester, C. and Salter, D. (2011) *Manchester and Salter on Exploring the Law: The Dynamics of Precedent and Statutory Interpretation*, 4th edn, London: Sweet & Maxwell.

Marmor, A. (2008) 'The pragmatics of legal language', *Ratio Juris*, 21(4): 423–52.

Marmor, A. and Soames, S. (eds) (2011) *Philosophical Foundations of Language in the Law*, Oxford: Oxford University Press.

Matoesian, G. M. (1993) *Reproducing Rape: Domination through Talk in the Courtroom*, Chicago, IL: University of Chicago Press.

Mauet, T. A. (2002) *Trial Techniques*, 6th edn, New York: Aspen.

McAuliffe, K. (2012) 'Language and law in the European Union: the multilingual jurisprudence of the ECJ', in P. M. Tiersma and L. M. Solan (eds), *The Oxford Handbook of Language and Law*, Oxford: Oxford University Press, pp. 200–16.

McMenamin, G. (1993) *Forensic Stylistics*, Amsterdam: Elsevier.

McPeake, R. (2014) *Advocacy*, 17th edn, Oxford: Oxford University Press.

McQuail, D. and Windahl, S. (1993) *Communication Models for the Study of Mass Communications*, 2nd edn, London: Longman.

Mellinkoff, D. (1963) *The Language of the Law*, Eugene, OR: Resource Publications.

Mertz, E. (2007) *The Language of Law School: Learning to 'Think Like a Lawyer'*, New York: Oxford University Press.

Monaghan, N. (2015) *Law of Evidence*, Cambridge: Cambridge University Press.

Morley, I. (2009) *The Devil's Advocate*, London: Sweet & Maxwell.

Myers, G. (1994) *Words in Ads*, London: Edward Arnold.

Myers, G. (1998) *Ad Worlds*, London: Edward Arnold.

Ng, K. H. (2009) *The Common Law in Two Voices*, Palo Alto, CA: Stanford University Press.

Nolan, F., McDougall, K. and Hudson, T. (2013) 'Effects of the telephone on perceived voice similarity: implications for voice line-ups', *International Journal of Speech, Language and the Law*, 20(2): 229–46.

Northcott, J. (2013) 'Legal English', in B. Paltridge and S. Starfield (eds), *The Handbook of English for Specific Purposes*, Oxford: Blackwell, pp. 213–26.

O'Barr, W. M. and Conley, J. M. (1990) 'Litigant satisfaction versus legal adequacy in small claims court narratives', in J. N. Levi and A. G. Walker (eds), *Language in the Judicial Process*, New York and London: Plenum Press, pp. 97–131.

Office for Criminal Justice Reform (2005) 'The use of bilingual (English and Welsh-speaking) juries in certain criminal trials in Wales: a consultation paper'.

Office for Criminal Justice Reform (2010) 'The use of bilingual (English and Welsh-speaking) juries in certain criminal trials in Wales: response to consultation'.

Penman, R. (1987) 'Discourse in court: cooperation, coercion and coherence', *Discourse Processes*, 10: 201–18.

Phillipson, R. (1997) 'Realities and myths of linguistic imperialism', *Journal of Multilingual and Multicultural Development*, 18(3): 238–48.

Pollock, F. and Maitland, F. W. (1895) *The History of English Law*, reissued with a new introduction and selected bibliography by S. F. C Milsom, 2 vols, Cambridge: Cambridge University Press.

Powell, R. (2008) 'Bilingual courtrooms: in the interests of justice?', in J. Gibbons and M. T. Turell (eds), *Dimensions of Forensic Linguistics*, Amsterdam: John Benjamins, pp. 131–59.

Preston, I. (1994) *The Tangled Web they Weave: Truth, Falsity and Advertisers*, Madison, WI: University of Wisconsin Press.

Pupavac, V. (2012) *Language Rights: From Free Speech to Linguistic Governance*, Basingstoke: Palgrave Macmillan.

Quinn, F. (2011) *Law for Journalists*, 2nd edn, Harlow: Pearson.

Remez, R. E., Fellowes, J. M. and Rubin, P. E. (1997) 'Talker identification based on phonetic information', *Journal of Experimental Psychology: Human Perception and Performance*, 23(3): 651–66.

Riley, A. and Sours, P. (2014) *Common Law Legal English and Grammar: A Contextual Approach*, Oxford: Hart.

Rogers, R., Hazelwood, L. L., Sewell, K. W., Harrison, K. S. and Shuman, D. W. (2008) 'The language of Miranda warnings in American jurisdictions: a replication and vocabulary analysis', *Law and Human Behaviour*, 32(2): 124–36.

Rosch, E. (1978) 'Principles of categorization', in E. Rosch and B. Lloyd (eds), *Cognition and Categorization*, Hillsdale, NJ: Lawrence Erlbaum Associates, pp. 27–48.

Rothman, L. (2013) 'J. K. Rowling's secret: a forensic linguist explains how he figured it out', *Time Entertainment*, 15 July, available at: http://entertainment.time.com/2013/07/15/j-k-rowlings-secret-a-forensic-linguist-explains-how-he-figured-it-out/ (accessed 28 February 2014).

Šarčević, S. (1997) *New Approach to Legal Translation*, The Hague: Kluwer Law International.

Šarčević, S. (2012) 'Challenges to the legal translator', in L. Solan and P. Tiersma (2012) *The Oxford Handbook of Language and Law*, Oxford: Oxford University Press, pp. 187–99.

Scalia, A. (1997) *A Matter of Interpretation: Federal Courts and the Law*, Princeton, NJ: Princeton University Press.

Scalia, A. and Garner, B. (2012) *Reading Law: The Interpretation of Legal Texts*, Berkeley, CA: Thomson/West.

Schane, S. (2006) *Language and the Law*, London: Continuum.

Schauer, F. (ed.) (1993a) *Law and Language*, Aldershot: Dartmouth Press.

Schauer, F. (ed.) (1993b) 'Rules and the rule-following argument', in F. Schauer (ed.), *Law and Language*, Aldershot: Dartmouth Press, pp. 313–18.

Searle, J. (1969) *Speech Acts: An Essay on the Philosophy of Language*, Cambridge: Cambridge University Press.

Shuy, R. (1993) *Language Crimes: The Use and Abuse of Language Evidence in the Courtroom*, Oxford: Blackwell.

Shuy, R. (2003) *Linguistic Battles in Trademark Disputes*, Basingstoke: Palgrave Macmillan.

Shuy, R. (2010) *The Language of Defamation Cases*, New York: Oxford University Press.

Shuy, R. (2012) *The Language of Sexual Misconduct Cases*, New York: Oxford University Press.

Solan, L. (2009) 'Statutory interpretation in the EU: the Augustinian approach', in F. Oslen, A. Lorz and D. Stein (eds), *Translation Issues in Language and Law*, Basingstoke: Palgrave Macmillan, pp. 35–54.

Solan, L. (2010) *The Language of Statutes: Laws and their Interpretation*, Chicago, IL: University of Chicago Press.

Solan, L. and Tiersma, P. (2005) *Speaking of Crime: The Language of Criminal Justice*, Chicago, IL: University of Chicago Press.

Solan, L. and Tiersma, P. (eds) (2012) *The Oxford Handbook of Language and Law*, Oxford: Oxford University Press.

Sperber, D. and Wilson, D. (1995) *Relevance: Communication and Cognition*, 2nd edn, Oxford: Blackwell.

Stephan, C. W. and Stephan, W. G. (1986) 'Habla Ingles? The effects of language translation on simulated juror decisions', *Journal of Applied Social Psychology*, 16(7): 577–89.

Stone, M. (2009) *Cross-Examination in Criminal Trials*, 3rd edn, London: Tottel.

Swales, J. (1990) *Genre Analysis: English in Academic and Research Settings*, Cambridge: Cambridge University Press.

Symonds, A. (1835) *The Mechanics of Law-Making*, London: Edward Churton.

Tabory, M. (1980) *Multilingualism in International Law and Institutions*, Alphen aan den Rijn, Netherlands: Sijthoff & Noordhoff.

Tannen, D. (1999) *The Argument Culture: Changing the Way We Argue*, New York: Virago.

Tanner, D. C. and Tanner, M. E. (2004) *Forensic Aspects of Speech Patterns: Voice Prints, Speaker Profiling, Lie and Intoxication Detection*, Tucson, AZ: Lawyers & Judges Publishing Co.

Tiersma, P. (1990) 'The language of perjury: "literal truth", ambiguity, and the false statement requirement', *South California Law Review*, 63: 373–431.

Tiersma, P. (1999) *Legal Language*, Chicago, IL: University of Chicago Press.

Tiersma, P. (2000) *The Nature of Legal Language*, available at: www.languageandlaw.org/NATURE.HTM (accessed 20 November 2015).

Tiersma, P. (2002) 'The language and law of product warnings', in J. Cotterill (ed.), *Language in the Legal Process*, London: Palgrave Macmillan, pp. 54–71.

Tiersma, P. (2008) 'The nature of legal language', in J. Gibbons and M. Turrell (eds), *Dimensions of Forensic Linguistics*, Amsterdam: John Benjamins, pp. 7–25.

Tiersma, P. (2009) 'What is language and law? And does anyone care?', in F. Olsen, A. Lorz and D. Stein (eds), *Law and Language: Theory and Society*, Loyola-LA Legal Studies Paper No. 2009–11.

Times Higher Education (2014) 'Sinister buttocks? Roget would blush at the crafty cheek', 7 August, available at: www.timeshighereducation.co.uk/news/sinister-buttocks-roget-would-blush-at-the-crafty-cheek/2015027.article (accessed 20 November 2015).

Turell, M. T. (2008) 'Plagiarism', in J. Gibbons and M. T. Turell (eds), *Dimensions of Forensic Linguistics*, Amsterdam: John Benjamins, pp. 265–99.

Twining, W. and Miers, D. (2010) *How to Do Things with Rules: A Primer of Interpretation*, 5th edn, Cambridge: Cambridge University Press.

Varó, E. A. (2008) 'Legal translation', in J. Gibbons and M. T. Turell (eds), *Dimensions of Forensic Linguistics*, Amsterdam: John Benjamins, pp. 95–111.

Vickers, B. (2002) *In Defence of Rhetoric*, Oxford: Clarendon Press.

Visconti, J. (ed) (forthcoming) *A Handbook of Communication in the Legal Sphere*, Berlin: de Gruyter.

Waelde, C., Laurie, G., Brown, A., Kheria, S. and Cornwall, J. (2014) *Contemporary Intellectual Property: Law and Policy*, 3rd edn, Oxford: Oxford University Press.

Warburton, N. (2009) *Free Speech: A Very Short Introduction*, Oxford: Oxford University Press.

Wells, G. (1992) 'Naked statistical evidence of liability: is subjective probability enough?', *Journal of Personality and Social Psychology*, 62(5): 739–52.

Welsh Language Use in Wales, 2013–15, Welsh Government and Welsh Language Commissioner.

White, D. (1989) *Trials and Tribulations: An Appealing Anthology of Legal Humour*, North Haven, CT: Catbird Press.

Wilson, D. and Carston, R. (2007) 'A unitary approach to lexical pragmatics: relevance, inference and ad hoc concepts', in N. Burton-Roberts (ed.), *Pragmatics*, Basingstoke: Palgrave, pp. 230–59.

Woolard, K. and Schieffelin, B. (1994) 'Language ideology', *Annual Review of Anthropology*, 23: 55–82.

Woolf, the Right Hon. Lord, Master of the Rolls (1996) *Access to Justice – Final Report*, available at: www.dca.gov.uk/civil/final/index.htm (accessed 20 November 2015).

Woolls, D. (2012) 'Detecting plagiarism', in L. Solan and P. Tiersma (eds), *The Oxford Handbook of Language and Law*, Oxford: Oxford University Press, pp. 517–29.

Zander, M. (2015) *The Law-Making Process*, 7th edn, Cambridge: Cambridge University Press.

CASES CITED

Bailey v. United States 516 U.S. 137 (1995)

Bronston v. United States, 409 U.S. 352 (1973)

Chambers v. DPP [2012] EWHC 2157

Doston v. Duffy, 732 F. Supp. 857 – Dist. Court, ND Illinois 1988

Fonden Marselisborg Lystbådehavn v. Skatteministeriet Case C-428/02

Heydon's case (1584) 3 Co Rep 7a, Moore KB 128, 76 ER 637, 21 Digest (Repl) 652, 1424

Lucasfilm Ltd v. Ainsworth [2008] EWHC 1878 (Ch); [2011] UKSC 39; [2012] 1 AC 208.

McBoyle v. United States 283 U.S. 25(1931)

McDonald's Corporation v. Quality Inns International US District Court for the District of Maryland, Civil Action No. PN-87-2606

Muscarello v. United States, 524 U.S. 125 (1998)

New York Times Co. v. Sullivan 376 U.S. 254 (1964)

Perrier Group of Canada Inc. v. Canada [1996] 1 F.C. 586

R (Ghai) v. Newcastle City Council [2010] EWCA Civ 59

State of Illinois v. Nathan Leopold & Richard Loeb [1924]

GLOSSARIAL INDEX